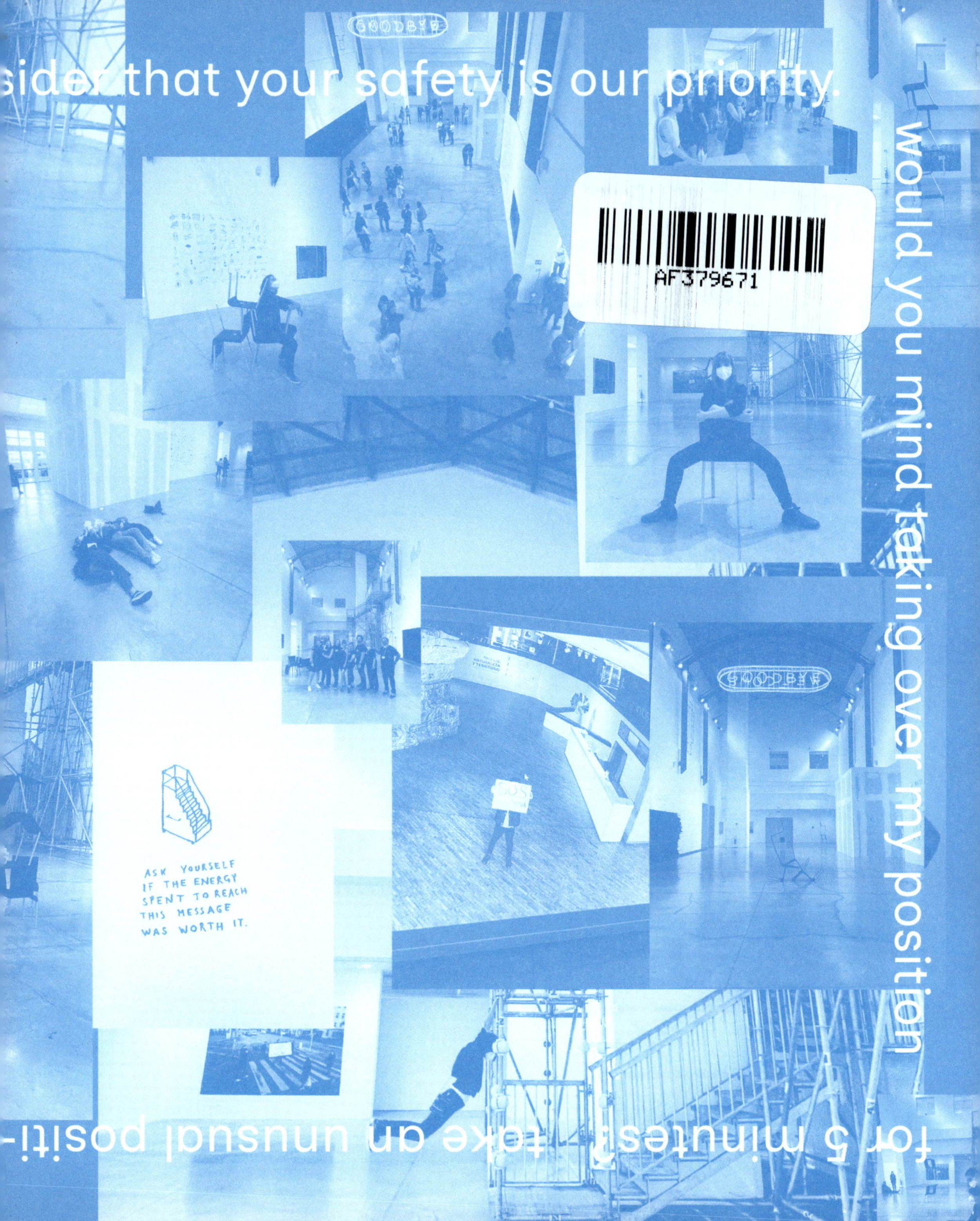

...sider that your safety is our priority.
would you mind taking over my position
for 5 minutes?   take an unusual positi-
GOODBYE
ASK YOURSELF
IF THE ENERGY
SPENT TO REACH
THIS MESSAGE
WAS WORTH IT.
AF379671

the
upside - down
museum

don't let anyone tell you what to do!

practice-based institutional critique,
working up from the actual museum floor,
by artist aldo giannotti

if you break the rules, please do it unnoticed.

if you are planning to take a risk,

B 5.17 MONTAGGIO NEON

- Montaggio in quota, tramite cavetti in acciaio, di n. 02 strutture
  in alluminio contenenti neon.
- Posizionamento di n. 04 trasformatori da allocare in quota in luogo
  da concordare.
- Collegamento elettrico.
- Fornitura cavo elettrico per neon mt. 25.

Descrizione
- n. 02 struttura + neon, larghezza mt 5x1 circa, peso complessivo kg 40.
- n. 04 trasformatori 10000V/25mA
- montaggio struttura a h mt 8 circa da terra
- fissaggio cavi h mt 13 circa

I cavi di appendim
agli appositi perni
presenti a soffitto.
Ogni arco porta k

cavo elet

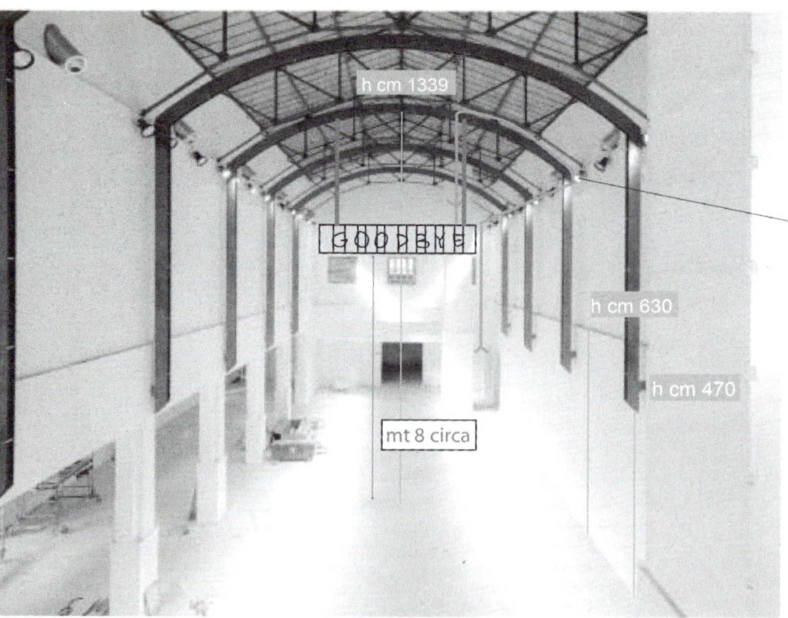

H mt 11.75
base dell'a

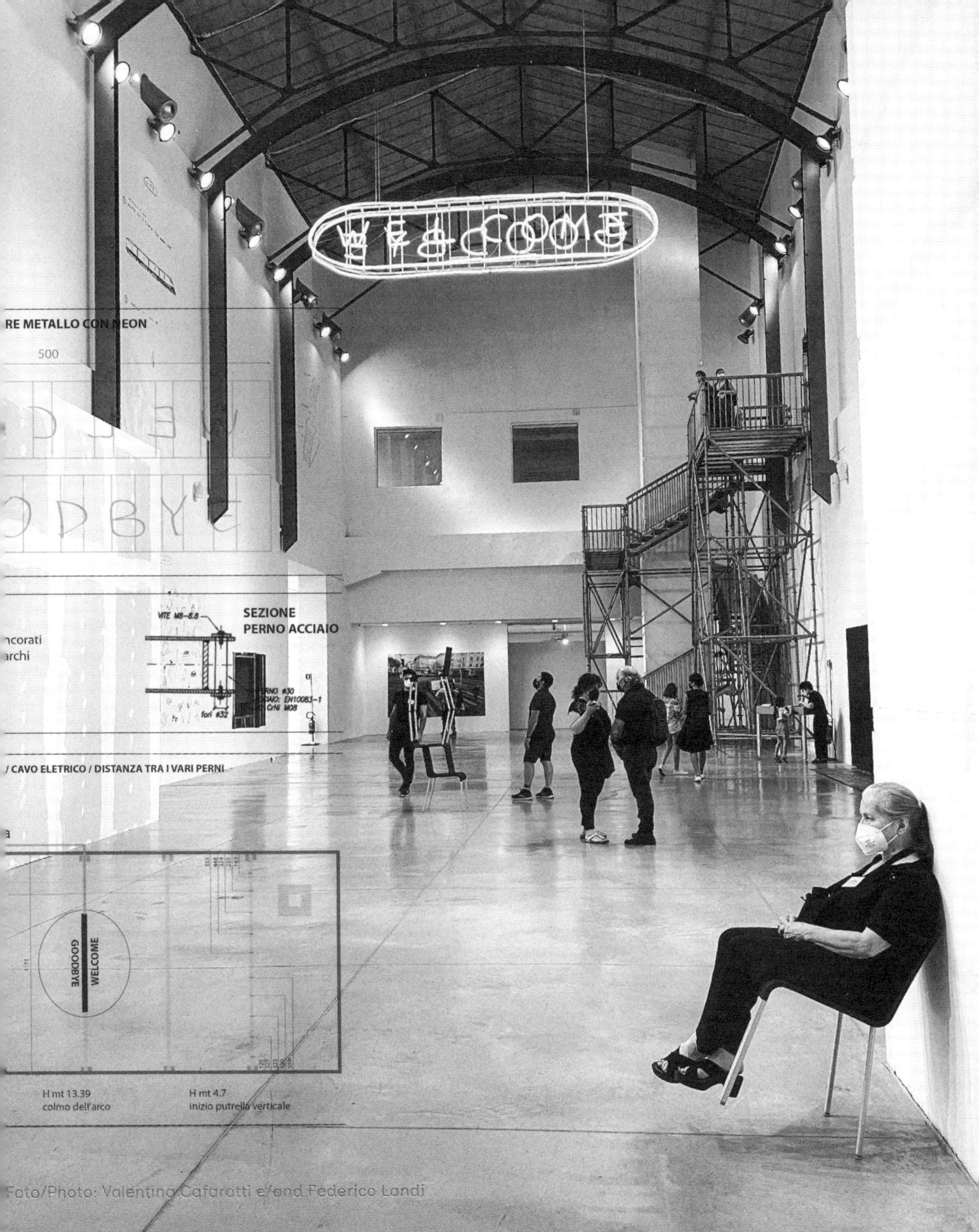

Foto/Photo: Valentina Cafarotti e/and Federico Landi

by means of
introduction

By Andrea
Steves and
Freek Lomme

The space museums take, and arguably their being, is defined by power and architecture: most notably by security cameras and guards, by the building itself and the exhibition narrative, by the codes of conduct, and social hygiene.

The imposing word "MUSEUM" hovers above the grand edifice of the museum building, bestowing an air of grandeur and conveying authority. As visitors we pass beneath this signage, confirming its authority. We enter a central hallway, reminiscent of a sacred space which exudes an aura of paternalism, its purpose veiled in subtlety. As we proceed through subsequent halls, the intensity of the often white surroundings may become so overpowering they distort the normal perception of depth and space, challenging our understanding of the environment.

Here the grandeur is to be admired in non-reciprocal communication, preferably while walking with hands gently held together behind the back, an expression of submission to the code of conduct at large, and the one of "not touching anything in particular". If the visitors wish to examine something up close, their hands should *remain* pinned behind their backs. They should try and move their head as near to the object as possible, being cautious not to stumble forward, and lean over as necessary to read the small caption telling them what the hell they're looking at, or whether it's cool to touch or not cool to touch that very thing.

together.   please consider that your

In these halls, shadows emerge, resembling figures that have just stirred and could be trailing you like zombies. These entities within the museum are referred to as guards, yet they differ significantly from the guards we encounter elsewhere in the world. They appear to embody a state of near-absence, moving in slow motion, almost as if gliding on what might be just about three socks per foot. Their hushed whispers reinforce the unspoken rules: visitors should make every effort to avoid being present in an attempt to embody something greater than anyone who has breathed within this space. The guards, mere interlopers to be ignored, are actually impossible to ignore: these shadows are constantly on the watch, waiting to shepherd the ignorant and misbehaving visitor through carefully laid-out pathways, ensuring the transfer and preservation of this building called MUSEUM.

This is the infrastructure of authority, set in codes and set in stone, enduring like a monument long after its post-war, privileged patrons have passed. Once Aldo Giannotti starts to mess around with the level set by codes and/or stones the full infrastructure of codes of conduct, cameras, safety measures, etc. are opened up as a creative toolbox. The established bar transforms into a tangible instrument, as creative adaptability underpins individuals' ability to embody the marvel of possibility, engaging with established norms and challenges. This process democratizes authority, embracing mutual responsibility and urging the liberation of inherent creativity. This is what actual art is about.

safety is our priority. would you mind taking

over my position for 5 minutes; take an

Aldo Giannotti's occupation is capturing the essence of the world before him and the institutions surrounding him, through sketching a multitude of new possibilities that expose the cracks and fill the gaps.

Initiating from sketches and driven by tangible reality while nurtured by autonomy, these works propel critical processing of the very elements before us, including institutional frameworks. These drawings also scale up and gain weight beyond the intimacy of the drawings, where Giannotti appropriates the role of the engineer and architect to actually redraw places and spaces, like the museum. Participants in Giannotti's work often find themselves suddenly engaged, sometimes evolving into performers for others, momentarily forgetting they are within the confines of the museum.

The result of this practice of redrawing and opening is not that it immediately leads to some institutional dismantling or perma-nent reconfiguration, and Giannotti is certainly not so idealistic as to have this expectation. But the work is destabilizing, and perhaps that is what it takes to make people start to see the potential: that even something as seemingly fixed as a museum could be cut open, and in this potential we can see paths towards overturning the museum and remaking it in a new way.

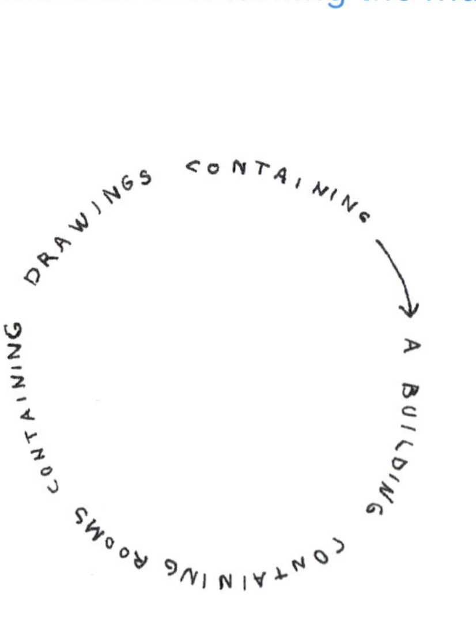

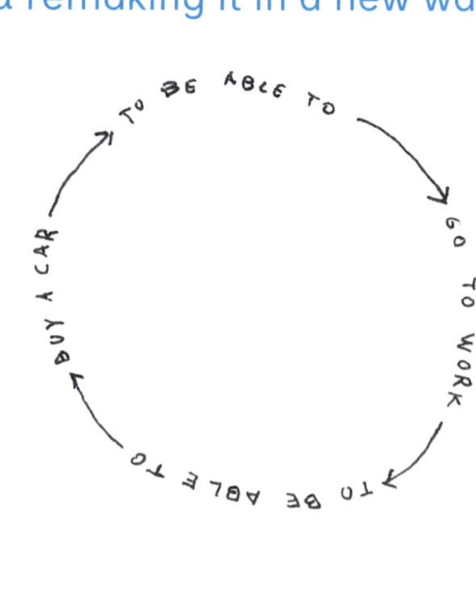

4

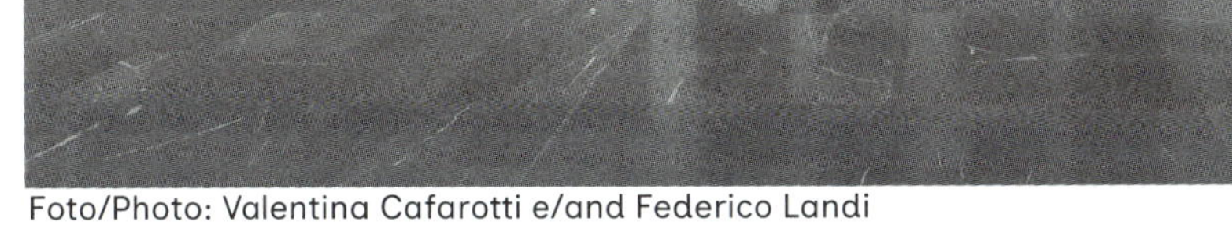

Aldo Giannotti **Safe and Sound**
a cura di / curated by Lorenzo Balbi con l'assistenza curatoriale di / with the curatorial assistance of Sabrina Samorì

Foto/Photo: Valentina Cafarotti e/and Federico Landi

unnoticed.   If you are planning to take

mind taking over my position for 5 minutes?

your safety is our priority.   would you

Disclaimer: *The pieces featured in this exhibition were actualized at MAMbo (Museo d'Arte Moderna di Bologna/Museum of Modern Art Bologna) in 2021, constituting Aldo Giannotti's solo exhibition, Safe and Sound. These works both operate as a standalone presentation but are also designed to comment on and resonate with museums on a broader scale.*

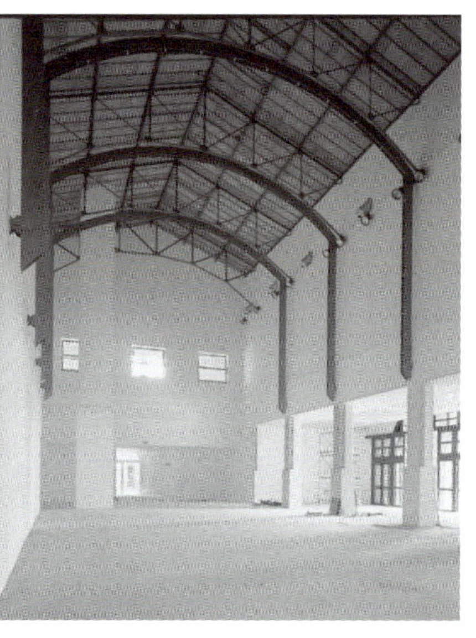

These site-specific works were created with particular attention to contextual elements such as the architecture.

If you have not visited the building, you might not know it has a huge central hall, almost like a white cube, with corridors and stairs beyond that hall leading to the permanent collection and more exhibitions.

This central hallway served as the genesis for a multitude of social and spatial interventions that engaged in forms of institutional critique. This critique quite literally unfolded from the exhibition floor and extends upward.

On the left is an image of this central hall.

This map was drawn on the wall, an imagined path for visitors..

"The Breach"

Layers of history are peeled away in an archeological and architectural act.

During a restoration of the building in the second half of the Nineties, architect Aldo Rossi envisioned a staircase ascending from the ground floor to the floor of MAMbo's collection. As soon as this staircase was constructed, it was dismantled. In his research for the exhibition, Aldo Giannotti stumbled upon the original drawing and the precise location where the door had initially existed in the architect's original plans.

The Breach reopened this once closed-off space to the heart of the entire museum, connecting the past and the present; staircases and doorways were rendered as more inviting and expansive. A substantial scaffold was added in the middle of the space, imposing, cutting a straight path between the main hall and the permanent collection.

The scaffold asserted a resolute "why not?" spirit—typical of builders—into the imagination of the space. The work extended the architectural evolution of the site from Aldo Rossi's initial concept to the transformation into a central white cube to Aldo Giannotti's recent intervention. This shows the various needs of the art museum in each of their respective times.

9

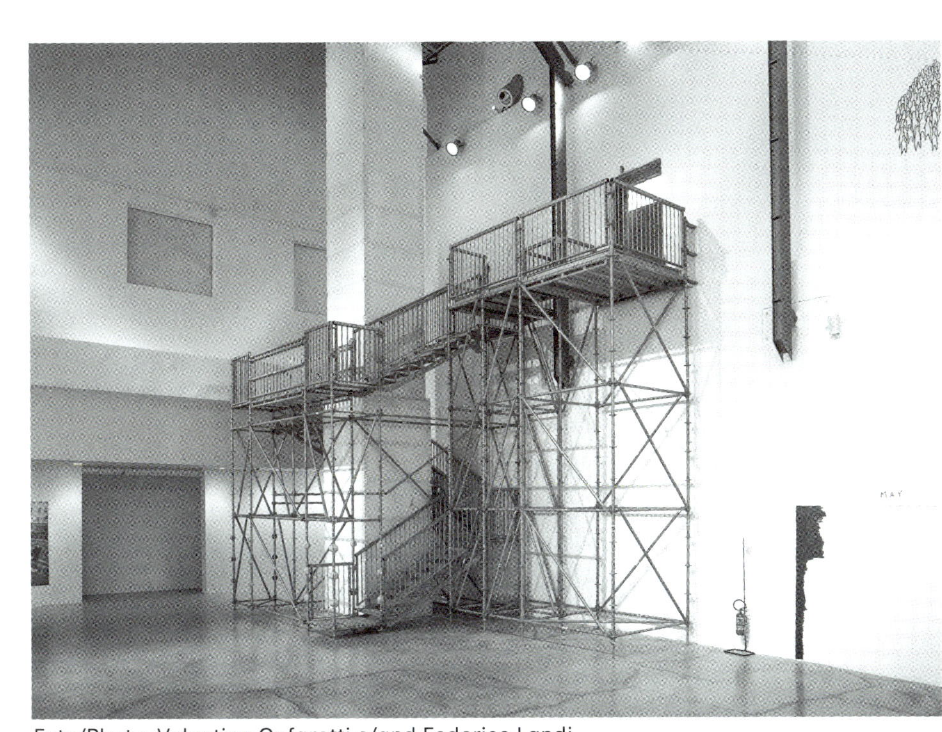

Foto/Photo: Valentina Cafarotti e/and Federico Landi

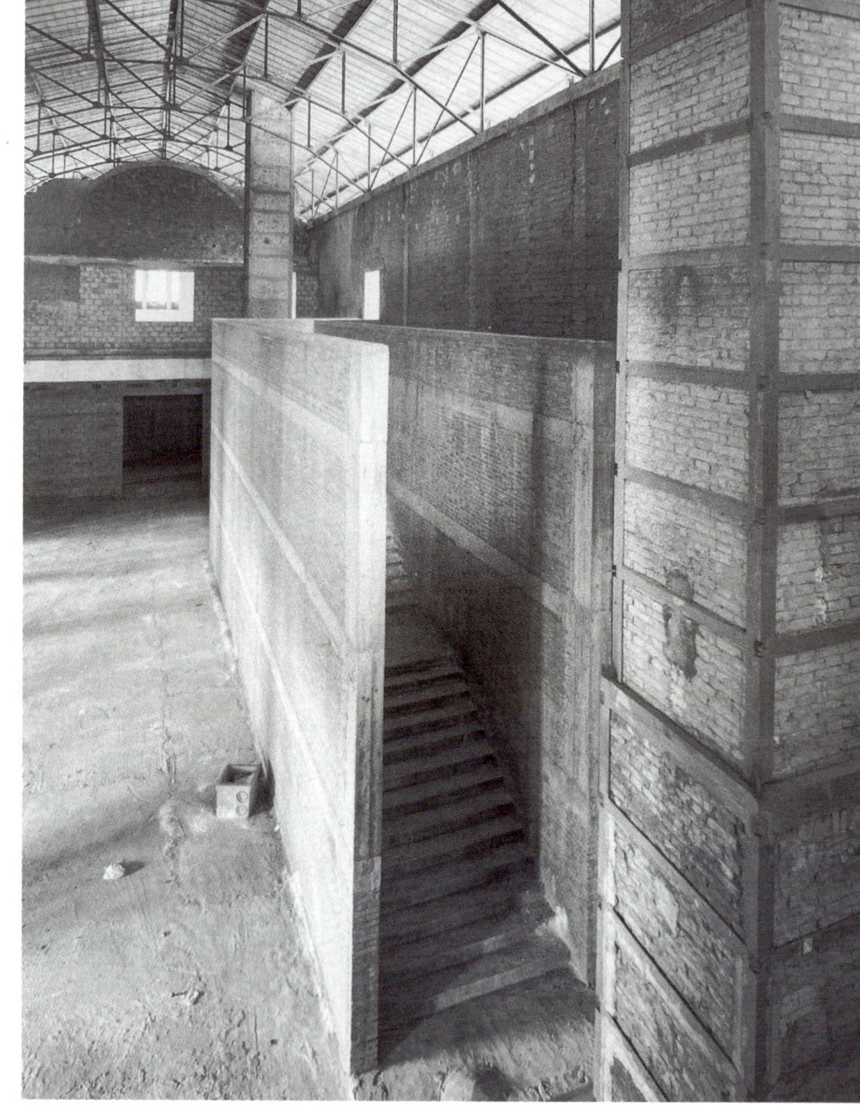
Staircase
conceived
by Aldo Rossi
during the
restoration of
the building.

half full hour in the main hall to sociali-

please consider

hall to socialize all together.

meet at every half full hour in the main

...e all together. If you break the rules, please do it unnoticed. If you are planning to take a risk, please involve me.

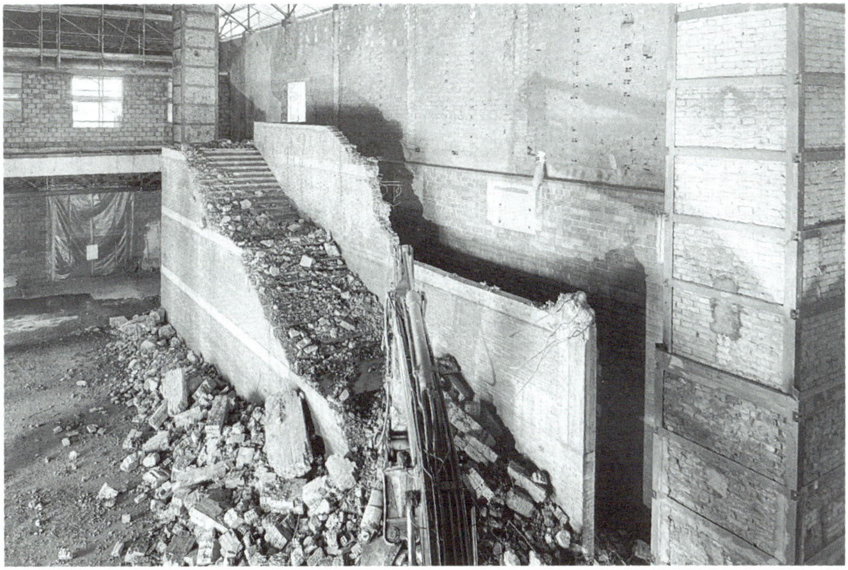

Aldo Rossi's stairs taken out, his door turned into wall.

that your safety is our priority.

Semi-permanence as a proposition to supposedly permanent architecture, while stretching creative imagining.

The extensive scaffold presented before, equipped with staircases that ascend to the third floor, led up to a deliberate breach in the wall created by Aldo Giannotti. This breach was the only place legally allowed within the wall, where formerly a door was situated within the original Aldo Rossi architecture.

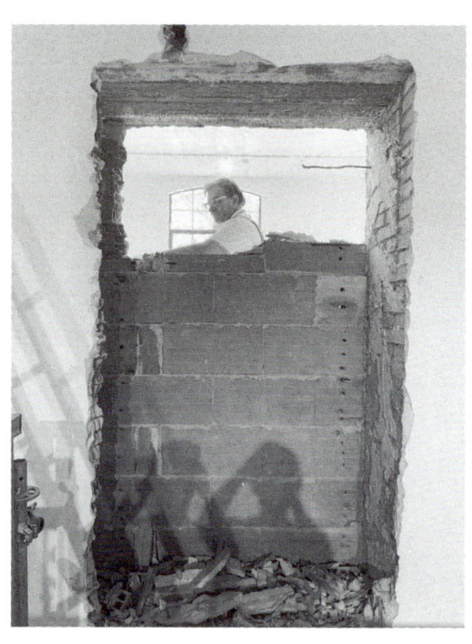
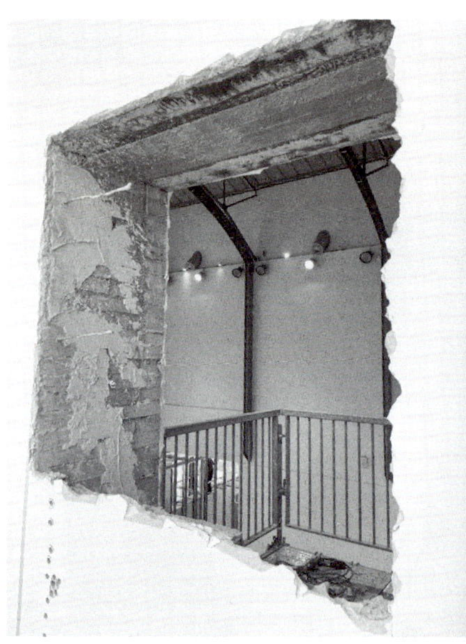

exhibition. draw "string drawings" and engage

please remember me as part of this

would you mind taking over my positi-

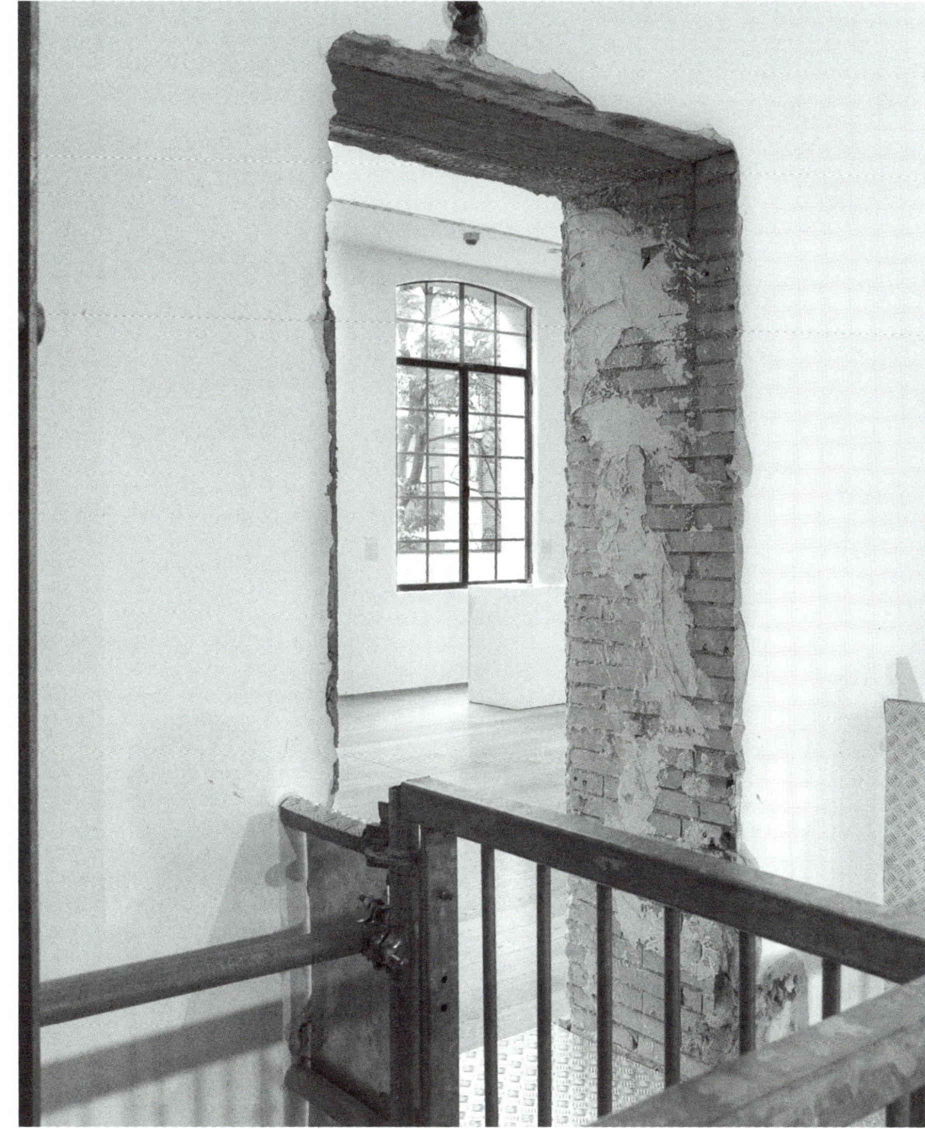

Foto/Photo: Valentina Cafarotti e/and Federico Landi

if you are planning to take a risk,

(2)

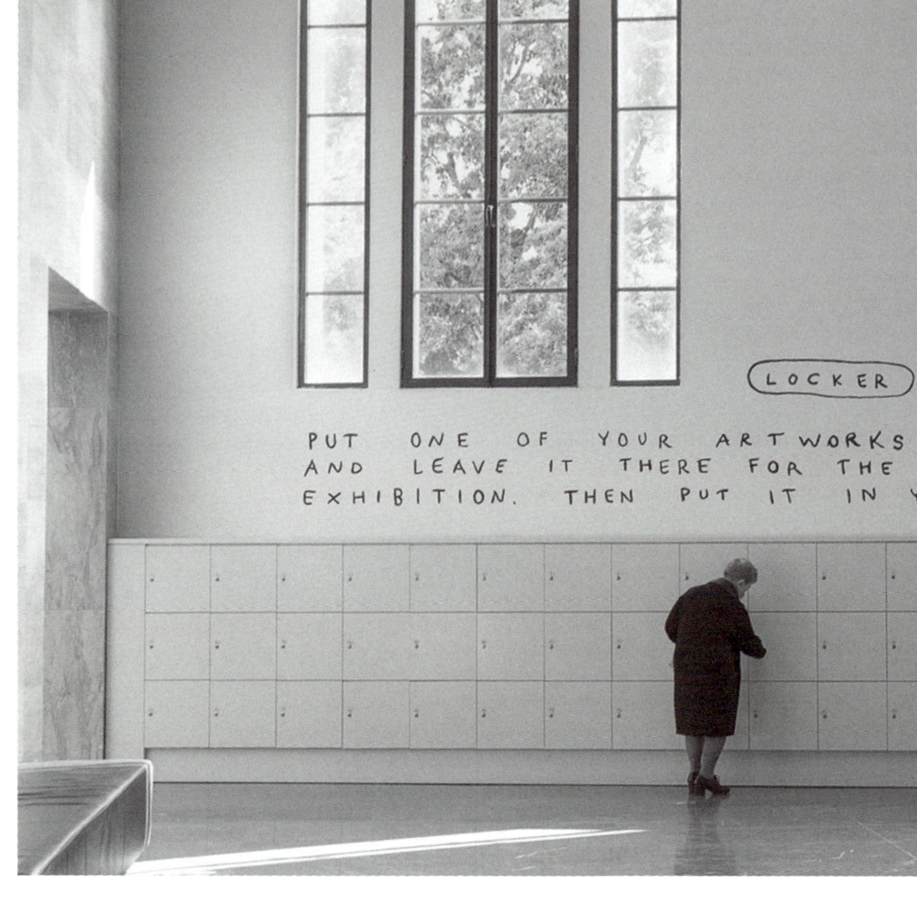

unnoticed.

if you break the rules, please do it

sculpture using all chairs in the center of the space. meet at every half full hour in the main hall to socialize all together.

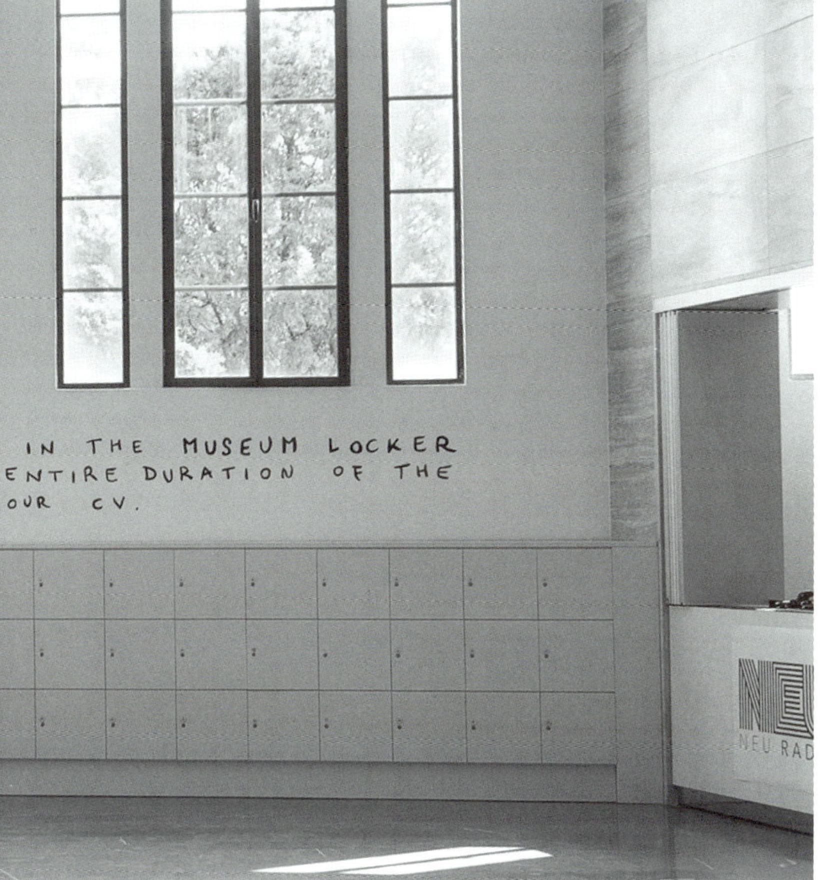

please involve me.   meet at every

VISIT A MUSEUM GUARD AND
PAY YOUR RESPECTS.
OPTIONALLY OFFER A GIFT.

...half full hour in the main hall to sociali-

ze all together. please consider that your

safety is our priority.   would you

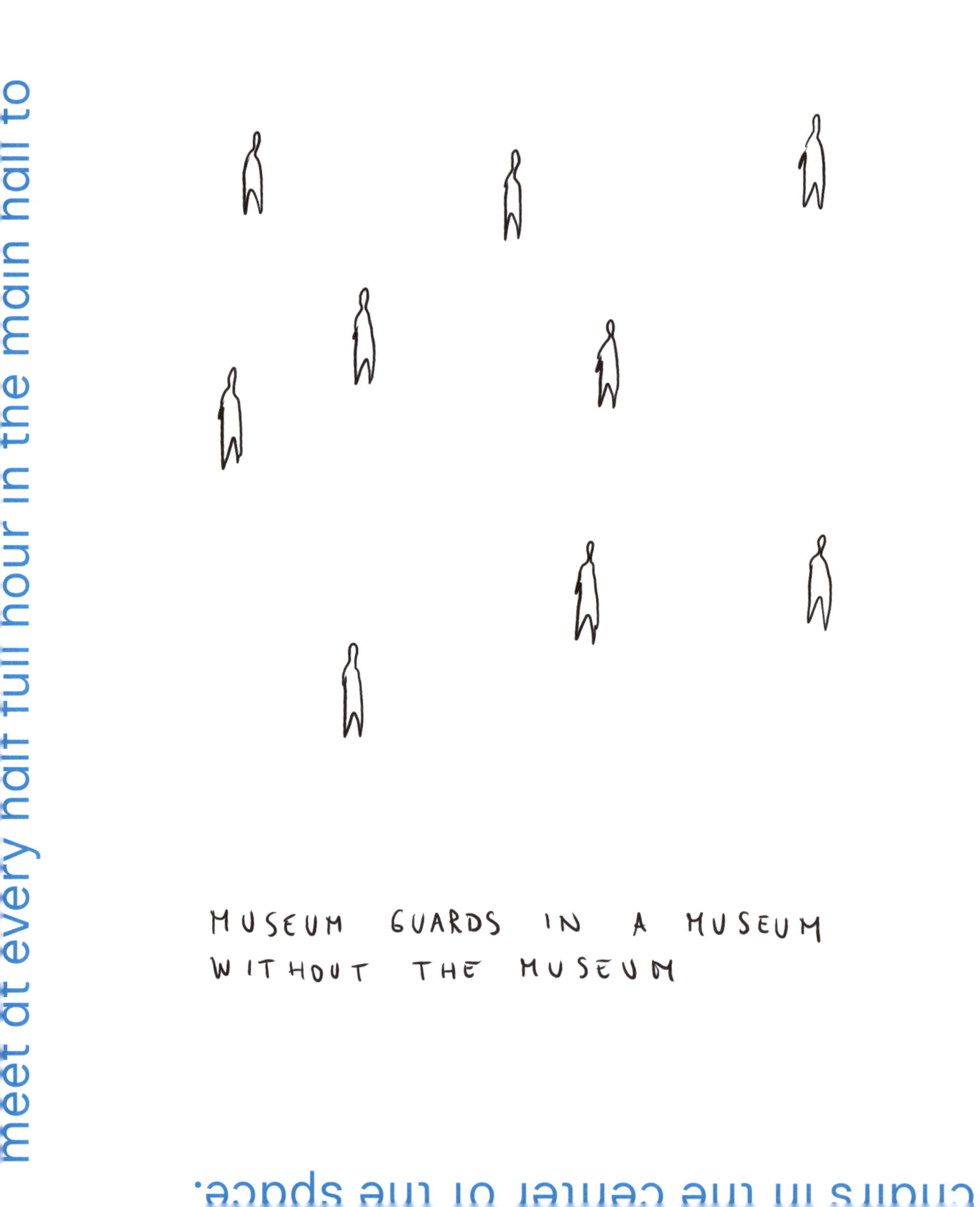

hi my name is .... please remember
meet at every half full hour in the main hall to
MUSEUM GUARDS IN A MUSEUM
WITHOUT THE MUSEUM
guards in the center of the space.

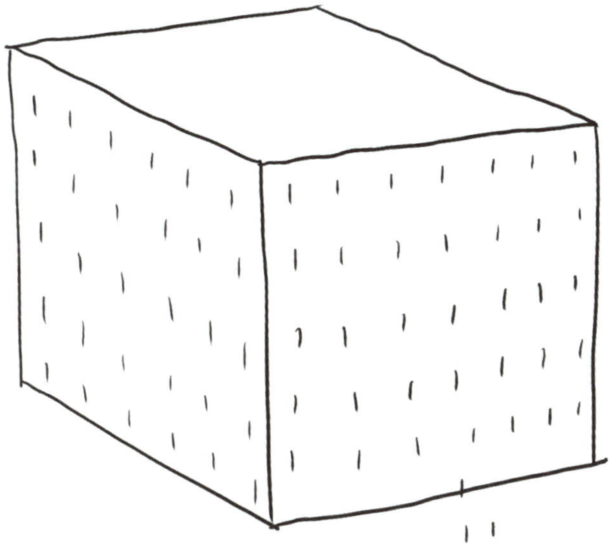

MUSEUM GUARDS PROTECTING
THE MUSEUM FROM THE MUSEUM
ITSELF

socialize all together.   if you break

please consider that your safety is our priority.

the main hall to socialize all together.

the rules, please do it unnoticed.

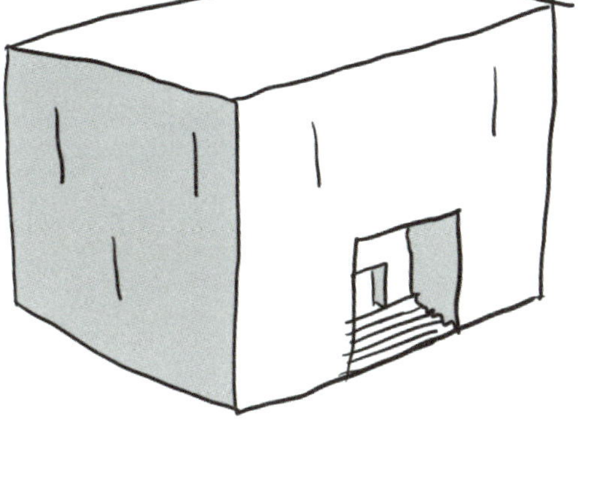
MUSEUM LOOKING FORWARDS

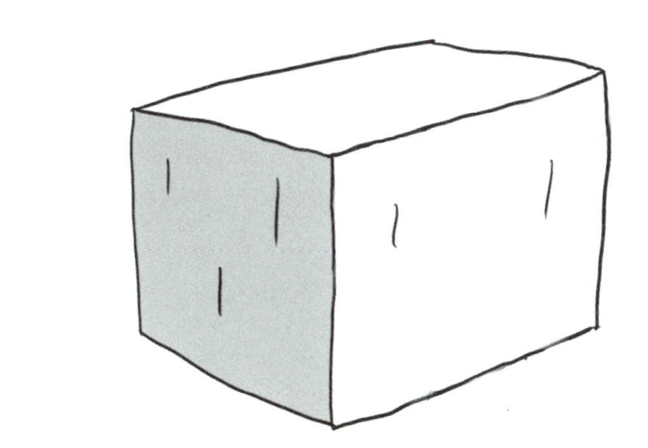
MUSEUM LOOKING BACKWARDS

If you are planning to take a risk, please involve me.

meet at every hair turn turn in
me.

Lorenzo Balbi:
(museum director, curator of the show)

Aldo's proposal was completely different…first of all, the idea of involving the real guards, not having a "performance," right? That's a complete shift, and was super interesting. I remember asking Aldo, "But you are going to, you know, make workshops for performers, and then do casting and ask them if they have specific skills, etc.?" And Aldo was saying, "No, no, no, that's not what I am thinking. It's the real guards; I want to work with them. I want you to provide me with a list of the workers…and I want to interview them without you…" So this process of making became an intervention on the structure of the museum.

Andrea Steves:
(editor)

What do you mean by the structure?

LB:

Whereas we might immediately think that an intervention on the structure of the museum is focused on the architectural structure, or maybe ideal structures of the operations, when Aldo works within the museum structures, he thinks about the museum structure not only as an architectural building or the pieces like ticketing, or the procedures… of course these are all a part of it, but the structure is also inclusive of the people working here: as guards, as the receptionist, the people in the bar and so on. All of these are components of the museum, and that's a very interesting thing. So it became an intervention within the structure of the museum, and thinking about guards as structural parts of the institution.

AS: Right. So Aldo wanted to work with the guards as a key component of the structure of the museum, as some of the closest mediators within the museum. So how did their assignments within *Safe and Sound* using Aldo's scores depart from their previous roles?

LB: We of course had involved the guards in things like educational events. We thought about how they were the ones that have the most direct feedback: they are our face in front of the visitors. But we didn't have a real or formal approach in which they took such an active role…that's what I was actually surprised about and very happy with. Where as before people were trained to ignore the guards, we shifted their position to the center, an active place where they become co-creators or partners, co-authors or allies. That is the difference. And this is very different from, for example, Tino Sehgal's approach or this or that way of using the image of a guard. Or just for a performative role. The guards were conceived to be co-authors, instead of just a subject of the work. It's not that Aldo is only using their role or their image, or their place inside the show to do work for him, to perform. He was actually asking them to just be themselves.

AS: Ok, so the attempt is to bring the guard to the forefront, to give them more agency and play with the hierarchies within the institution. Then the question for me becomes: what shifts did this bring about in the actual role of the guard within the institution and what possibilities for the future did this create?

ture using all chairs in the center of the

LB: Very large question. To start, the role of guards in contemporary art museums is often very different museum by museum. I was used to working in a museum where there were not any guards, there were just cultural mediators: students of contemporary art (including me, at one point) whose role was to educate visitors on the contents of the exhibition, not guards at all. Of course we were monitoring the visitors, and if they would approach too close to the works, we would ask them, "Please don't touch." But our role was really to kind of mediate the contents of the exhibition or the ideas coming from it and the immediate feedback and personality of the visitors....

AS: So more like an interpreter, or a docent?

LB: Yes, like a cultural mediator, docent...So a work like the one Aldo suggested would not have been as attractive in that other context, where the guards are already taking an active role as a cultural mediator or docent. It wouldn't be a shift. But here at MAMBO the proposal was completely different and made a lot of sense.

The first thing to know is that our group of guards here is composed of people hired through a cooperative of services, which includes different services like reception or guarding the exhibition space. So let's say half of them are from this cooperative. And the other half, which is maybe even more interesting, are volunteers. These again come from an association and include people in retirement

meet at every half hour.

please involve me.

if you are planning to take a risk,

space. meet at every half full hour in

looking to stay active and to continue having a rhythm of life and a workplace: meeting people, not staying at home every day. Guards are hired as programs for community service or reintegration.

So coming to the museum becomes a way of working, having a schedule for the day. We were already trying to involve them a bit in the exhibition process; it's not like we just tell them, "Stand there, and if someone gets too close to the work, you have to say, 'Don't touch.'" We would have training and meetings with them to introduce the show, the kind of work, and the artist. But their role during the day is very passive, you know, mostly checking what's happening there, checking tickets, checking what visitors do in the show. So then when Aldo came and said, I have this idea, I'm making a work asking you to have a role, an active role, their reaction was immediately positive. This was the first time they were asked to be active, not passive. It was a choice to participate, if they didn't want to, they could move their assigned position from Aldo's exhibition to working in the permanent collection…but most wanted to participate.

AS: And after the exhibition was over?

LB: The guards were super nostalgic. They were asking us, asking me when we will do that again. It enabled them to have a better understanding of their daily practice, and what is missing….

the main hall to socialize all together. If you

break the rules, please do it unnoticed.

hour in the main hall to socialize all to-

AS: I can imagine. It became a different kind of work, a
different energy within the museum.....

LB: The nostalgia was a common feeling even for the public.
The main theme, let's say, of the exhibition was breaking
rules, you know, breaking attitudes, norms. If you go to the
museum, you have to stay quiet, not touch, not run...not...
not...not sit...not...not dance, not make noise. And the
exhibition itself and all the installations and works in the
exhibition, they were all reflecting about rules, about
breaking rules, about the possibility of leaving the spaces,
leaving your attitude in the space in a new way. And so, like
after six months, people started to adjust, to be engaged in
this mode....so when we had a new show and they couldn't
dance or run, people were asking, "Why do you turn back to
the old way?"

AS: And what did you answer?

LB: I said that was part of the show that was interesting. That
was an installation. The fact that you were running was part
of the show. Right? That's another show now, right?

AS: So it also reflects on how we like to react against rules, and
break them....if the rules really were not there in the first
place, then it wouldn't be nearly as sexy to break...right?

LB: Yeah, that was for the guards too. They changed after that.
They thought before that we were asking them to have a

very cold presence...you know, static and quiet and severe. Right after the exhibition, I noticed they continue to speak more with people, with visitors. Before it was mostly instructions, intrusive,
"Can you show me your ticket?"
But then they started thinking about what it means to welcome….
"We are happy to have your here."
That was a shift.

AS: The exhibition was conceived before the COVID-19 pandemic, through which we gained a heightened awareness of security, procedures, and protocols in our daily lives. But the exhibition was planned well beforehand, and this was more of a coincidence, not a response, right?

LB: Right. We planned the concept of the exhibition by May 2020, at least the key themes, the concept and the works. So the idea of reflecting on the thematic of security was already there before the pandemic, before so many procedures became very evident in our daily life. But from the beginning, the show was exposing the borders between the thing that you can do and the thing you can't; forcing us to confront this border.

AS: Can you then talk a bit about the process through which the exhibition developed. How did you bring Aldo in, how did you decide what to include?

LB: I really think that working within an institution means to ask the artists to be here. So this idea of working with the structure and on the borders of what you can do and what you can't do, what was made and what we can make, it's really interesting in the way of dealing with an institution. And so when I asked him for a solo presentation, I knew there would be many ideas, and I remember having meetings with the staff to warn them to be ready, there would be many ideas that would challenge the institution. We will have problems. We will have problems with our safety engineers. We will have problems with people working in the show. But that is really the work.

AS: I am sure there were, as ever from Aldo, many ideas…

LB: Yeah, Aldo was proposing, as always—because it is his way of working—a thousand different ideas. Immediately he started to send me hundreds and hundreds of drawings he had made. It was almost endless.

AS: This is his process, right? The proliferation. Taking all of the parts and rearranging them, in every configuration. Just an endless set of possibilities, and see which moves forward, which opens something, which ends up not working. Many of the unrealized ideas and sketches made it into the lobby, but there was probably a lot of work that was left unseen….

LB: Not even just sketches. I mean, maybe we can take mails and correspondence with the engineers as a work by Aldo.

He was asking us in many ways what was possible, and we were performing, performing a work by him. This was also his way of working with the structure of the museum, forcing the rules, even the work of the registrars and the person in charge of the display. All of these possibilities and questions were works, and sometimes we couldn't find a solution. Some ideas were really impossible.

AS: Tell me more about the pieces that were impossible.

LB: Actually, nothing was really impossible. I think one of the main challenges was to build the room inside the museum, The Column, that would be open for 24 hours a day, mostly for safety. The Column shared a wall with the museum in which there are paintings worth millions. Right on the other side of the wall. And then meanwhile you have somebody chainsawing a piece off that wall, if you really put two and two together, it was kind of craziness. In terms of pushing rules, there was quite a bit of destruction: opening a hole in the first floor, connecting it, allowing people to enter without a ticket, for example. So I suppose he broke the main things that could be broken.

AS: In Aldo's previous book, *Welcome and Goodbye*, you did an interview with him, a sort of reverse artist statement where Aldo interviews you about himself as an artist. And one of the questions that he asks you is "Do you think I'm a political artist?" You answer that in a way, every artist is sort of making a political statement. Do you remember this?

please do it unnoticed.   if you are

LB: Yes, yes, I remember.

AS: Ok, good. I am curious if after the experience of working on
      this exhibition with Aldo, you would still answer in the same
      way, or if you would add anything. Is Aldo a political artist?

LB: Is Aldo a political artist? This is the question of the decade.
      I mean, what does it mean to be a political artist? I'm still
      completely convinced about the fact that being an artist is
      already a political statement. But the thing that I can add
      that at the time I wasn't thinking about is in relation to the
      art system or the art market. Aldo's relation—or lack of
      relation to this system—is really a political approach and
      position taken by Aldo.

      In a system where if you don't sell work…or if you don't
      make work that is even possible to sell, it's difficult to
      survive, right? And this is really a political statement. For
      sure, I'm really interested in this kind of art, this way of
      making art that is not focused on selling. A reaction against
      the common way of thinking and conceiving of art as only
      suitable for a market, as only a product. This is critical,
      because if we don't give space to this kind of thing, it's
      going to die. So I can add this. I'm still convinced about
      what I said, but I want to add this.

would you mind taking over my position for 5

consider that your safety is our priority.

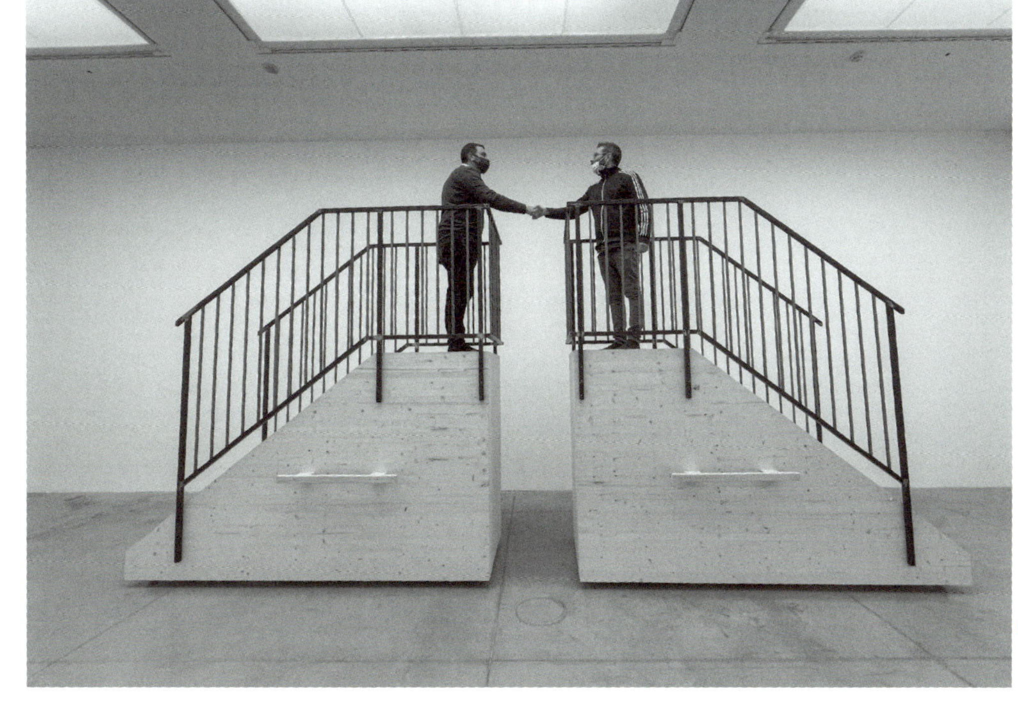

A firm handshake
between Lorenzo Balbi and Aldo Giannotti
(As practiced in the framework of the 'Mobile Staircase' work.)

(15)

THE MUSEUM SCORE

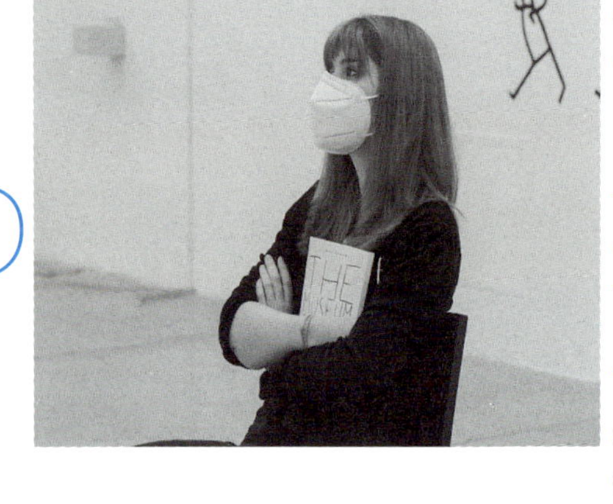

(4)

The familiar becomes unfamiliar, and the expected is disrupted, compelling visitors to reevaluate their relationship with the art, the museum space, and each other.

The Museum Score served as both a compendium and a transformative tool to reimagine the role of the guard.

Designed and illustrated by Giannotti himself, this document came to life through specially trained museum guards, positioned throughout the exhibition. Instead of blending into the background, the guards became key protagonists, both an integral part of the exhibition's material and a commentary on the invisible labor in the museum.

These guards were instrumental in shaping visitors' experiences (as guards often are unintentionally), by introducing a radically different set of guidelines governing visitor behavior and attempting to shift the normal social conventions and corresponding behavioral patterns inherent in a traditional museum setting. The guards' gesture of welcome was one of many that aimed to make visitors feel comfortable while challenging the standard role of the unwelcoming guard, the scolder, or the surveiller.

The Museum Score consisted of instructions to engage visitors in conversations and provocations.

Aldo Giannotti:

DON'T LET ANYONE TELL YOU WHAT TO DO!

IF YOU BREAK THE RULES, PLEASE DO IT UNNOTICED.

IF YOU ARE PLANNING TO TAKE A RISK, PLEASE INVOLVE ME.

MEET AT EVERY FULL HOUR IN THE MAIN HALL TO SOCIALIZE ALL TOGETHER.

PLEASE CONSIDER THAT YOUR SAFETY IS OUR PRIORITY.

WOULD YOU MIND TAKING OVER MY POSITION FOR 5 MINUTES?

TAKE AN UNUSUAL POSITION IN SPACE.

HI, MY NAME IS .... PLEASE REMEMBER ME AS PART OF THIS EXHIBITION.

DRAW "STRING DRAWINGS" AND ENGAGE VISITORS IN THE ACTIVITY.

CREATE A SCULPTURE USING ALL CHAIRS IN THE CENTER OF THE SPACE.

a report from
the floor
(sort of)

By Andrea
Steves

The Museum Score cut through the inherent tensions in the role of the museum guard: the space they occupy within museum bureaucracy, tasked as enforcers, asserting museum rules and regulations, yet facing structures of control and discipline themselves; a space in which guards carry out their orders and model behavior.

What emerged through interactions with the artist was a sense of self-reflection and observation within the guards. In interviews, the guards talked about how their work felt different than "usual": they were given agency to improvise, to make connections, and to help visitors forge connections to the works in the space—that is, when people were willing. I asked a few of the guards what they thought the biggest barrier was to visitor participation. One of the guards told me, "Well, I think people are afraid, because we're not used to being told that anything is possible." *The Museum Score* offered the guards a means to challenge visitors' expectations, to create a space where rules can be reshaped, refomed, or broken. Yet encouraging this very break from the conventions, which are deeply embedded through constant training and conditioning, proved to be a difficult sell. It's not straightforward to convince people to break the silence in a museum, to break the rules, to break the infrastructure; eventually to break through their own fear or expectations.

he main hall to socialize all together.

While in the exhibition, visitors somehow adjusted to the guards even in their slightly idiosyncratic behaviors (sitting wide-legged on the floor, offering assistance, approaching with questions, etc.). But a way out of the museum was a one-way exit from two-story high scaffolding, inserted in the middle of the space. After climbing the loud, clanging metal staircase, visitors were ejected into the "real" part of the exhibition (the permanent collection) where they were met with "real" guards whose performance was more like what we might expect from a "real guard."

While some of Giannotti's work spilled into this "real" part of the exhibition—in the form of small boxes with cards that offered scores to visitors—the "real" part was accompanied with a shift in light, sound, and general mood: back in this real part of the museum, visitors might be subjected to the normal restrictions: no talking, no gum-chewing, and don't get too close to the works. It felt controlled, particularly in contrast with the atmosphere of the ground floor. Some visitors tried to turn around and go back to the fun part. But the interaction with the scripted guards might have been enough to encourage visitors to note the boredom on the real guards' faces, to think about what rules they could or should break.

If you break the rules, please do it unnoticed.

If you are planning to take a risk,

hour in the main hall to socialize all to-
please consider
together.
ll to socialize all together
meet at every half full hour in the main
hall to

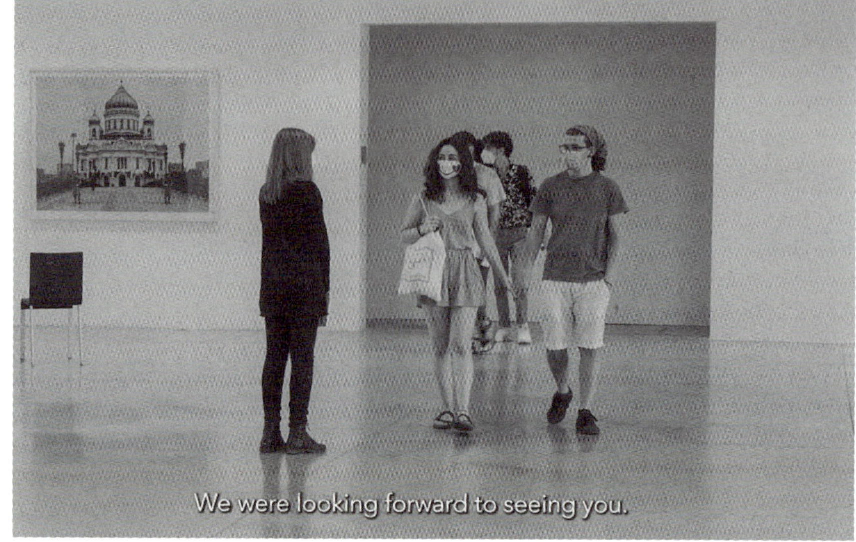

We were looking forward to seeing you.

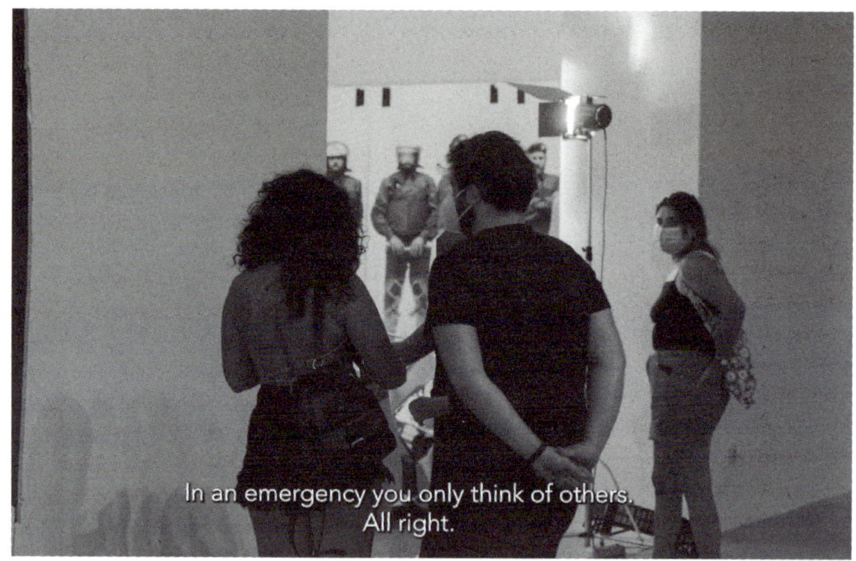

In an emergency you only think of others.
All right.

gether.   If you break the rules,

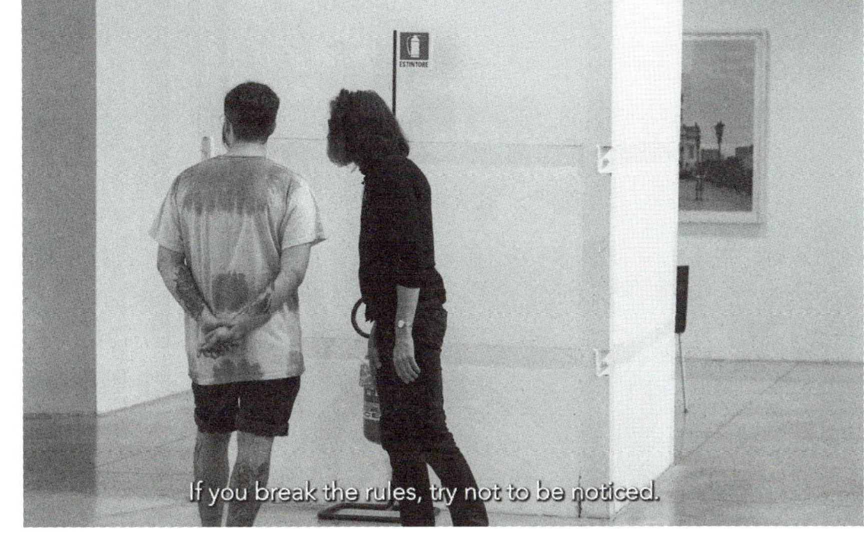

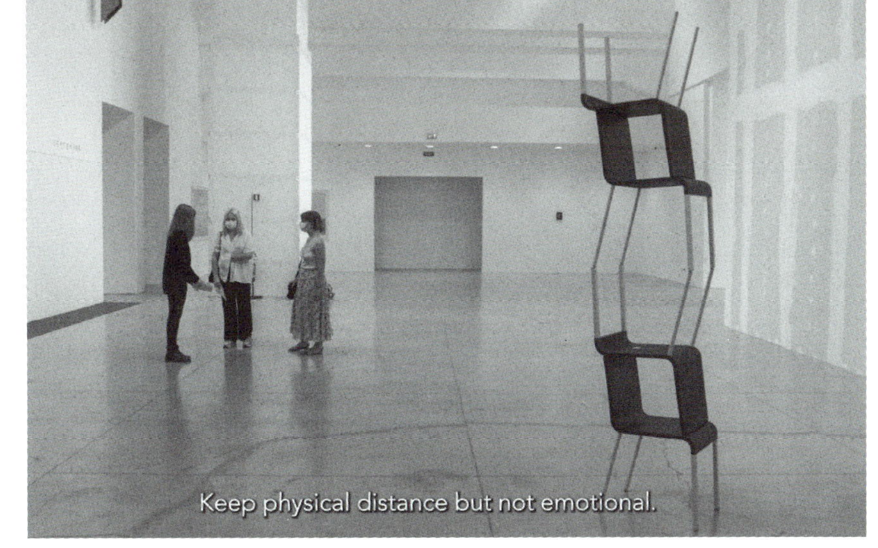

please do it unnoticed.   If you are planning

to take a risk, please involve me.

The guards

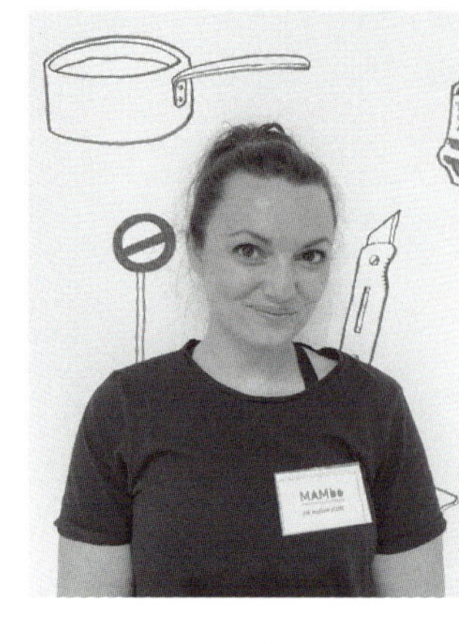 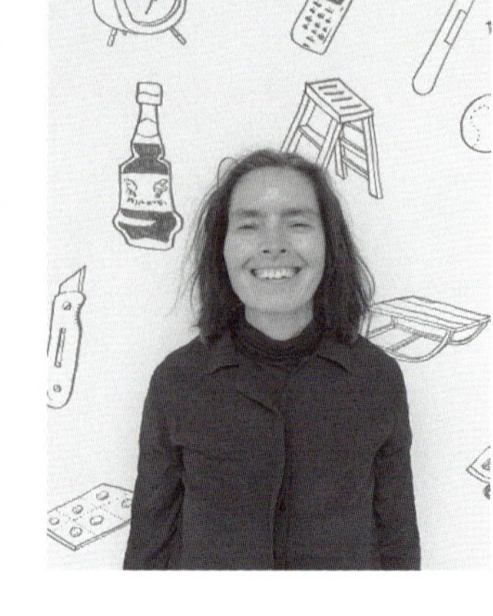 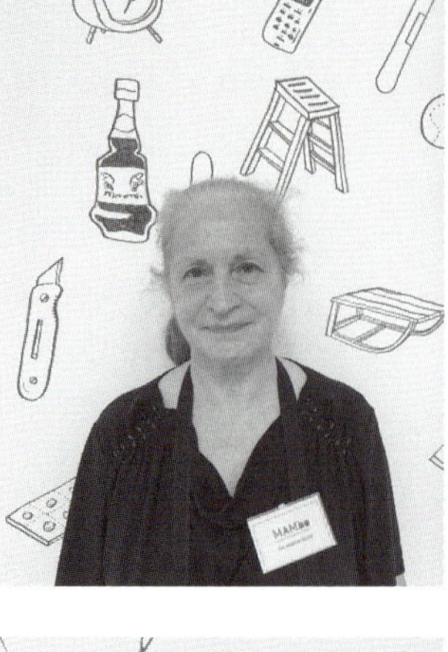

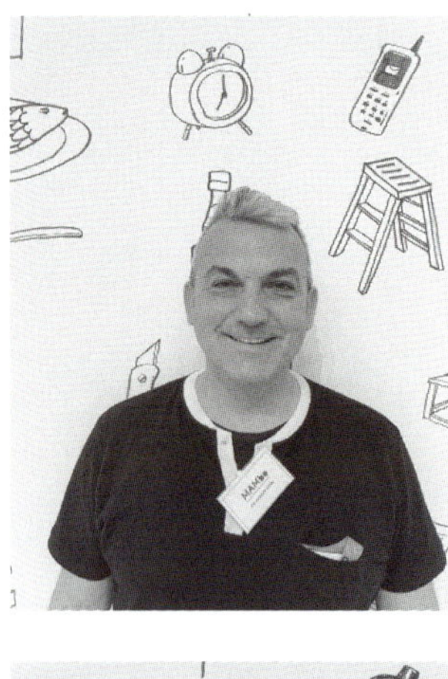 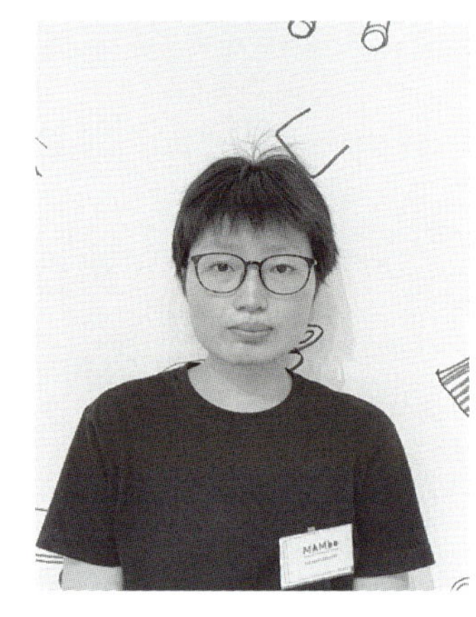 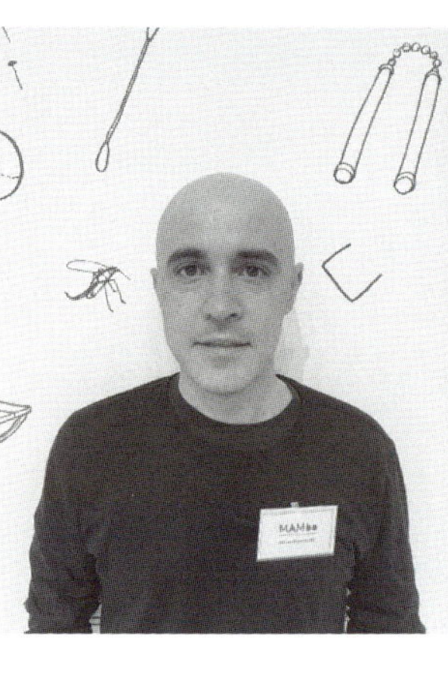

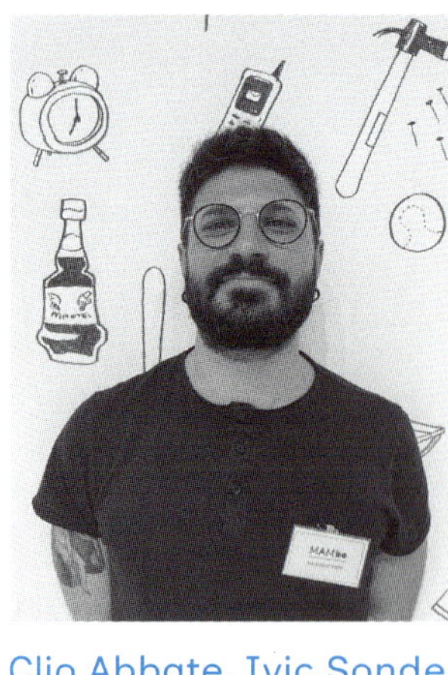 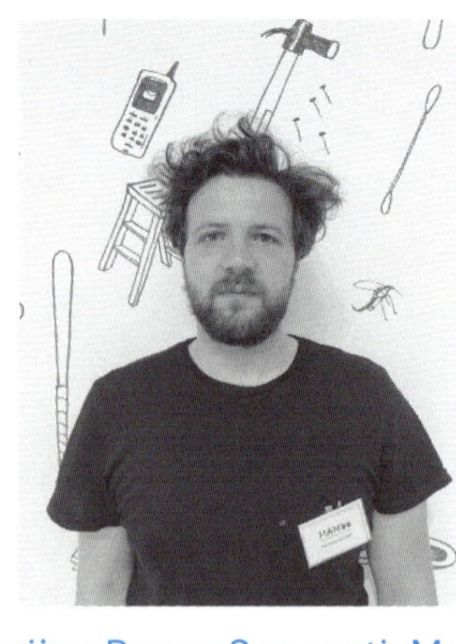 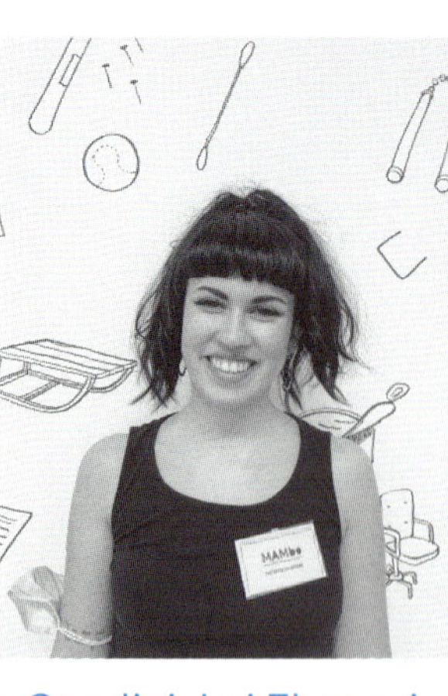

Clio Abbate, Ivic Sondermeijer, Renza Saccenti, Matteo Gandini, Lai Zhengyi, Fabio Cutraro, Giacomo Mogini, Tommaso Pioli and Elena de Robertis

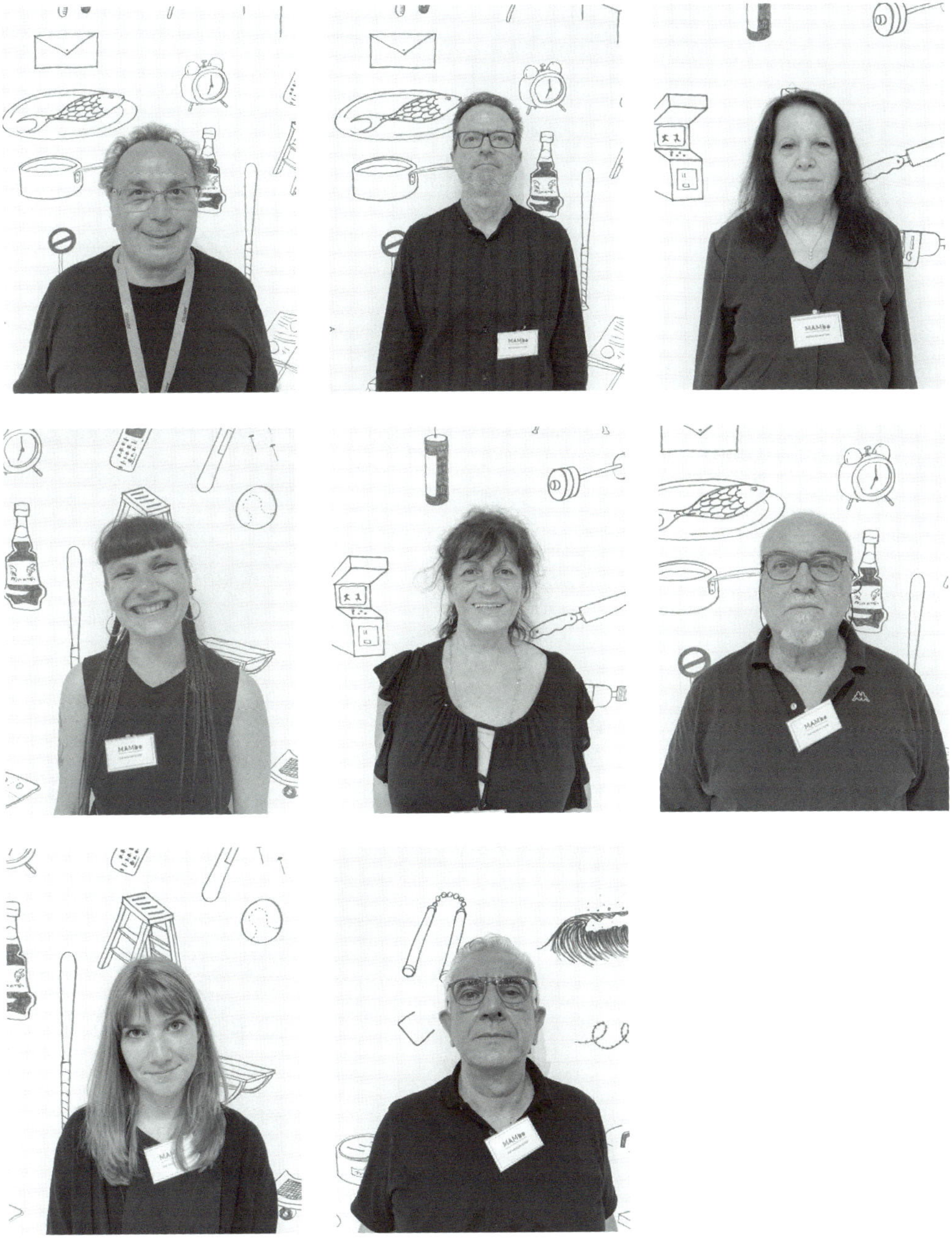

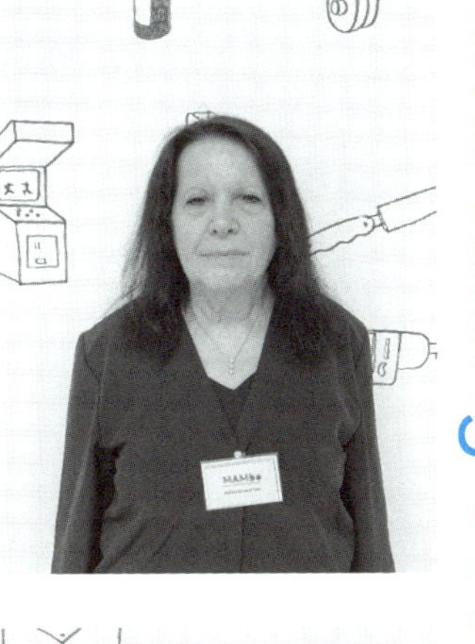
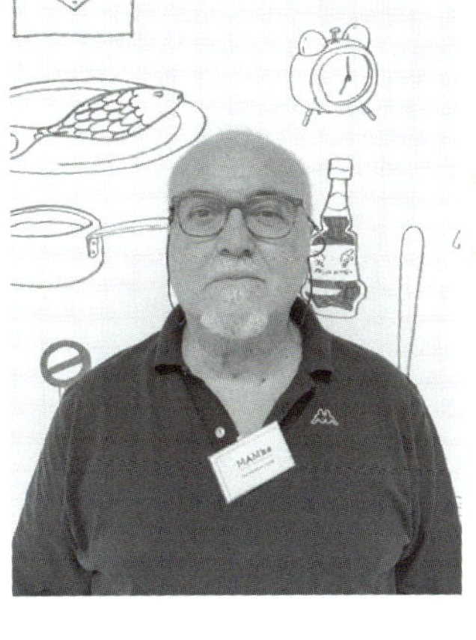
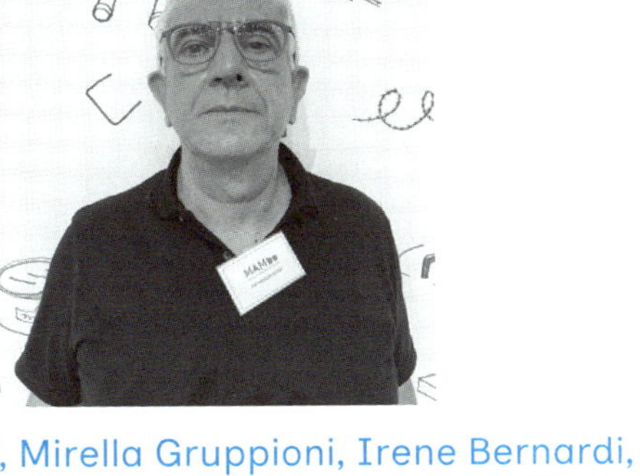

Vito Romano, Piero Tacconi, Mirella Gruppioni, Irene Bernardi, Clotilde Gallotta , Sergio Pajetti, Paola Spagnulo and Camillo Arlotti
Others, not pictured:
Alfredo Pellecchia, Donatella Tasini, Francesco Ruggeri and Loris Alessandri

mind taking over my position for 5 minutes? take

an unusual position in space.

please consi-

together.

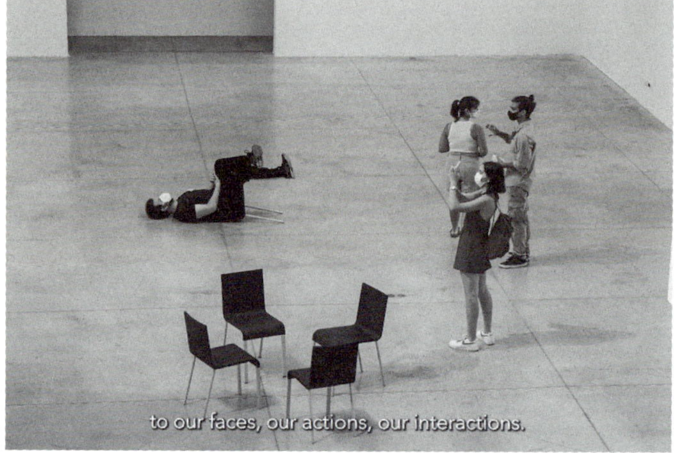

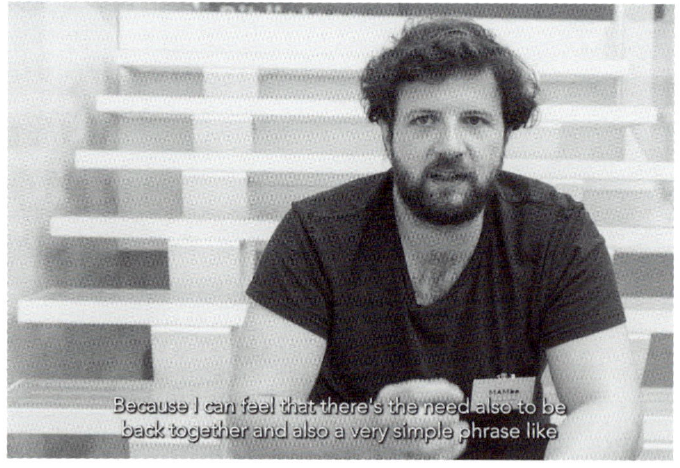

hall to socialize all togi-

...gether. if you break the rules, please do it unnoticed. if you are plan-ning to take a risk, please involve me.

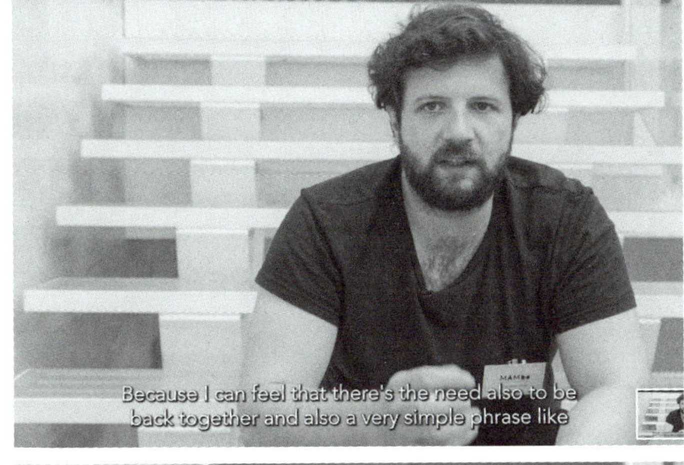

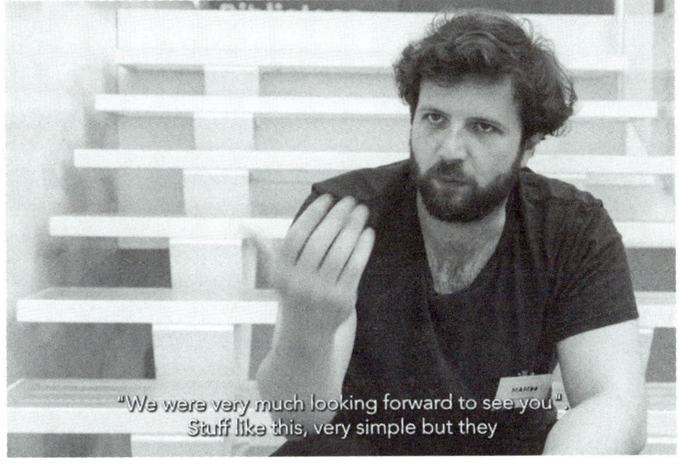

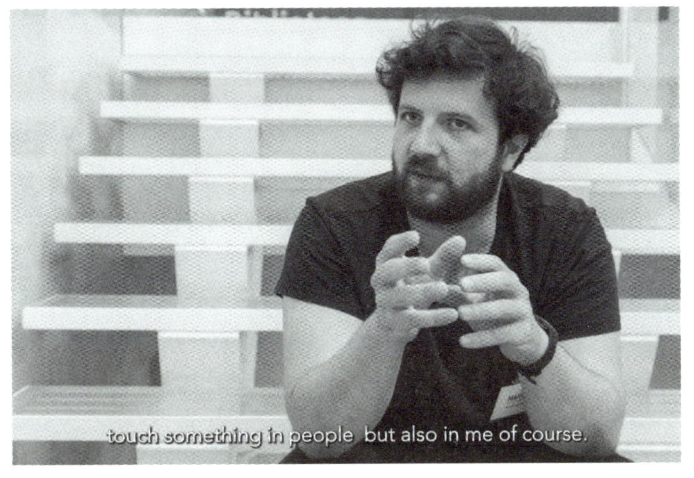

der that your safety is our priority.

draw "string drawings" and engage

exhibition.

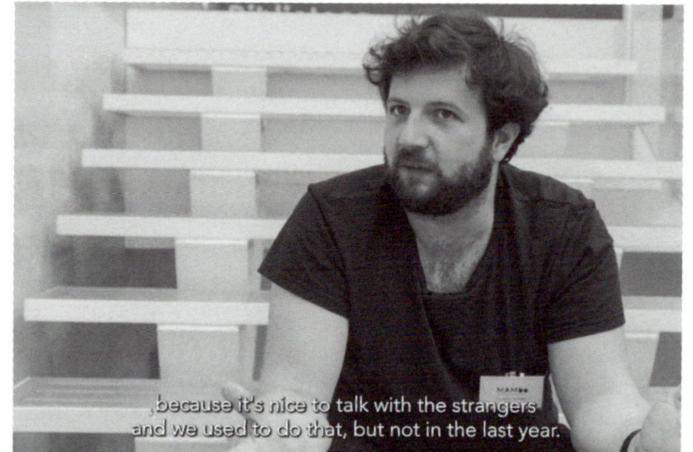

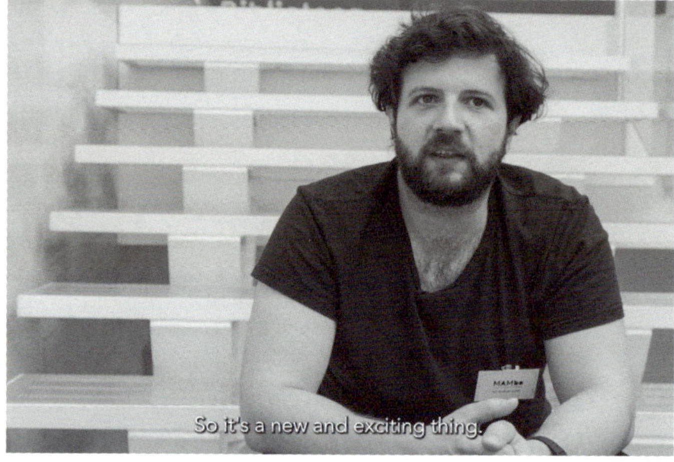

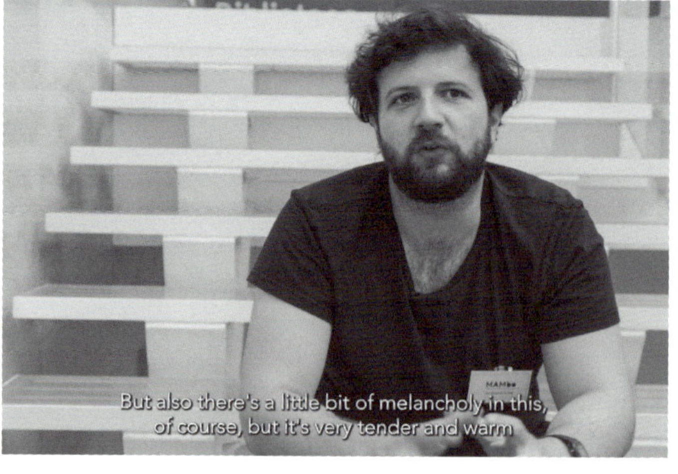

please remember me as part of this

would you mind taking over my position for 5 minutes?

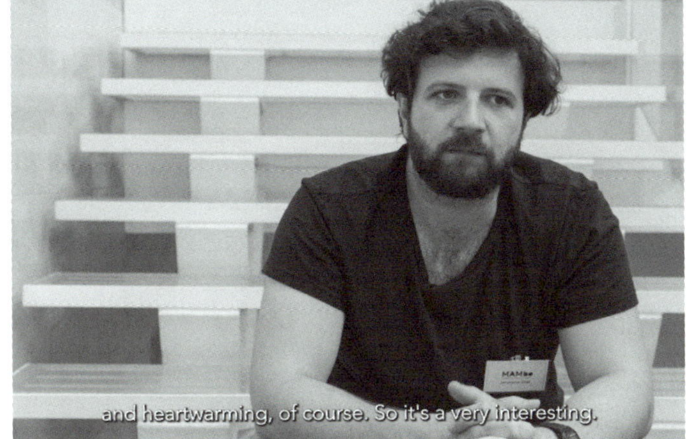

take an unusual po-
sition in space.

in my name is ....

and engage visitors in the activity.

if you are planning to

please do it unnoticed.

ALDO GIANNOTTI

THE
MUSEUM
SCORE

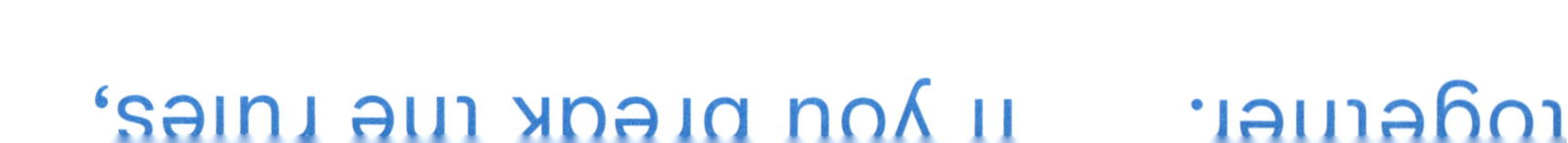
together.   if you break the rules,

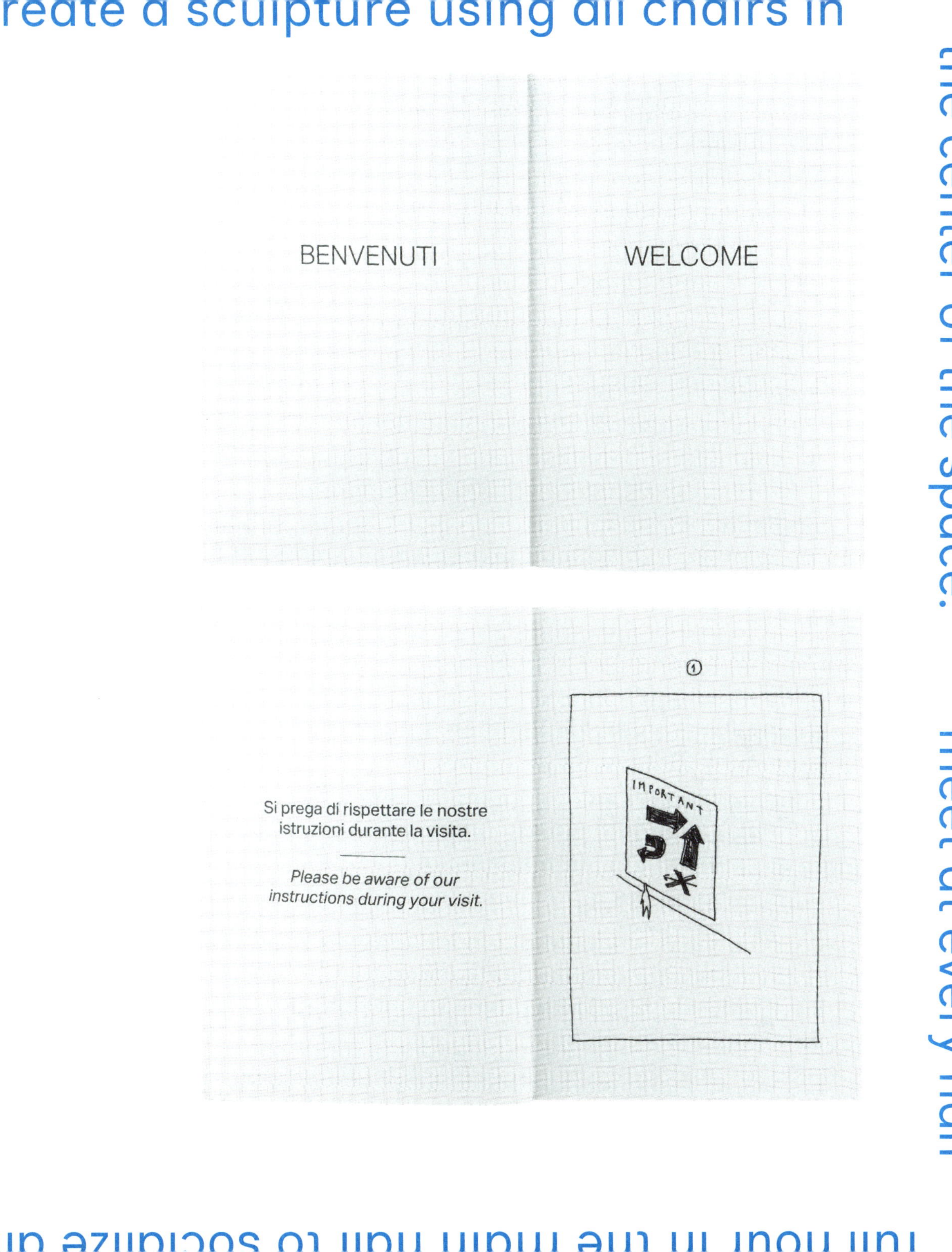

BENVENUTI

WELCOME

Si prega di rispettare le nostre
istruzioni durante la visita.

———

*Please be aware of our
instructions during your visit.*

Salve, mi chiamo ....
Sarò responsabile della sua
sicurezza durante la visita
di questa mostra.

————————

Hi, my name is ....
I will be in charge of your safety
during this exhibition.

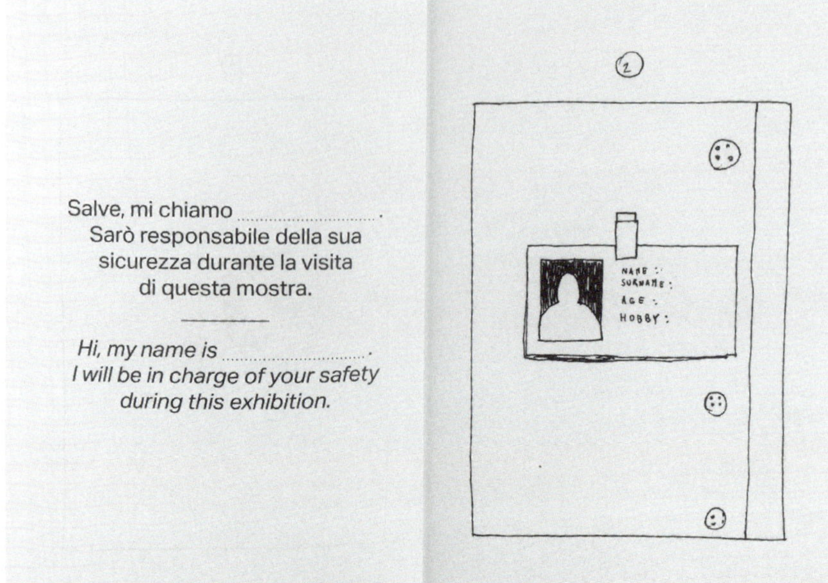

Non vedevamo l'ora di vederla.

————————

We were very much looking
forward to your visit.

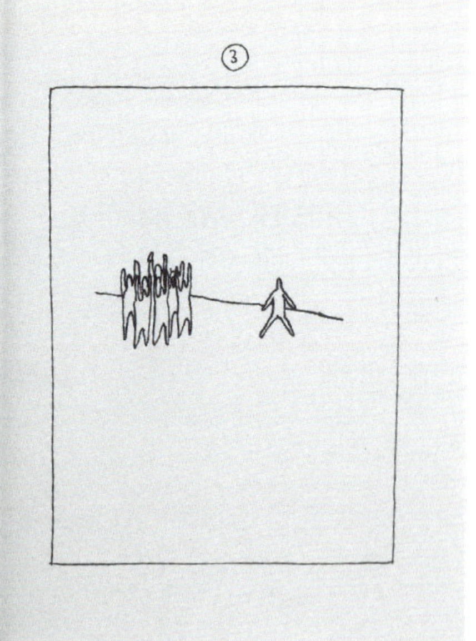

The restless gatekeepers, from Aldo Giannotti's Safe and Sound at MAMbo in Bologna

By Ivan Carozzi

Sitting on a regional train, a couple of days after visiting Aldo's Giannotti's exhibition at the MAMbo museum in Bologna, I discovered a photo on Instagram of a page from *The Last Landing*, a book by Hisham Matar. It is worth transcribing a passage, not only because the lines retrace the train of thought that each of us might have experienced while wandering through a museum, but because what Matar writes, with great calm and precision, could be an ideal epigraph for the Giannotti exhibition. The title of the chapter is "The Keepers of the Museum":

> "The rooms of the art gallery were mostly empty [...] The only stable presence was the museum guards. Most of them were women and they seemed to share something substantial, as if they were part of the same state of mind, united by the same emotional thread. Perhaps it is their loneliness that makes them seem that way, or perhaps all museum guards, no matter how busy the rooms are, feel that they are alone, standing or sitting, usually in a doorway, going about their working days observing halls that are constantly emptying out, where people arrive and

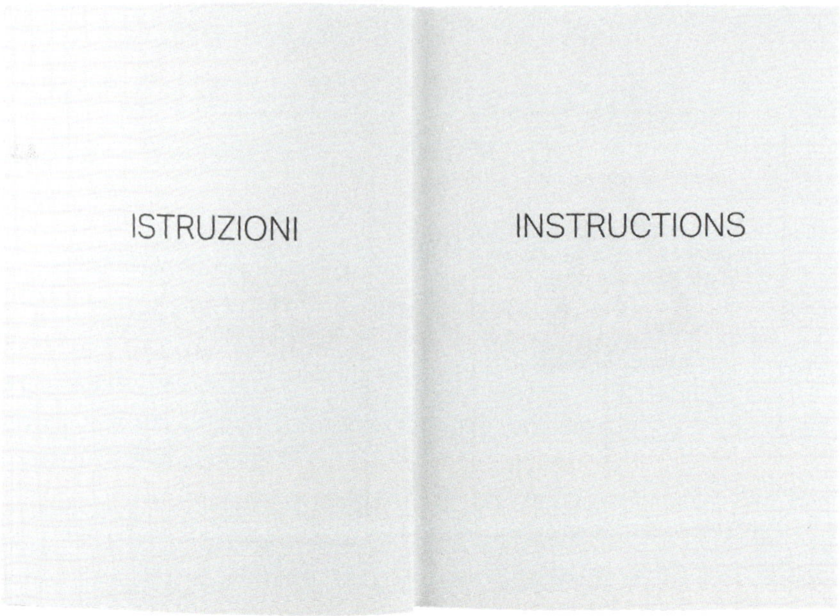

ISTRUZIONI

INSTRUCTIONS

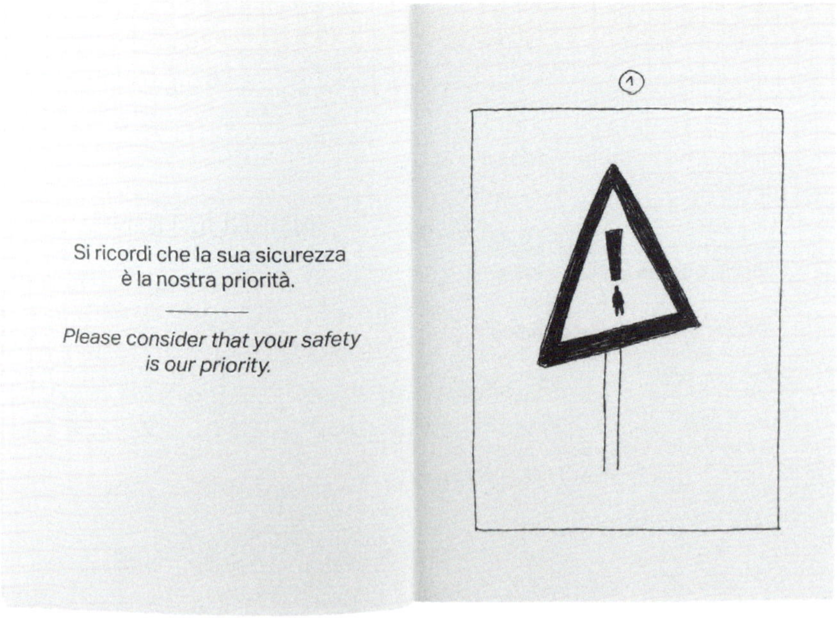

Si ricordi che la sua sicurezza
è la nostra priorità.

———

*Please consider that your safety
is our priority.*

almost immediately continue on to see something else, or to go to lunch, or simply to resume their lives. Don't we get the impression that these figures, in all the museums of the world, share the same secret regret, as if they had been disappointed by all of us?"

Giannotti involves those who work and spend time amidst the museum walls: the museum guards. A dialogue and a relationship develops between the artist and the guards, which takes the form of an illustrated booklet, *The Museum Score*. The guards have the opportunity to browse through the manual, which features images and phrases printed in a font size similar to that of Facebook cards. They select from a range of possible actions and gestures, along with helpful phrases and formulas for engaging with visitors. For example, the phrase "Would you mind holding my spot for five minutes?" prompts the attendant to step aside, possibly for a restroom break or a phone call, and a visitor temporarily takes their place.

Perhaps, as they become integrated into the exhibition project, the guards experience a newfound sense of freedom and expression, shedding the "loneliness" and "secret regret" mentioned by Matar. In this context, you might encounter a room attendant sitting cross-legged on the floor, singing, or playfully overturning the plastic chair they typically occupy for hours. The enigmatic quality, seen in the photos of the Castello di Rivoli roomkeepers, persists even with the uniforms designed by Alessandro Michele of

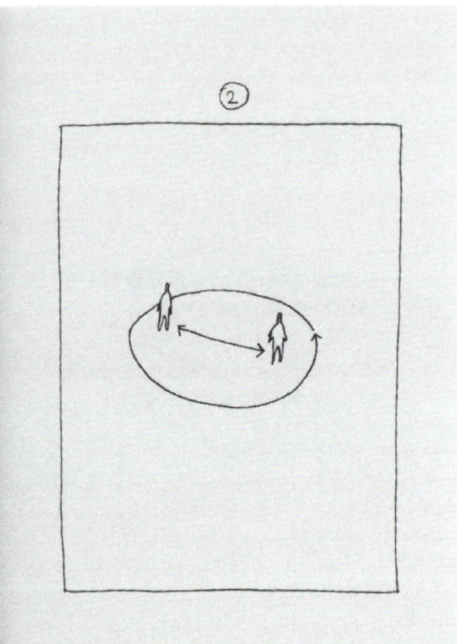

Si prega di mantenere la distanza
fisica, ma non quella emotiva.

————

*Please keep physical distance,
but not emotional.*

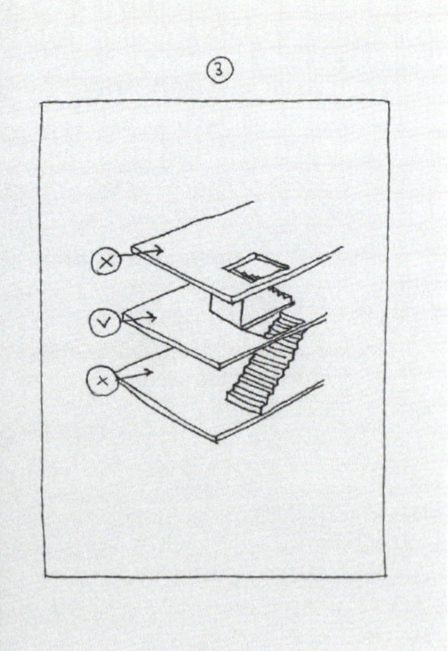

Il posto più sicuro di questo
edificio è al secondo piano.

————

*The safest place in this building is
on the second floor.*

Gucci. However, in this latter case, the roomkeepers appear more passive, as if emptied and used, while the sage green uniform and Gucci aesthetics evoke images reminiscent of the corridors of asylums from the past.

I approached some of the MAMbo guards to strike up a conversation and took the opportunity to inquire about their professional backgrounds, their connection with art, and their experiences with *Safe and Sound.*

Ivic: *I was born in Rotterdam, and I earned my degree in European Studies from the Faculty of Arts at the University of Amsterdam. In 1998, I relocated to Bologna as a guest of a friend. It didn't take long for me to secure a job as a translator. Subsequently, after a brief internship in the consultancy sector, I began working as an economic and social research assistant on behalf of an institute in the Emilia-Romagna Region. In the following years, I assumed the role of assistant manager in the agricultural research sector. Both institutes underwent reorganization, prompting me to enroll in a regional course for tour operators.*
In 2007, I joined the team at MAMbo. A cooperative was actively seeking individuals with degrees, and my profile matched their requirements perfectly. I had just completed my studies at that time.

I've been working as a guard for approximately six years. My duties include checking tickets, overseeing exhibition spaces and artworks, welcoming visitors, offering

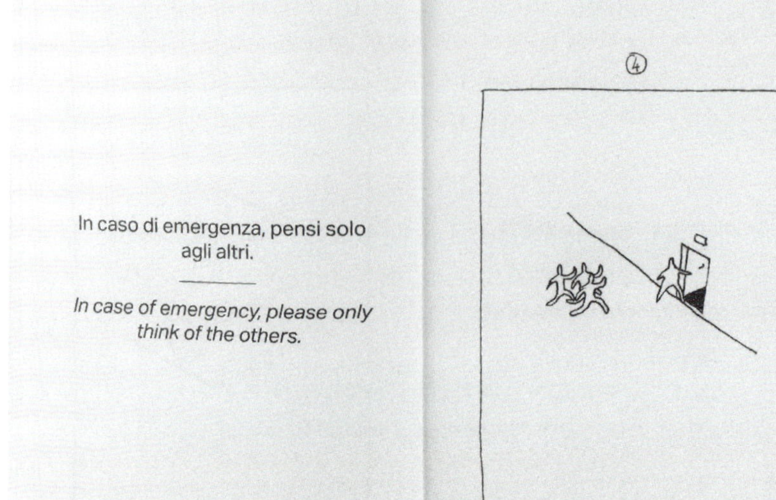

In caso di emergenza, pensi solo
agli altri.

———

*In case of emergency, please only
think of the others.*

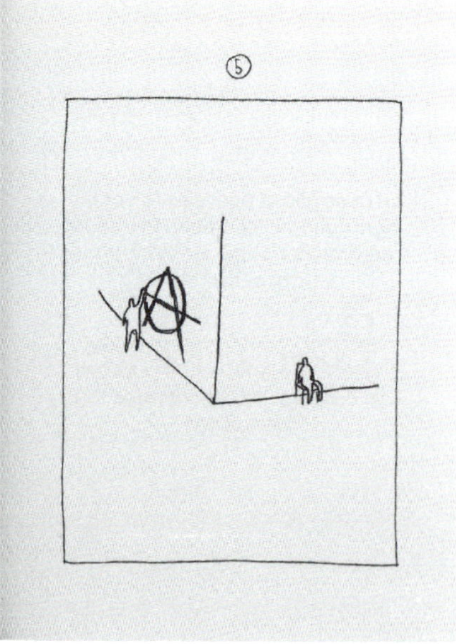

Se infrange le regole, cerchi di
non farsi notare.

———

*If you break the rules, please do it
unnoticed.*

information about the exhibition layout, the artworks, services, and the museum's activities. It's a role that doesn't demand any specific skills, apart from language proficiency and the ability to be attentive to people. The work tends to be somewhat static, passive, and at times, monotonous. Passing the time can be challenging, and on days with very few visitors, it feels like time stands still. Providing assistance and information is a welcome relief when visitors ask for it. I miss the social interaction, the dynamism, and engaging with the public, as well as the camaraderie of teamwork.

In the winter of 2020, the management approached me to participate in a project led by a new artist, Giannotti. Aldo was seeking guards for interviews, and I was selected because of my long tenure at MAMbo since its inception. It was an honor to be chosen. During the interview process, I noticed the questions were quite unique, and it became evident that this was a special project.

Now, I'm a performer, actively involved in the exhibition. It's a fantastic opportunity. As a performer, I take on a leading role in the exhibition. We play a crucial part in its operation, in itself becoming an integral component of the exhibition. We enrich the visitors' experiences with our presence. It's gratifying to be able to evoke emotions, make connections through the power of gaze, movements, and words. People are often surprised, amused, and sometimes even a bit intimidated.

Le consiglio di ricordarsi il volto di ogni guardia del museo in questo edificio. Potrebbe avere bisogno del loro aiuto più tardi.

—————

I advise you to remember the face of every museum guard in this building. You might need their help later.

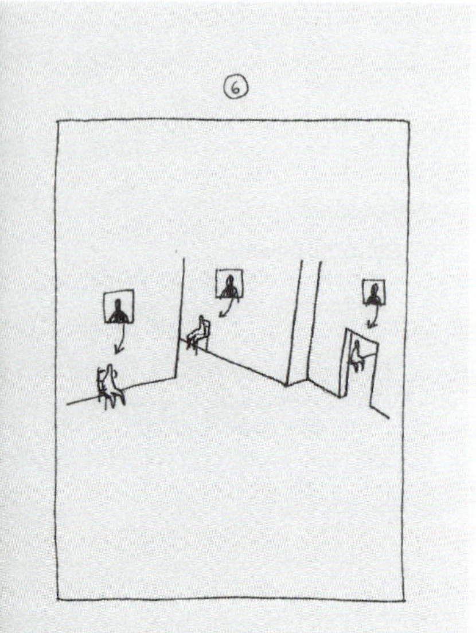

Salve, mi chiamo ....
La prego di ricordarsi di me nell'ambito di questa mostra.

—————

Hi, my name is ....
Please remember me as part of this exhibition.

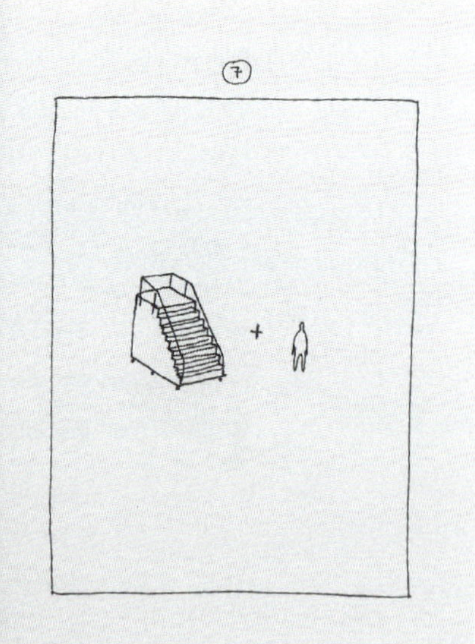

ne center of the space.   meet at

Giacomo: *I'm 33 years old, from the Marche province. I completed my undergraduate studies in Modern Literature in Urbino, and then I relocated to Bologna, where I've been living for the past 5 years. Besides having held various jobs, I also attended a couple of courses in the HR sector and a two-year comic screenwriting course at The Sign Academy in Florence. For a while, I divided my time between Bologna and Florence, which was demanding but highly stimulating. I collaborated with collectives and small comic book publishers, but everything changed with the pandemic. I'm currently working as a Museum Services Officer for the Giannotti exhibition at MAMbo.*

I don't really have a background as a guard. This is my first assignment, though it's not precisely a guard role but more of a performer. However, I had the chance to observe the work of the attendants in MAMbo's permanent collection. It strikes me as a challenging job, different from the labor of a warehouse worker or a researcher who studies twelve hours a day. The difficulty here lies in the slow passage of time. When you're tasked with monitoring a place without interaction, minutes feel like hours. I'm not sure how one can do this job for an extended period, but I imagine it requires great psychological balance. The privilege of working in a museum might not fully compensate for the boredom, especially when you don't have an active and concrete role as a guide or mediator but only exchange minimal information with visitors. Establishing a positive relationship with colleagues and being proactive and willing

every half full hour in the main hall to socialize

all together.   if you break the rules,

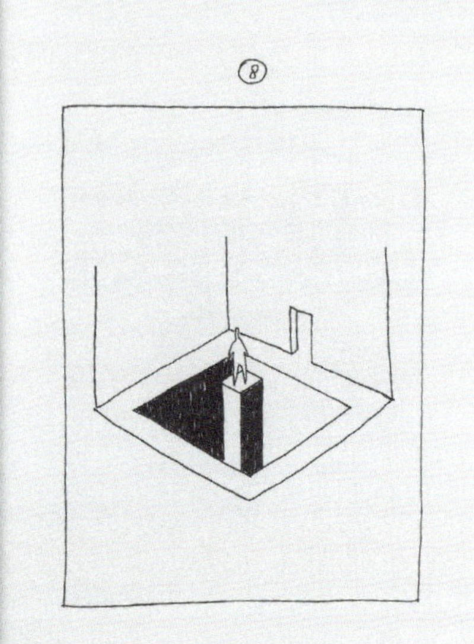

La posizione più sicura è al centro della stanza.

———

The safest position is in the center of the space.

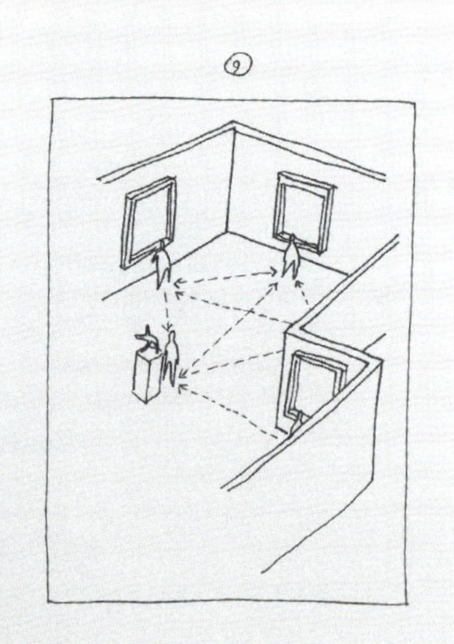

Si prega di cercare di mantenere sempre un metro di distanza dagli altri visitatori, al contempo avvicinandosi il più possibile alle opere d'arte.

———

Please try at all times to keep one meter of distance to the other visitors while getting as close as possible to the artworks.

to take on more responsibilities to diversify one's work are essential.

As for Aldo's exhibition... Initially, I was somewhat hesitant about an experiment that took me out of my comfort zone. It required getting involved and stepping into a character's shoes, something I had never done and for which I did not have a natural aptitude. However, I came to see it as a highly formative experience, especially through contact with other professionals involved.

It took me a while to grasp Aldo's exhibit. At first, I wasn't overly impressed. My perspective began to change as I listened to colleagues' impressions and interpretations and observed the enthusiastic reactions of visitors. There's a small room, my favorite, where a video of a crowd watching a fireworks display in Valencia is projected on one wall. The room exudes an incredible atmosphere, with its walls covered in black soundproofing material and a soft carpeted floor. During quiet moments, I like to sit there, relishing the room's intimacy and observing every individual, couple, or group watching the fireworks. I enjoy watching their reactions, interactions, and imagining their conversations. Perhaps there's a budding romance between two teenagers —one appearing disinterested while the other seeks their attention. But in my view, they may be sharing something precious.

Se ha intenzione di correre un
rischio, la prego di coinvolgermi.

———

*If you are planning to take a risk,
please involve me.*

⑩

Si invita a toccare tutto ciò che è
inorganico in questa mostra.

———

*You are welcome to touch
everything inorganic in this
exhibition.*

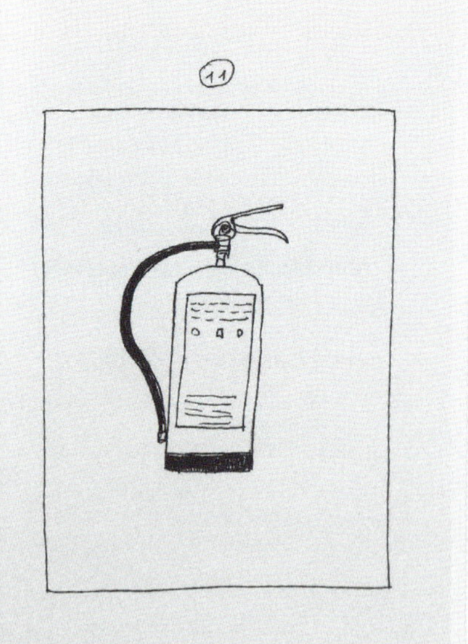

⑪

My relationship with museums, galleries, and art spaces is that of a curious and occasional visitor. I appreciate archaeological museums as much as contemporary art that manages to surprise me.

Clio: *I was born in Bologna and pursued studies in Nouveau Cirque and contemporary dramaturgy techniques. I work in the theater as an actress and acrobat, teach aerial acrobatics, write, read, and paint. I've always had an aversion to mere self-presentation. I believe that knowledge is most valuable when it's put into action and experienced. Otherwise, I feel self-conscious and I struggle to define myself without overjudging or underestimating. Additionally, I've often pondered why we tend to define ourselves primarily through our professions, neglecting other aspects of our identity. For my part, I can say that I'm inherently curious, enjoy observing, and personally find connecting with others fascinating. I'm passionate about body expressiveness, non-verbal communication, and the depths of psychology, both the dark and light aspects. I find the human being strange and captivating.*

I came to MAMbo as a volunteer, eager to contribute to a place I've always seen as a haven of peace, contemplation, sharing, and culture. Prior to this experience, I often thought to myself, "If I were a room attendant, I'd study the museum's works, engage with visitors to provide information, and seek to understand their perspectives." As a visitor, I greatly appreciated such attention, and when it

Non si faccia dire da nessuno
cosa fare.

———

*Don't let anyone tell you what to
do.*

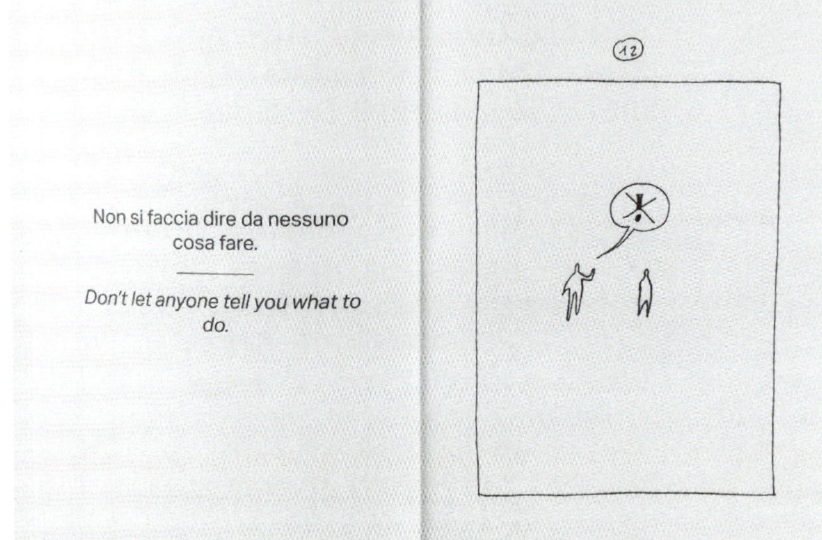

Le dispiacerebbe prendere il mio
posto per 5 minuti?

———

*Would you mind taking over my
position for 5 minutes?*

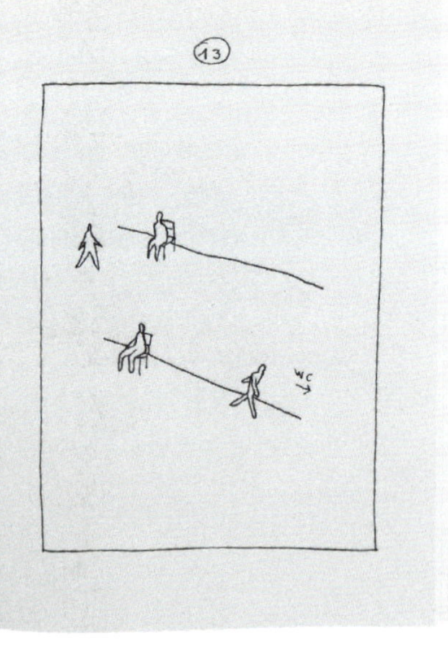

was lacking, I missed it. I firmly believe that it's people who make the difference, not the tasks they find themselves doing, while many may see it as monotonous work.

For Aldo's exhibition, I received a booklet called The Museum Score, which allowed me to choose from various actions and phrases to use when interacting with visitors. I find it stimulating to observe the amazed expressions on visitors' faces and the interactions we share. The real challenge lies in creating the right atmosphere.

The exhibition Safe and Sound prompts one to question, "What can I do with my freedom, and how can I use it if I feel like it?" There's no predetermined path. However, what's truly remarkable is the atmosphere, the level of attention, and the care. I'm delighted to be part of a collective effort that functions harmoniously.

One artwork from the exhibition struck a chord with me, Things that hurt me (a large wall designed by Giannotti). It rekindled a cascade of personal memories, making me reflect on the universal nature of pain. It made me realize that there are things that hurt both me and others in similar ways, and the gravity of pain can't be measured as more or less serious or important. When something hurts, it hurts, period.

Art has always been a presence in my family.
My mom painted, shared stories of artists, and took me to

mind taking over my position for 5 mi-

create a sculpture

sitors in the activity.

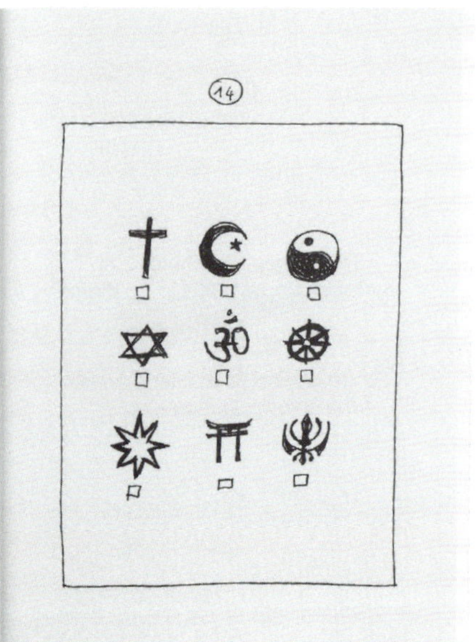

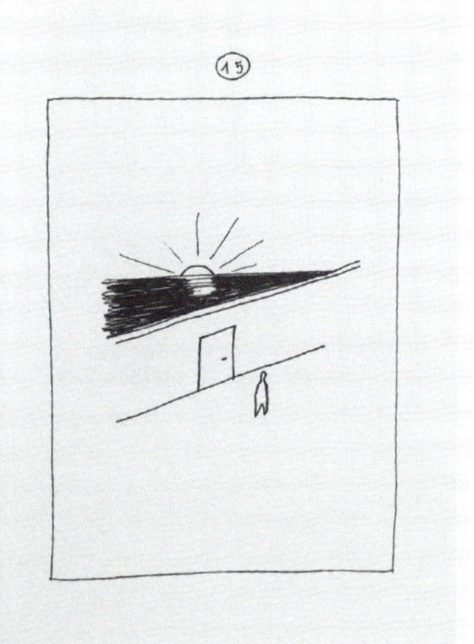

In caso di emergenza la prego di rivolgersi alla sua divinità, nel caso l'avesse.

———

In case of emergency please refer to your own god or goddess, if any.

Trovi una porta chiusa e si immagini il posto più sicuro dietro di essa.

———

Find a closed door and imagine the safest place behind it.

draw string drawings and engage viappreciate nature. My grandmother, on the other hand, had a deep passion for opera, music, and theater. This infusion of art into our lives has always been part of our cherished family experiences. My love for art has never waned; it's a vital nourishment for my mind and spirit. When I stand before a work of art, I often ask myself, "What do I feel? Does it move me? Does it speak to me?" From there, I embark on intricate inner journeys that sometimes drive me to the brink of obsession. Art is an infinite resource of inspiration and sustenance

Tommaso: I'm 31 years old. After earning a degree in Literature from the University of Pisa, I found myself in Bologna, where I made the decision to enroll in an actor training program at the Alessandra Galante Garrone Theater School.

While working as an actor, taking on the role of a guard is a novel profession for me. I've held various jobs that involved interacting with the public, ranging from waitstaff to bellboy and club security, but there's a distinct relationship with the dimension of time in this role. Listening to the tales of more seasoned colleagues, I understand that time tends to move slowly, and there's ample room for contemplation but limited interaction, as silence is typically maintained in a museum.

I was instantly enthused for Safe and Sound because the commitment required aligned with a multitude of skills I had already honed throughout my career. This includes

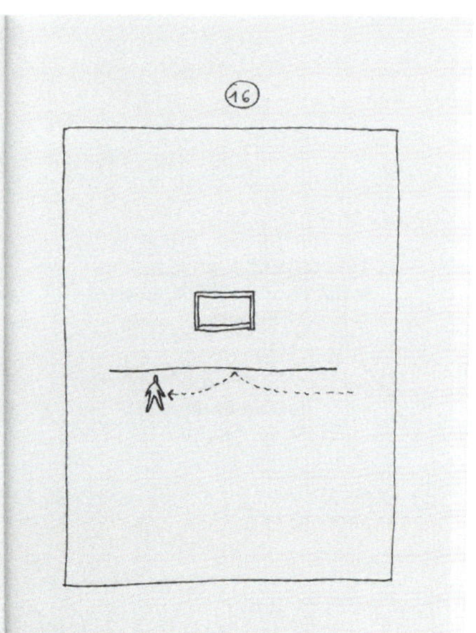

Si prega di fare tutto al contrario
per i prossimi 10 minuti.

———

*Please do everything backwards
for the next 10 minutes.*

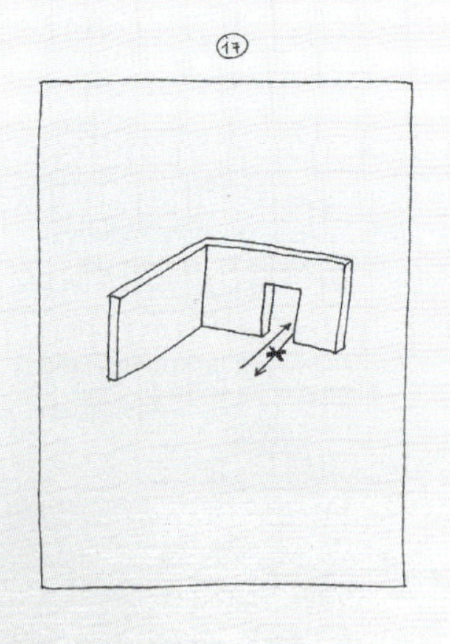

Una volta che lascia questa
stanza, non potrà più tornare
indietro.

———

*Once you exit this room you won't
be able to return.*

interacting with visitors, often in a playful and enigmatic manner, and utilizing my body as a form of expression, such as assuming unconventional positions within the exhibition space. The project places significant emphasis on energy, both mental and physical, that when collectively harnessed with colleagues, helps create that quirky, alienating yet inviting atmosphere—which I dare say is one of the aims of Aldo's work. I was struck by how this project delves into themes of closeness and distance, security and freedom; it carries a sense of irony, making us all feel smaller, and as a result, equal and united. The visitor is encouraged to engage, participate, and communicate. Witnessing people's reactions to our provocations is truly enjoyable, as there is a palpable desire for communication and play.

Cinema has always held a special place in my heart, and during my childhood, I was passionate about comics and drawing. In recent years, I've ventured into the world of theater, but music has been a constant presence in my life. On the other hand, my relationship with art history is somewhat complicated, possibly because my mother is an art history teacher, and I certainly wouldn't classify myself as an expert. However, if there's one form of art that excites me more than any other, it's undoubtedly comic art, understood in the broadest sense—art that makes people laugh and traverses a multitude of languages. Laughter has always been a prevalent element in my family, and from a young age, I viewed it as a means of connecting with others. Through laughter, I've learned many of the few things I know.

Non è permesso stare in silenzio nella stanza in cui si sta per entrare.

———

It is not allowed to be quiet in the room you are about to enter.

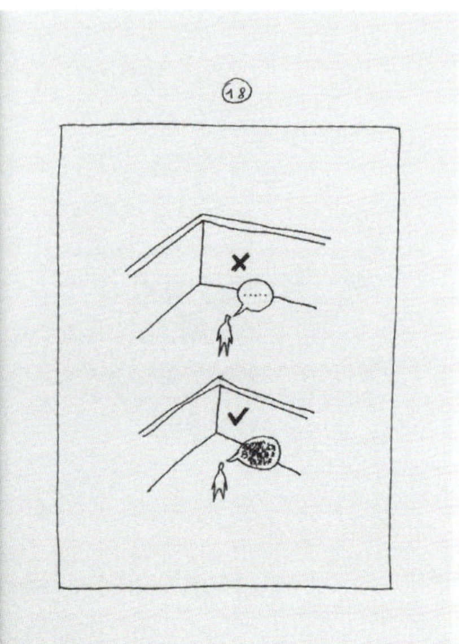

La prego di condividere la sua opinione su quello che ha visto con più persone possibili.

———

Please share your opinion of the show with as many people as possible.

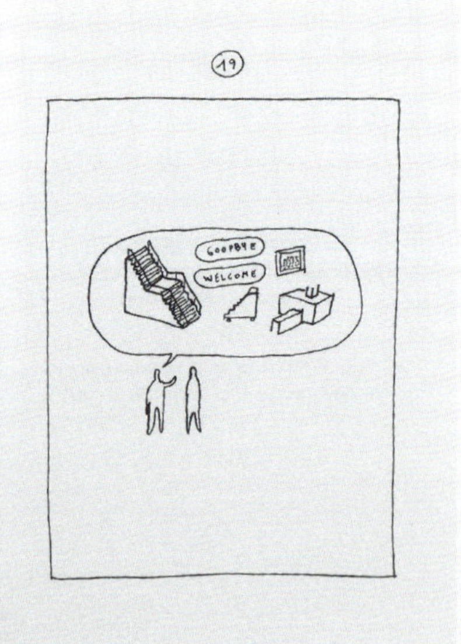

È consentito e perfino
incoraggiato correre all'interno
della sala espositiva.

———

*It is allowed and even encouraged
to run inside the exhibition hall.*

Lei è libero/libera di usare la mia
sedia per riposarsi in qualsiasi
momento.

———

*You are welcome to use my chair
to rest at any time.*

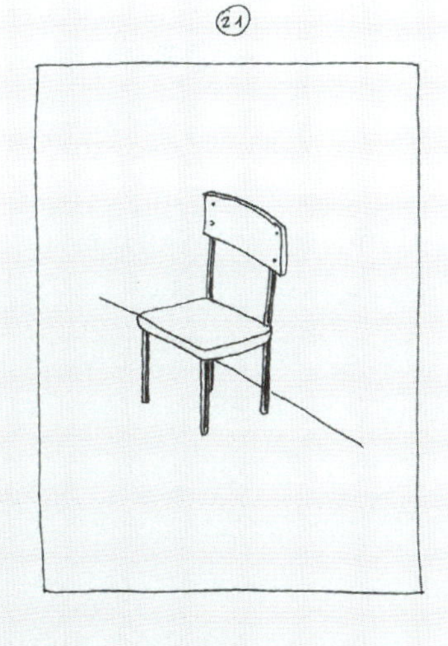

Non è permesso fare più di 1200 passi durante la visita di questa mostra.

——————

It is not allowed to take more than 1200 steps during the visit of this exhibition.

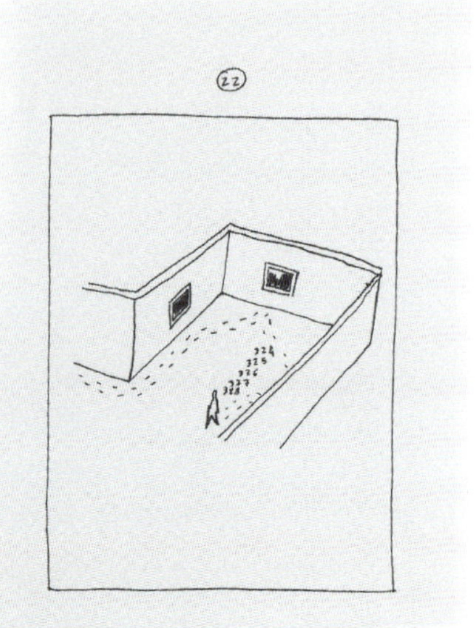

Si prega di camminare vicino alle pareti.

——————

Please walk close to the walls.

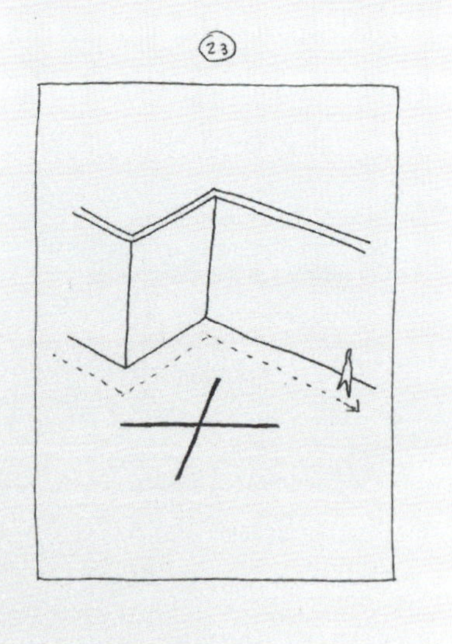

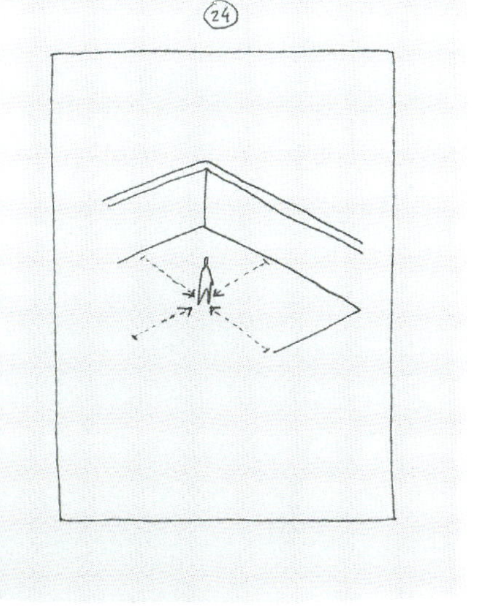

Si prega di provare a rimanere al centro di questa stanza.

———

Please try to stay in the center of the space.

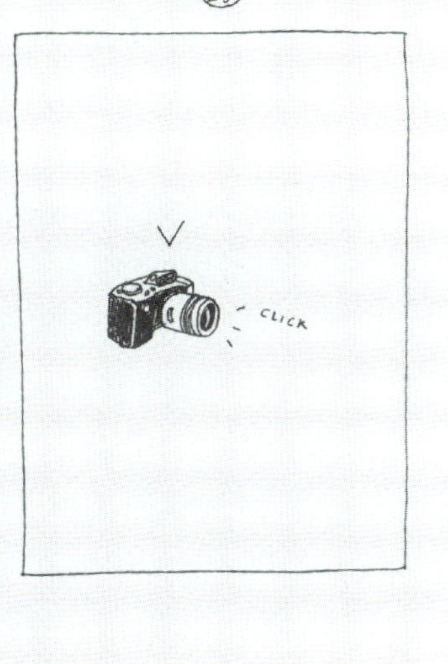

È vivamente consigliato scattare foto.

———

Taking pictures is highly recommended.

Si prega di taggare l'artista in ogni
foto che posta.

———

*Please hashtag the artist with
every picture you post.*

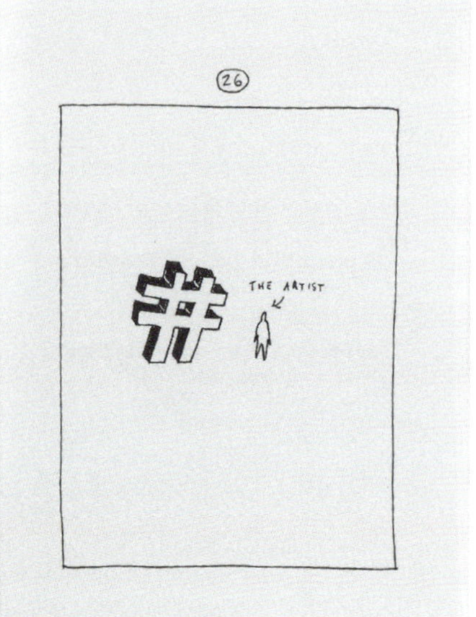

Si prega di immaginare questo
spazio senza il tetto.

———

*Please imagine this space without
the roof.*

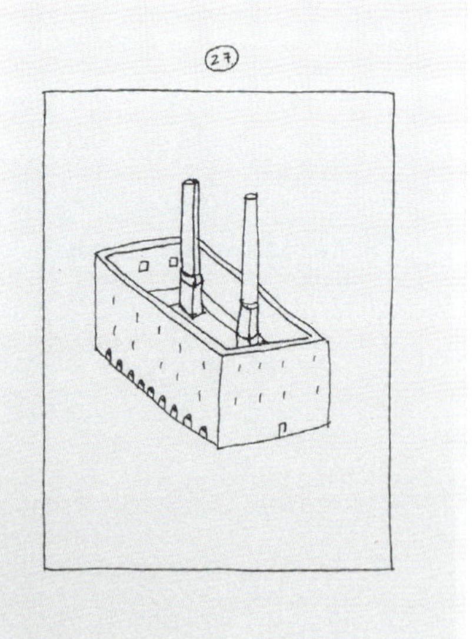

Se è emozionato/a da un'opera
d'arte specifica, gridi "yay"!

If you feel excited about a specific
art piece, shout "yay"!

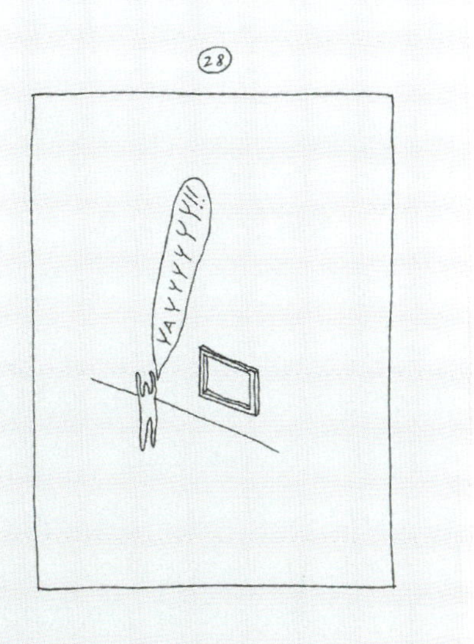

INTERATTIVO

INTERACTIVE

Mi è stato detto di mostrarle
la mia opera d'arte preferita
all'interno della mostra.

———

*I'm instructed to show you my
favorite piece in the exhibition.*

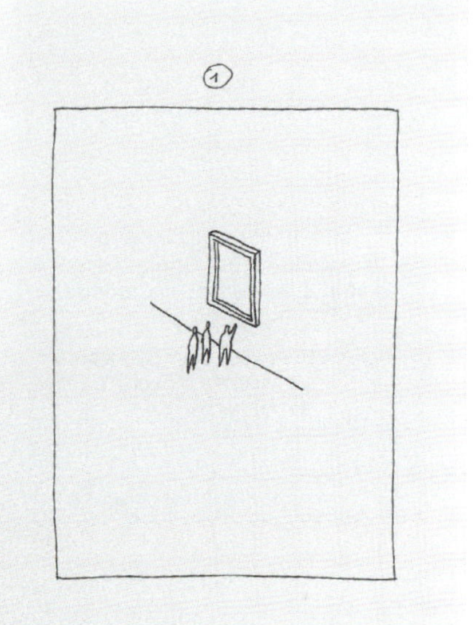

Mi è stato detto di venire
a guardare la sua opera d'arte
preferita all'interno della mostra.

———

*I'm instructed to come and watch
your favorite artwork
in the exhibition.*

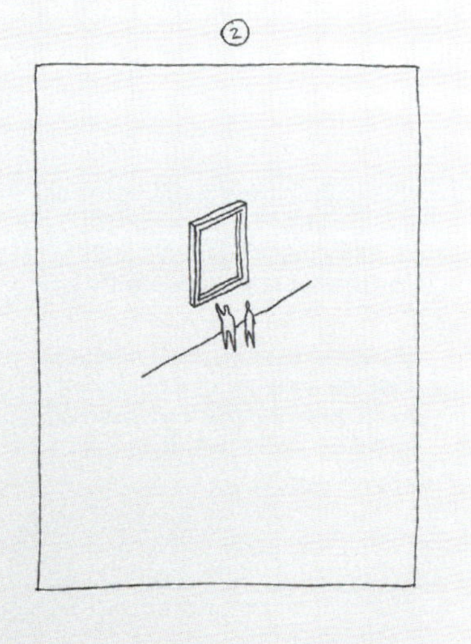

Si senta libero/a di chiedermi di
mostrarle tutte le uscite
di sicurezza dell'edificio in
qualsiasi momento della visita.

———

*Feel free to ask me to show you
all the emergency exits in this
building at any point of your visit.*

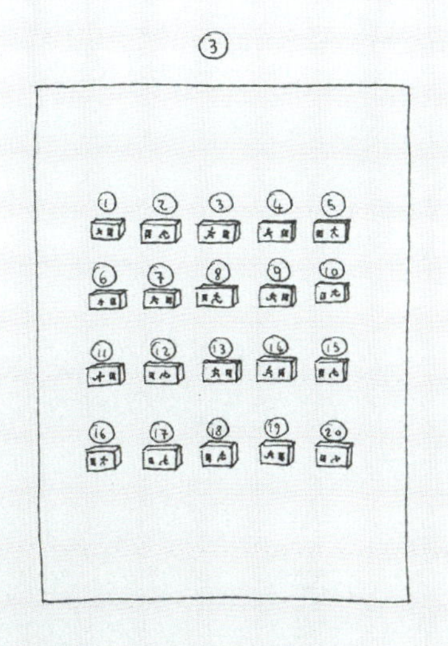

Se le rimane qualche domanda
sulla mostra, posso darle
il numero di telefono dell'artista.

———

*If you have any remaining
questions about the exhibition,
I can give you the artist's phone
number.*

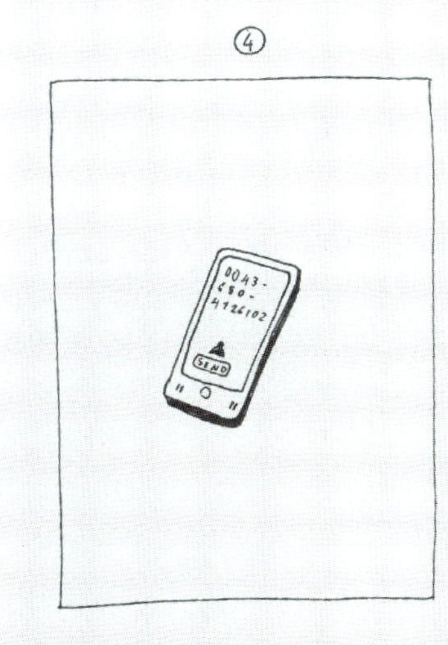

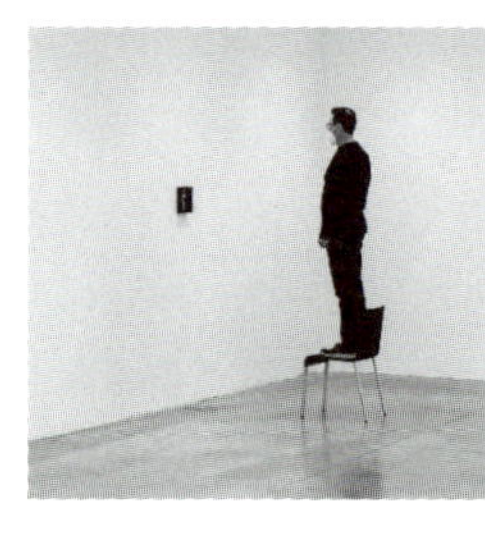

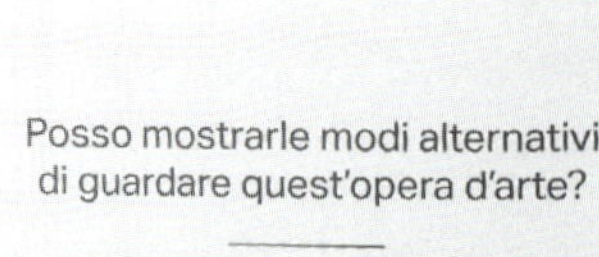

Posso mostrarle modi alternativi
di guardare quest'opera d'arte?

———

*May I show you alternative ways
to watch this artwork?*

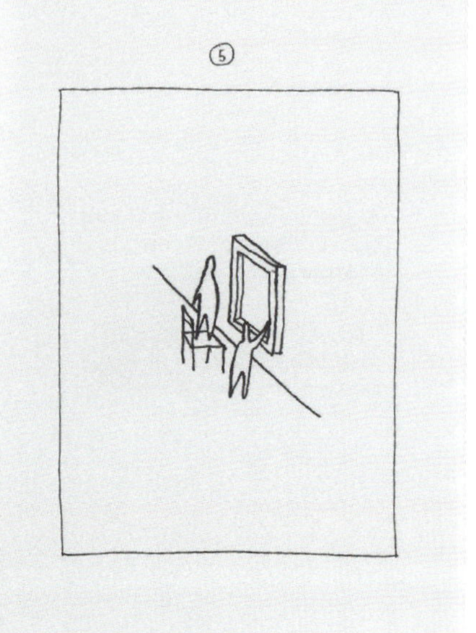

Vorrebbe aiutarmi a svolgere
questo compito? (il compito si
riferisce a "occupare il tempo")

———

*Would you like to assist me
executing this task? (the task
refers to the work 'filling time')*

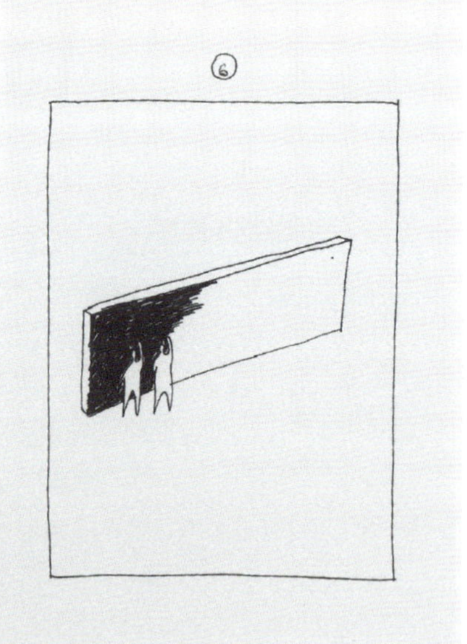

AZIONI

ACTIONS

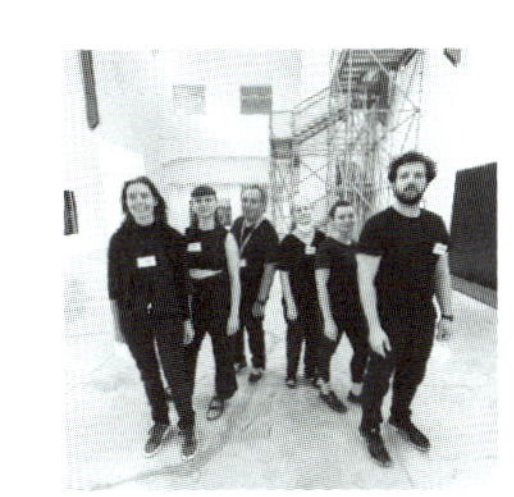

Allo scoccare di ogni ora, fatti trovare nella sala principale per socializzare tutti assieme.

Meet at every full hour in the main hall to socialize all together.

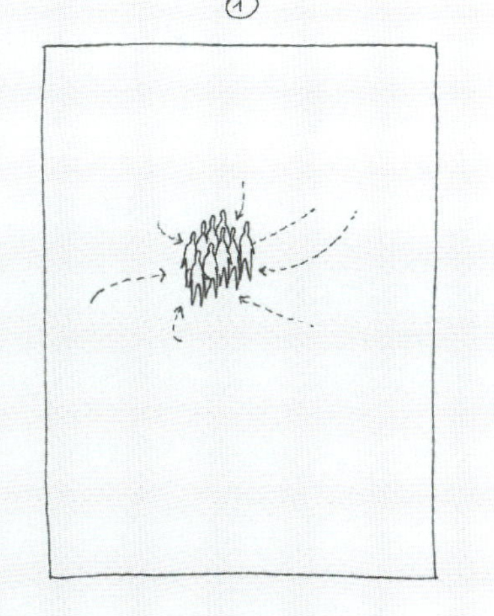

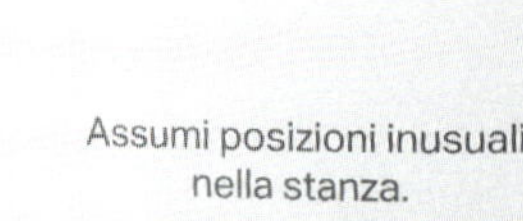

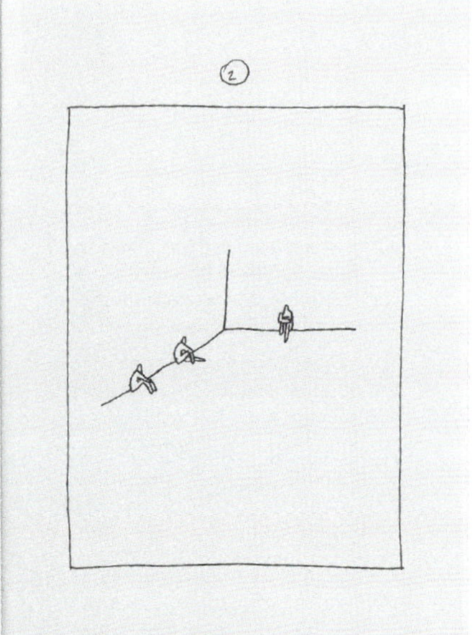

Assumi posizioni inusuali
nella stanza.

———

Take unusual positions in space.

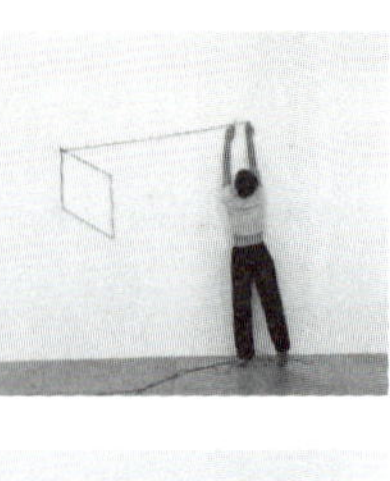

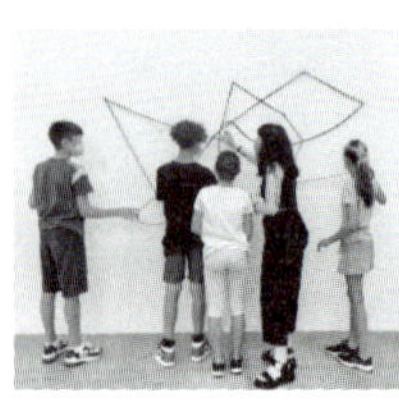

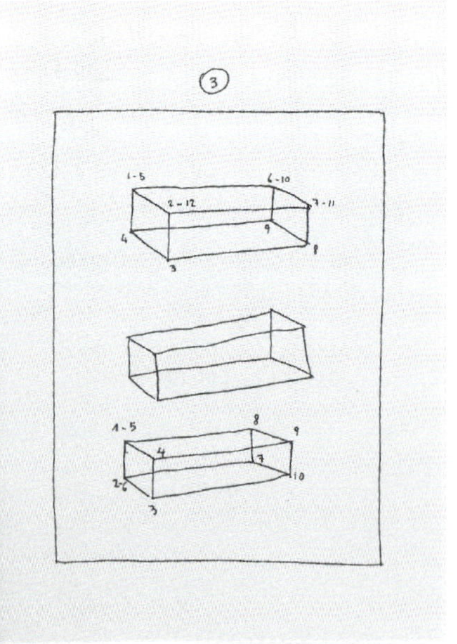

Crea una 'string art' (un disegno
fatto con fili di tessuto) e
coinvolgi i visitatori nell'attività.

———

Draw 'string drawings'
and engage visitors in the activity.

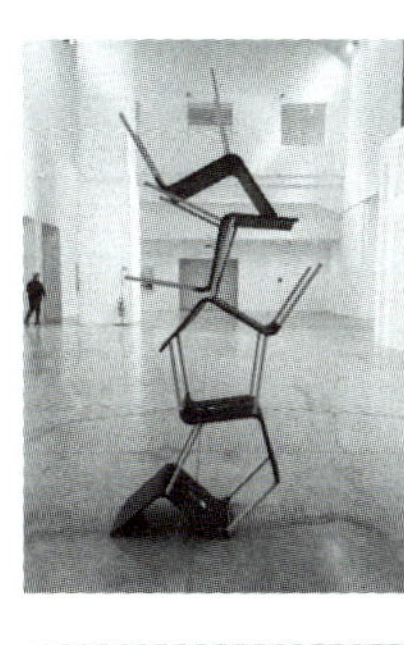

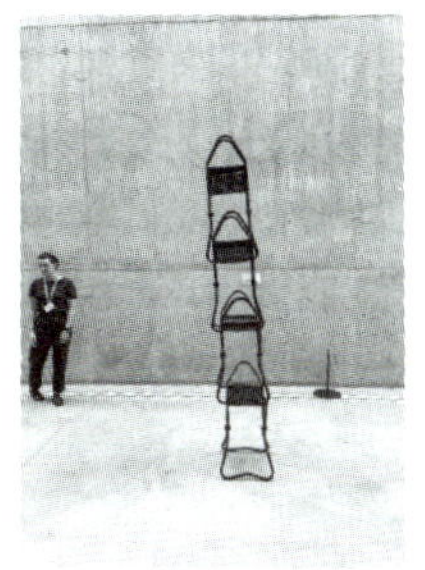

Crea una scultura al centro della stanza usando tutte le sedie.

Create a sculpture using all chairs in the center of the space.

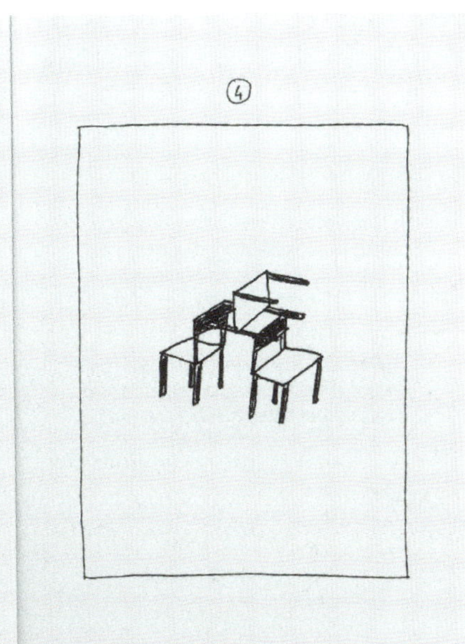

Una volta all'ora, cammina per tutta la mostra riproducendo un "mambo" con un sistema audio portatile.

Once per hour walk through the entire exhibition space equipped with a portable sound system, playing a "mambo".

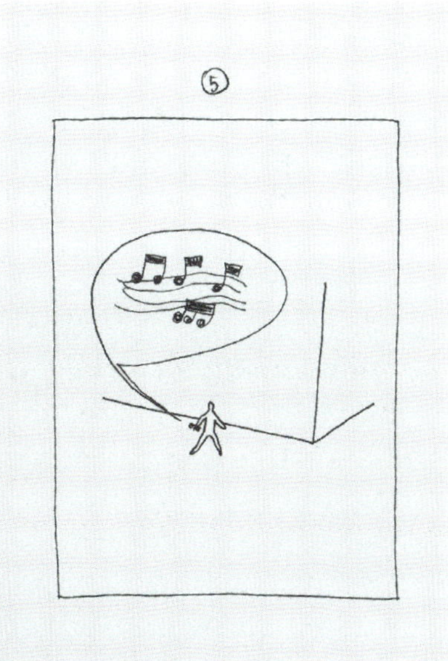

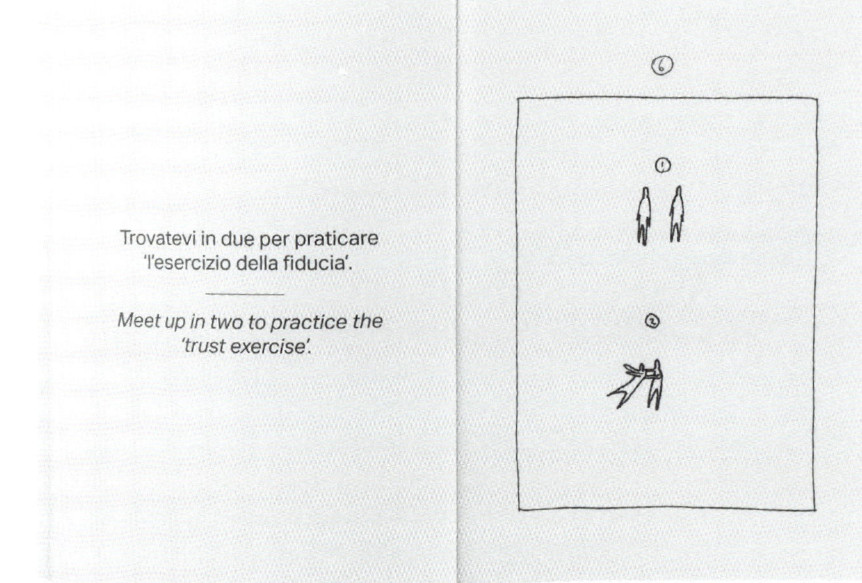

Trovatevi in due per praticare
'l'esercizio della fiducia'.

———

*Meet up in two to practice the
'trust exercise'.*

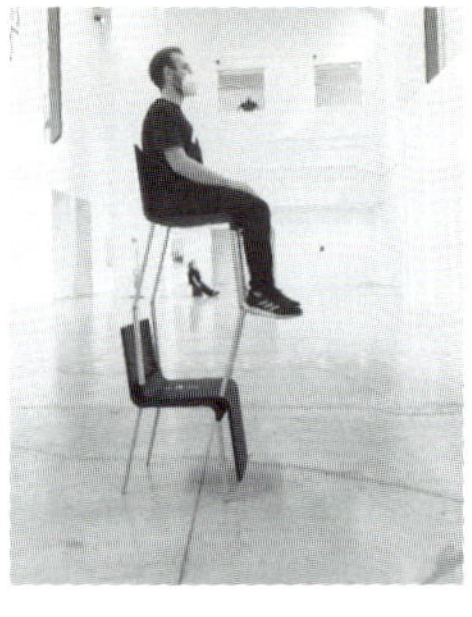

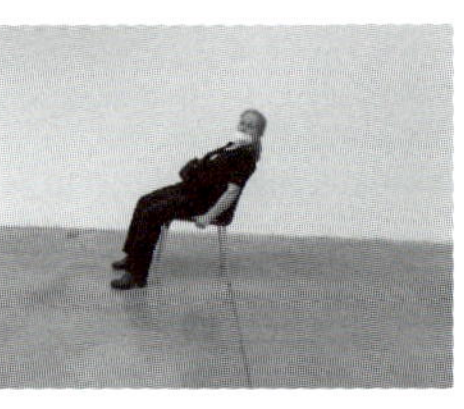

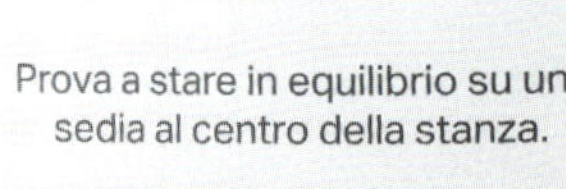

Prova a stare in equilibrio su una
sedia al centro della stanza.

———

*Try to balance on a chair in the
middle of the space.*

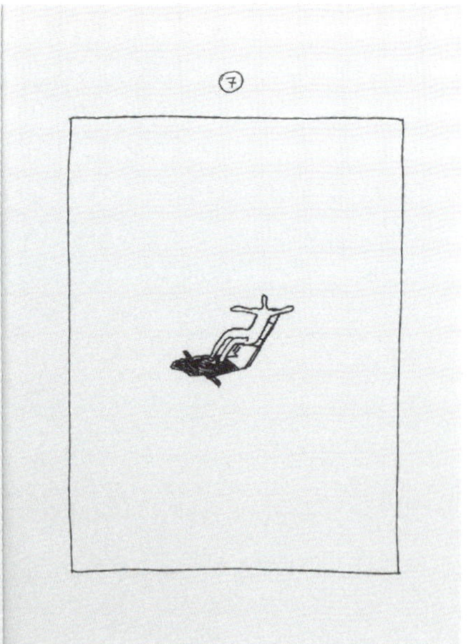

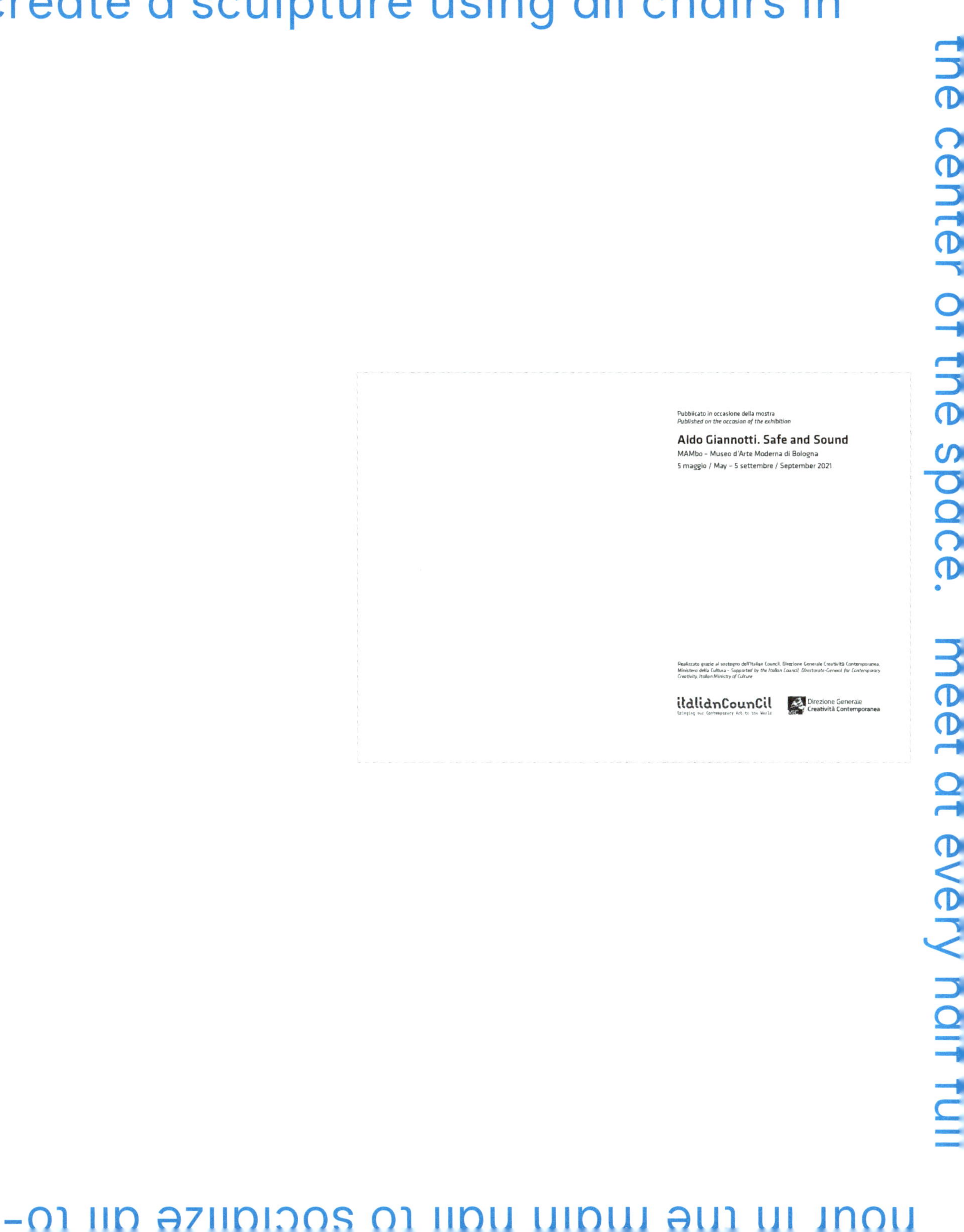

Pubblicato in occasione della mostra
Published on the occasion of the exhibition

Aldo Giannotti. Safe and Sound
MAMbo – Museo d'Arte Moderna di Bologna
5 maggio / May – 5 settembre / September 2021

Realizzato grazie al sostegno dell'Italian Council, Direzione Generale Creatività Contemporanea, Ministero della Cultura - *Supported by the Italian Council, Directorate-General for Contemporary Creativity, Italian Ministry of Culture*

italianCouncil
Bringing our Contemporary Art to the World

Direzione Generale
Creatività Contemporanea

IN ROTATION, ALL THE INSTITUTION'S STAFF SPENDS ONE DAY AS A MUSEUM GUARD.

GUARDS' EMPOWERMENT:
SELF-ORGANIZATION AND PUBLIC SAFETY

The working conditions of guards are difficult: long hours on their feet, low pay, strict movements and stiff uniforms. And in fact, the role of the guard often extends beyond enforcing rules and protecting objects and serves to enforce a dated vision of the museum: as a technology of power (after Bennett and Foucault[1]), or an instrument for the democratic education of the "masses", or the "citizen", where there is a divide between the experts or "educated" content producers and the consumers of knowledge[2].

Gianotti's engagement with the guards was not just turning "normal" guards into performers. The guards were selected through a process in which the artist presented his work from an open call, offered the guards a raise to take on additional responsibilities, and then worked with them in advance and throughout the exhibition. But even within the exhibition, the artist embedded commentary on the economic asymmetry within the museum—for example, with *Redistribution*: a wall drawing, the artist required the director of the museum to paint the following proposal on the wall.

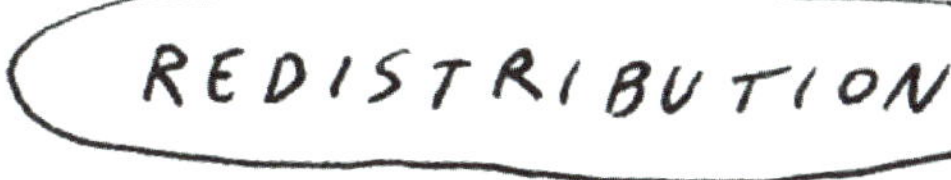

THE MONTHLY SALARIES OF THE APPROXIMATELY 160 PEOPLE WHO WORK AT THE INSTITUTION ARE ADDED UP AND DIVIDED EQUALLY BY THEIR NUMBER

One of the prompts within *The Museum Score* read: "Meet at every full hour in the main hall to socialize all together".

In the current context of museum labor unionization and museum workers organizing for better working conditions, the regular assembly of guards could pose a real threat to the institution, and among the guards, a possibility to organize, to build solidarity, or at least build friendships. Giannotti confronts the limits of what can be done within the constraints of an institutional commission: testing the museum's boundaries and patience, producing a capacity to demand more.

In the broader context of *Safe and Sound*, which explored themes of security and safety from both a practical and conceptual level, the guards became a performative interface, challenging definitions of rules and regulations, how security is implemented in society and its institutions, asking visitors to rethink what it is to feel "safe"—or who is protecting what from whom or what. Through the prompts in *The Museum Score*, guards commented on safety and security directly, opening potential conversations with visitors about museum conditions. And at a basic level, *The Museum Score* tried to demonstrate, through encounters, different modes of creating a welcoming or "safe" atmosphere: for instance, a simple welcome or round of applause probably contrasts starkly with the average encounter with a stern-faced museum guard, who you might expect to instead scrutinize your every move, tell you to put your camera away and stop standing so close to the art.

To Giannotti, who views the museum more as a field of play, the guards might actually be the key to troubling these conventions and breaking from them. Guards fill an important role as the public face of the museum, perhaps as the first or only people that visitors might encounter. Guards often field questions, serve as context providers, and of course spend all day watching people looking at art, granting them a potential position of understanding the range of responses and reactions to an exhibition—and that limiting the role of the guard to surveillance, without acknowledging their potential as experts on an exhibition, is perhaps a missed opportunity.

So perhaps Giannotti is getting us to think about guards as facilitators, who have the potential to advance the role of museums as "social spaces where cultures meet, clash, and grapple with each other, often in contexts of highly asymmetrical relations of power"[3], and through the prompts of *The Museum Score*, these asymmetrical power relations are brought to the foreground.

In order to reflect back on the conditions of the institution and the art world, the museum space is recast as a place of encounter between visitors and staff, which allows for negotiations and interactions. The prompts, carried out by the guards, confused the normal divide between passive and active, performer and spectator; and the guards extended and morphed the prompts in ways the artist never dreamed possible.

And for those of us who still believe in the utopian potential
of the museum space and the power of art, we might see
the expansion of the role of the museum guard as an
invitation to reimagine what possible interactions could
happen in a museum if museums felt less like spaces
where you are policed and more like spaces where you are
welcomed, brought in, engaged.

When I spoke to one guard about the conditions of their
work, he spoke about one particular piece, *Filling Time*.
The work consisted of a blank timeline which an attending
guard invited visitors to fill in with a black marker—*Would
you like to assist me in executing this task?*—activating the
labor of museum visitors. The museum is not just a space o
leisure or contemplation, but an arena of labor. Visitors to
the museum invest their time and resources, yet the value
generated is often obscured and unevenly distributed, and
though visitor participation can be engaging, often it is the
institution, in the end, that reaps its rewards.

Filling Time also reflects on the sense of boredom museum guards often experience: tasked with controlling, with
behavior constrained by rules, the minutes become hours.
Time barely passes. The passing of time, inscribed slowly
on the wall with thick, dark marker, became a visualizati-
on—representative of the individual condition of boredom,
gesturing towards a larger shared condition of boredom,
but also, an act that resists boredom. And perhaps even in
a museum space, with its accepted embedded rules,

you break the rules, please do it unno-

limitations, modes of conditioned behavior, as a space of control, confronting this boredom could encourage us to imagine new possibilities.

PROVOCATION

Simon O'Sullivan writes, "Art involves framing, the marking out of a territory, or the building of a house, but this house is always open to an outside… Art is a form of territorialisation that in turn allows for, and produces the conditions for, deterritorialisation."[4]. In the closing hours of the exhibition, the guards gathered in the exhibition hall, hugging like family, recounting visitor interactions. It made you wonder if these guards, understanding their potential, could really go back to being "real" guards, or if they might continue to organize hourly meetings with their co-workers, starting conversations with visitors, commanding attention with new tools which break expectations… and what all this could lead to.

It also left me wondering: since we make the museums we visit and inhabit, can redrawing the lines, just as Giannotti does, allow for us to rethink the institution's role in shaping our society? Can we redraw the lines of our world, just as Giannotti reconfigures the boundaries of the museum?

1. Bennett, Tony. 1990 The Political Rationality of the Museum. The Journal of Media and Cultural Studies.; Foucault, Michel. 1977: Discipline and Punishment: The Birth of the Prison.
2. Greenhill, Eileen Hooper. 1992. Museums and the Shaping of Knowledge. Routledge. P 190
3. Pratt, Mary Louise. 1991. "Arts of the Contact Zone." Profession, 33–40.
4. O'Sullivan, Simon. 2006. Art Encounters Deleuze and Guattari: Thought Beyond Representation. Palgrave Macmillan, London.

ticed. If you are planning to take a risk,

please involve me. meet at every

8

meet at every half full hour in the main

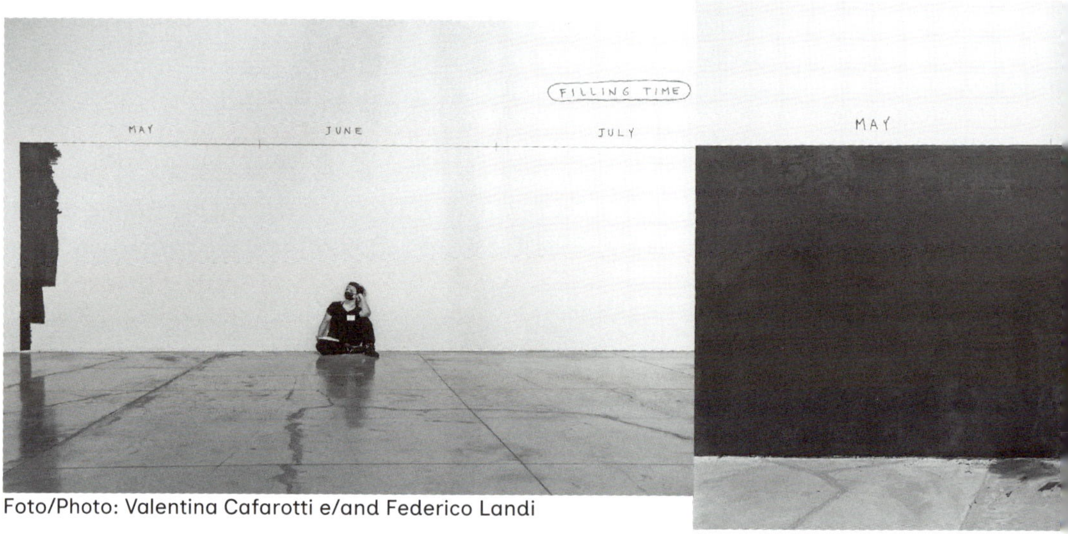

Foto/Photo: Valentina Cafarotti e/and Federico Landi

space.

using an chairs in the center of the

...ber me as part of this exhibition.

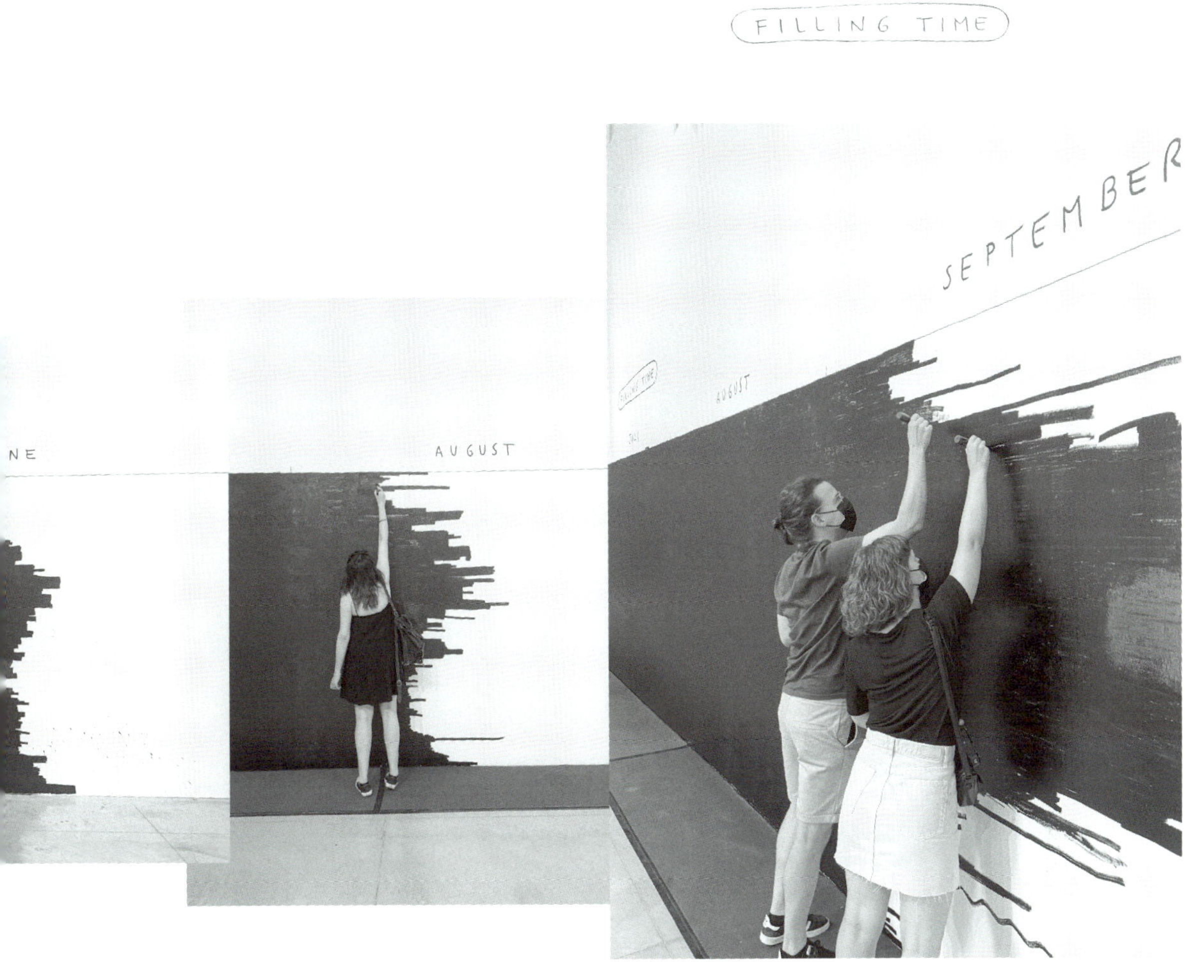

draw string drawings, and engage visitors in the activity.

create a sculpture

in the activity.

please consider that

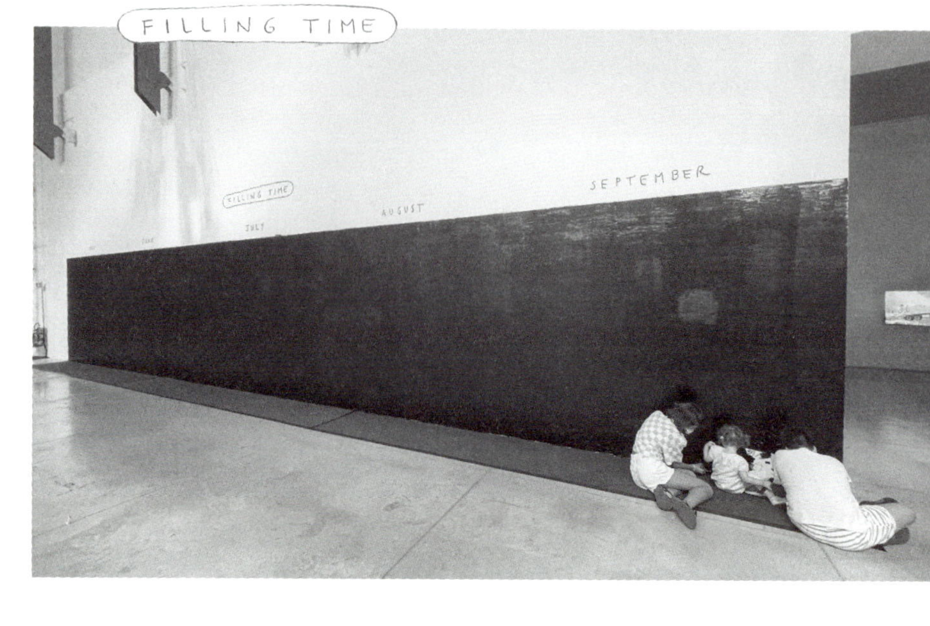

to socialize all together.

at every hall hour in the main hall

ou break the rules, please do it unno-

ticed.

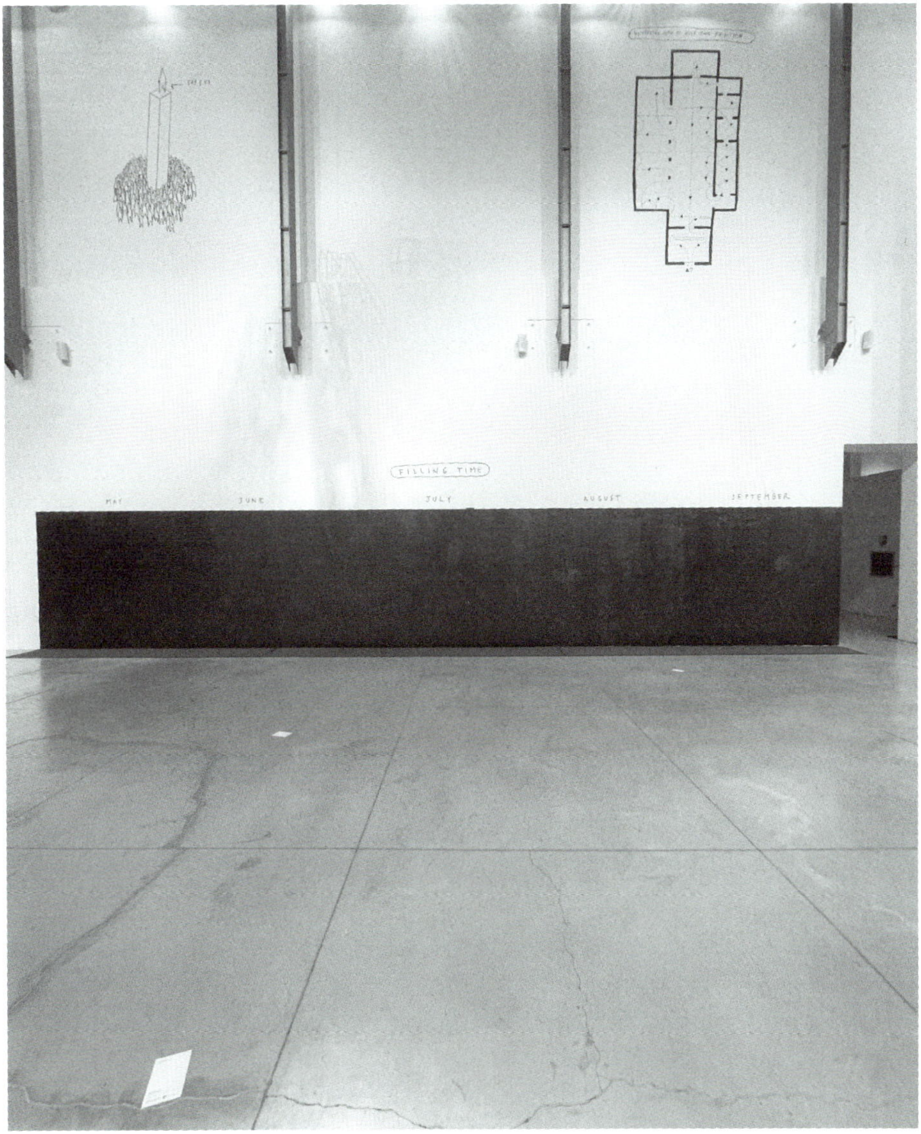

If you are planning to take a

risk, please involve me.

meet

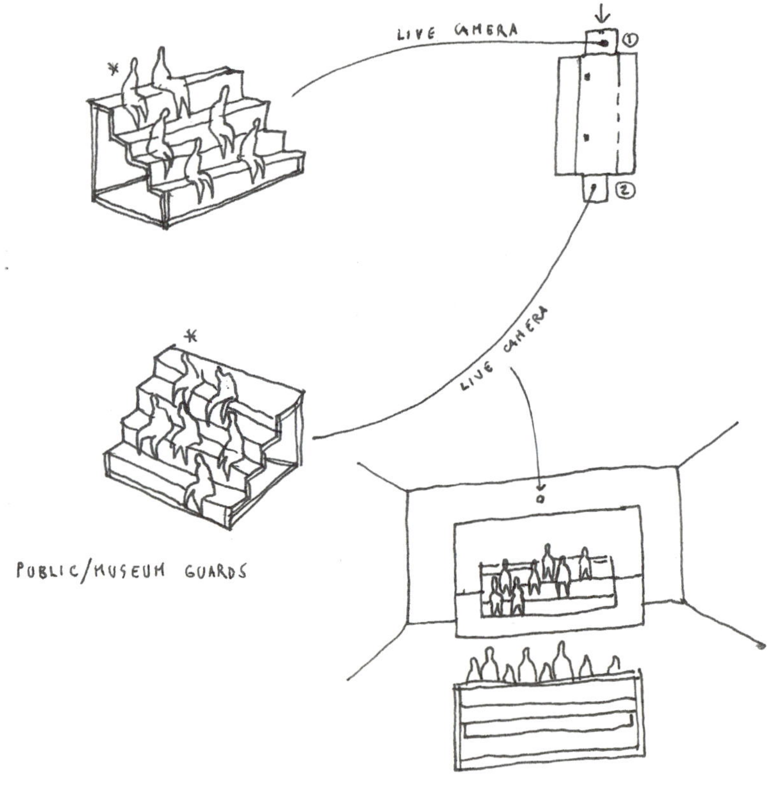

OPENING:
ALL THE MUSEUM GUARDS ARE POSITIONED IN THE
ROOM (2) AT THE BEGINNIG OF THE EXHIBITION OPENING.
THIS FOOTAGE IS PROJECTED IN ROOM (1). AT THE
SAME TIME THE FOOTAGE FROM ROOM (1) IS PROJECTED
IN ROOM (2). AT A LATER POINT THE GUARDS
ENTER THE MAIN HALL AS A GROUP. TO BE DECIDED
THEN THEY REPEAT THE SAME ACTION IN ROOM (1).

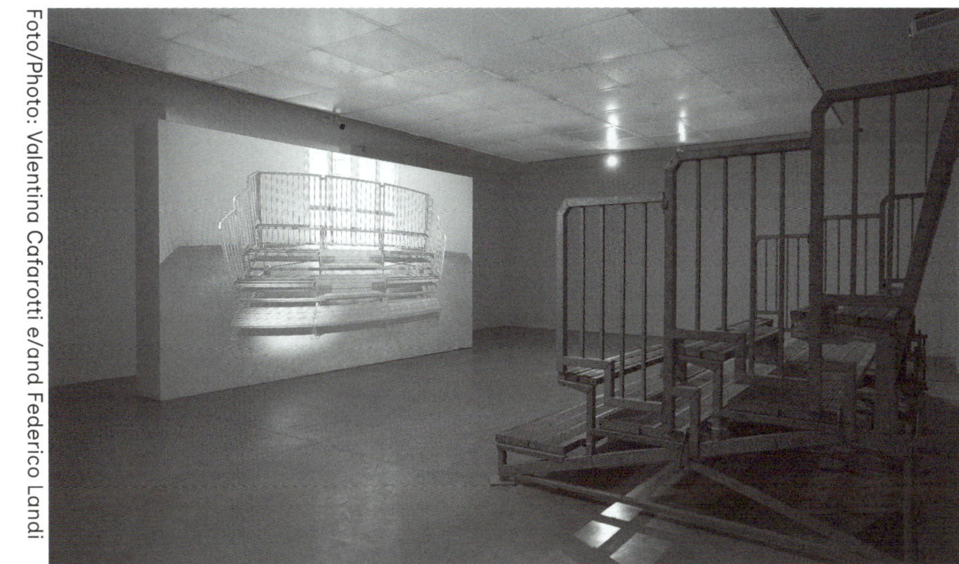

The first room people entered was a sort of rough cinema, looking at what appeared to be a recorded copy of an identical set-up.

Before entering *Safe and Sound's* central hall, visitors passed through a room with metal bleachers. Facing a wall projection mirroring the seating arrangement, a guard mimicked visitors' every move, subtly surveilling them. Some visitors, intrigued, began making increasingly dramatic movements— testing the limits of what the guard would replicate, such as standing on the metal railing, lying down on the benches, or jumping up and down.

the activity.   create a sculpture wu-

if you are planning to take a risk,

unnoticed.

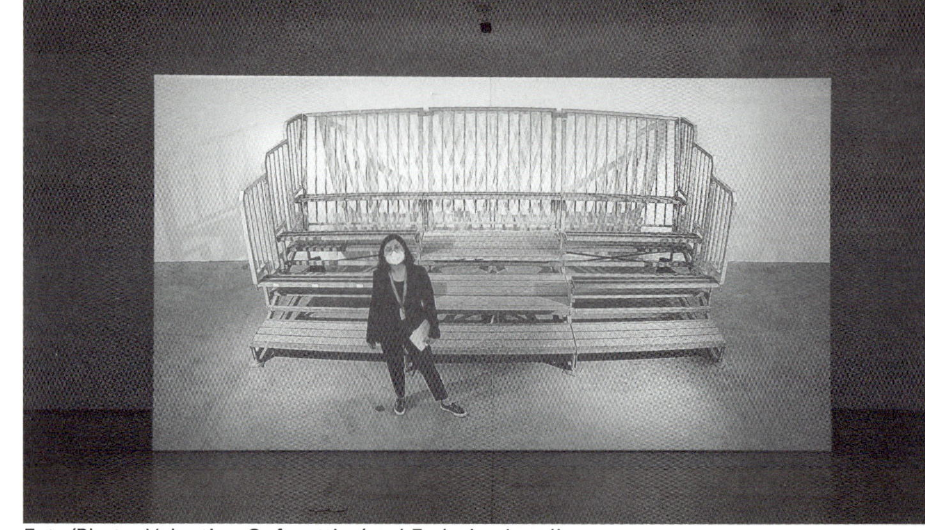

Foto/Photo: Valentina Cafarotti e/and Federico Landi

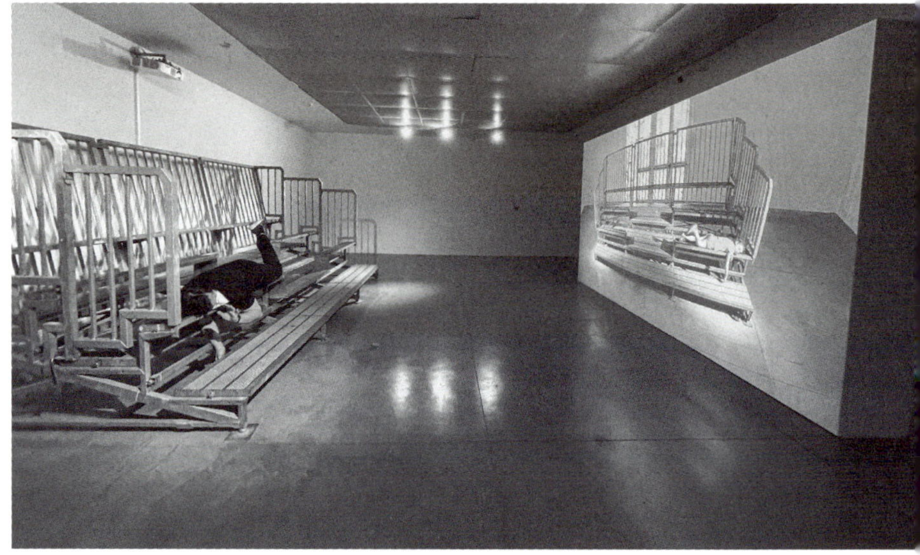

you break the rules, please do it

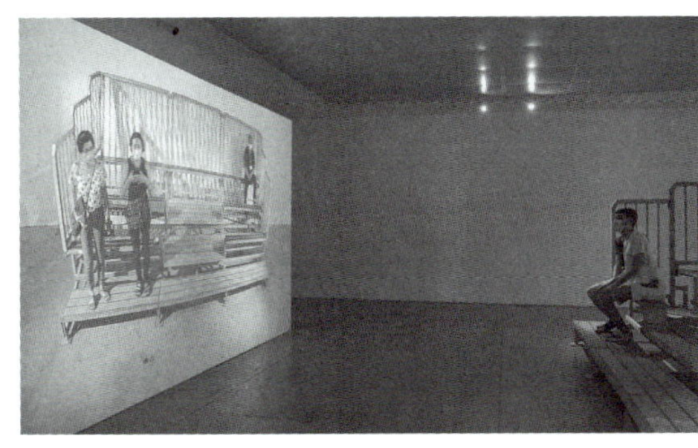

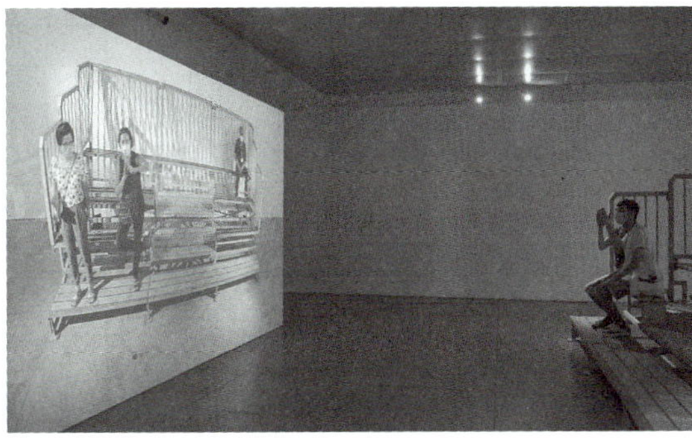

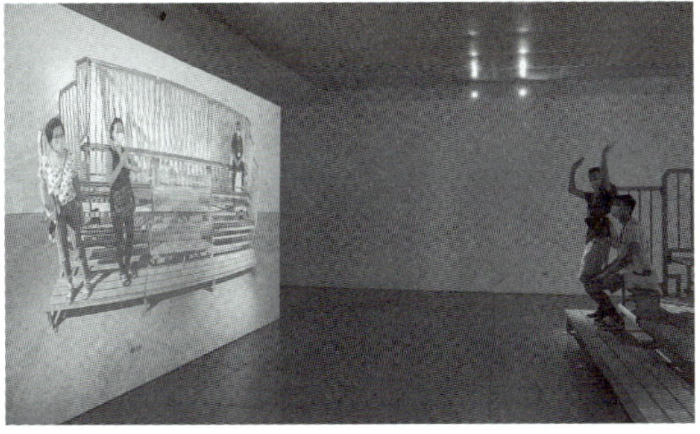

Upon leaving this initial space, visitors proceeded to the museum's expansive central hall, comprising the main part of the exhibition. It wasn't until the end of the visit that they found out the very last room at the end of the hall mirrored the first one. The guard in the projection was actually positioned on the opposite side of the exhibition, waiting for new visitors to sit down on the bleachers, allowing them to surprise the next visitor through this mutual act of surveillance.

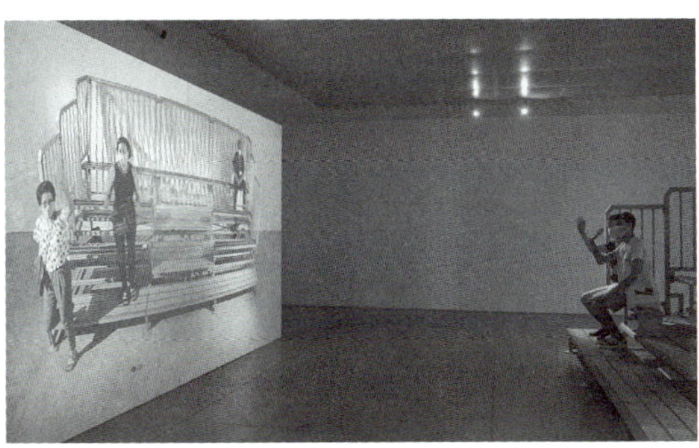

A room was filled with two mobile staircases.

Nearby guards would help visitors push the heavy staircases around the room. This allowed the visitors to ascend and view small elevated sketches at the top of the wall.

15

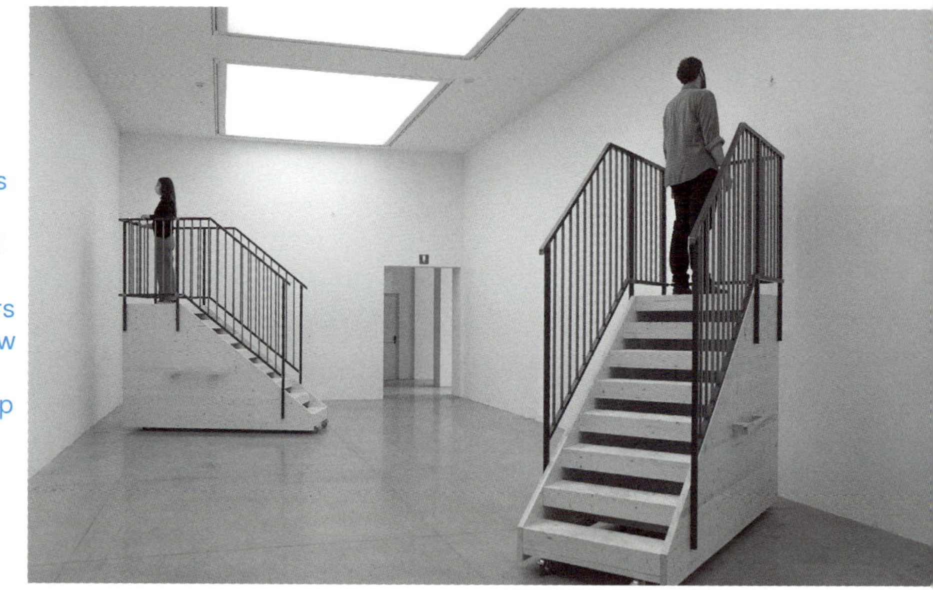

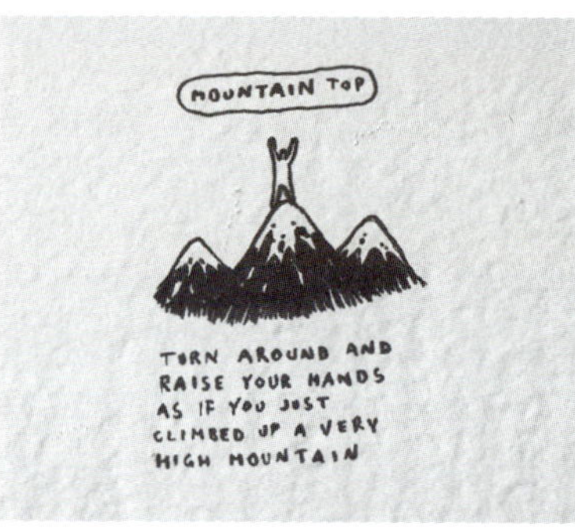

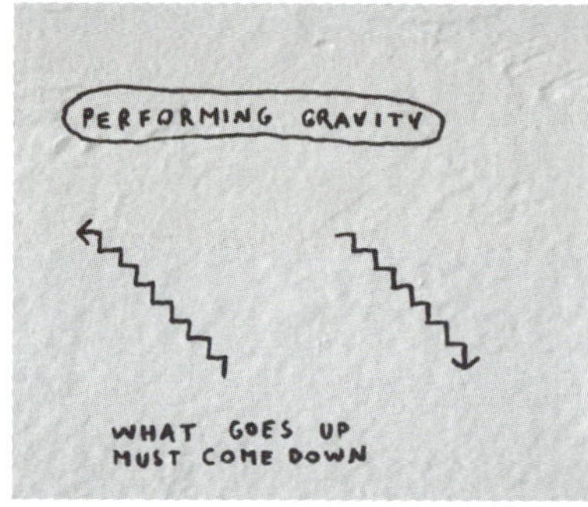

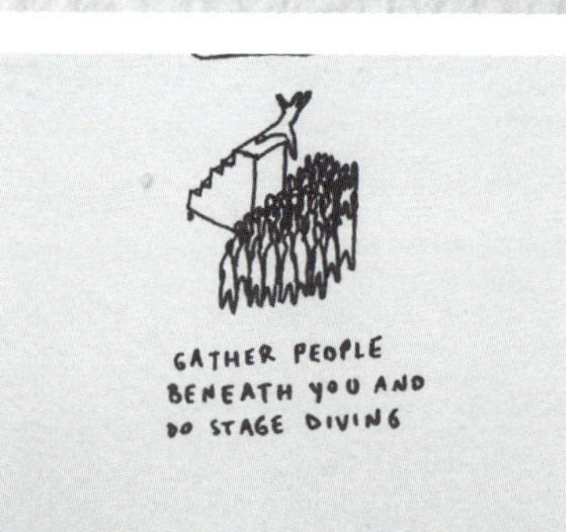

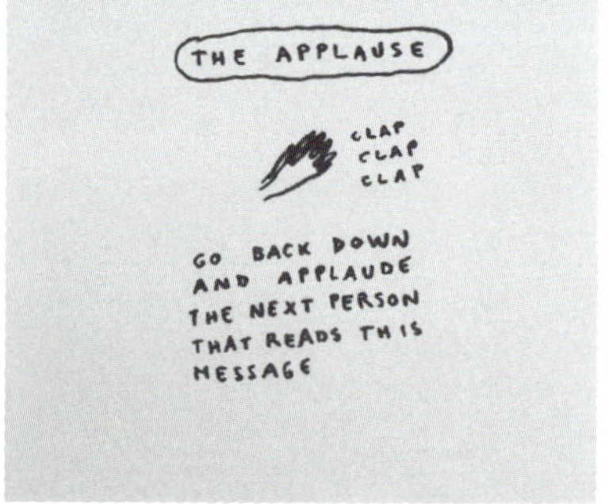

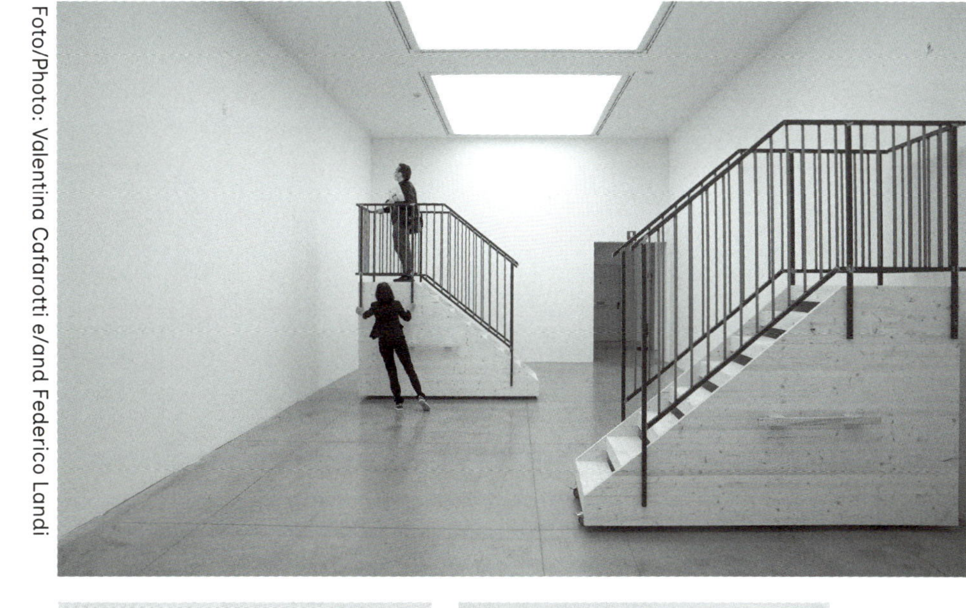
Foto/Photo: Valentina Cafarotti e/and Federico Landi

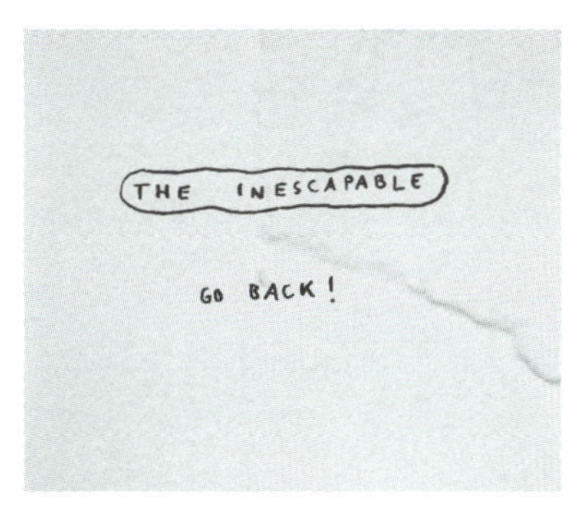

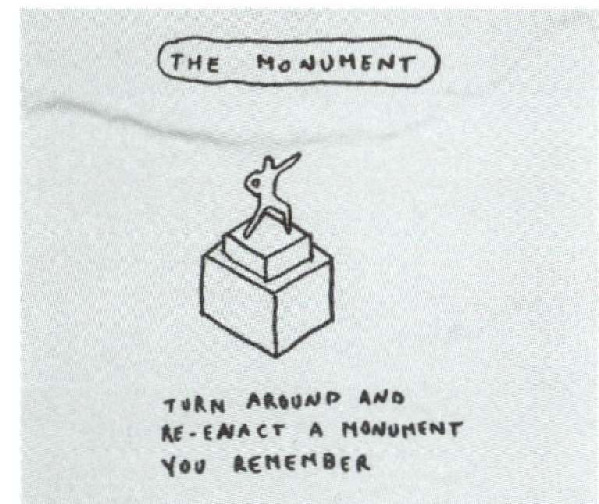

Details: small drawings, as drawn on the walls in this installation.

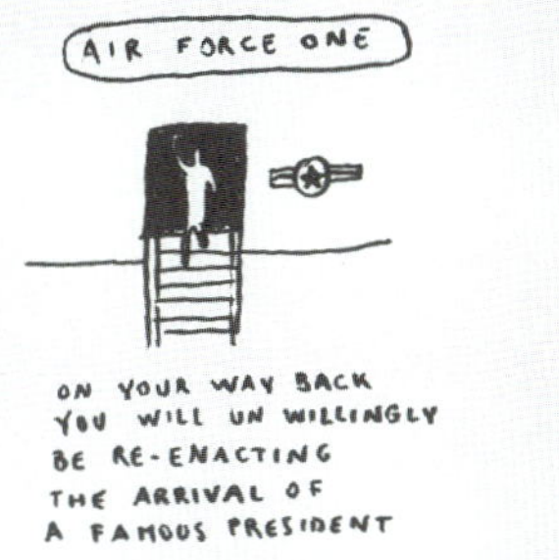

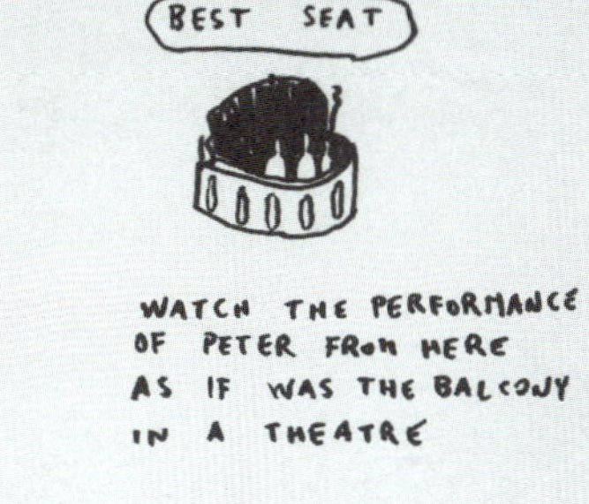

name is .... please remember me as

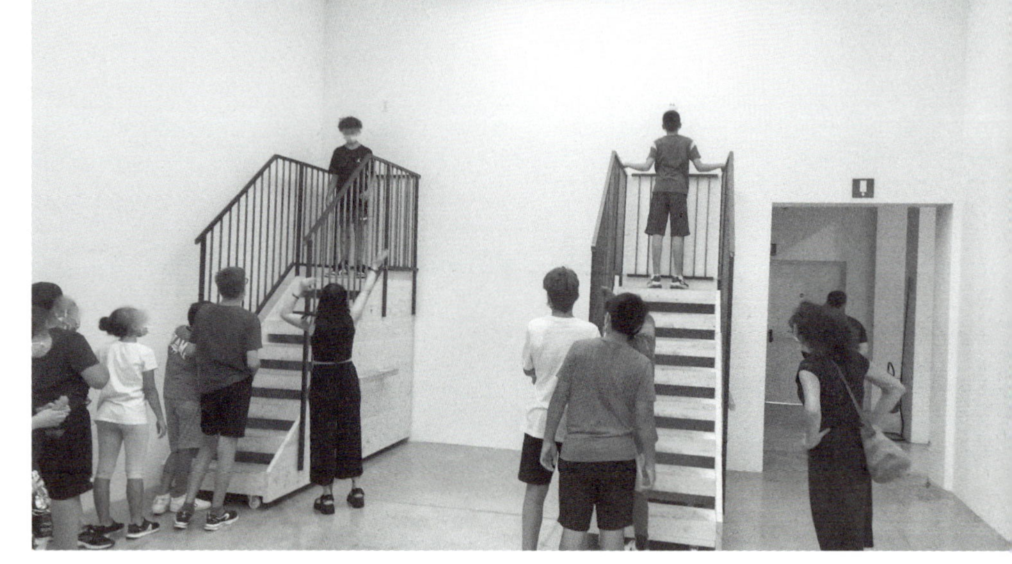

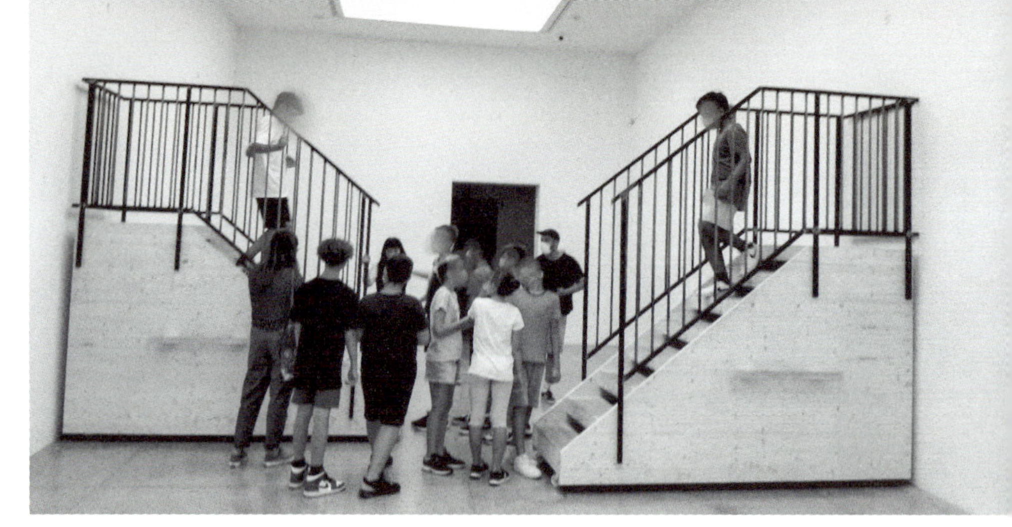

every half full hour in the main hall to socialize

meet at the center of the space.

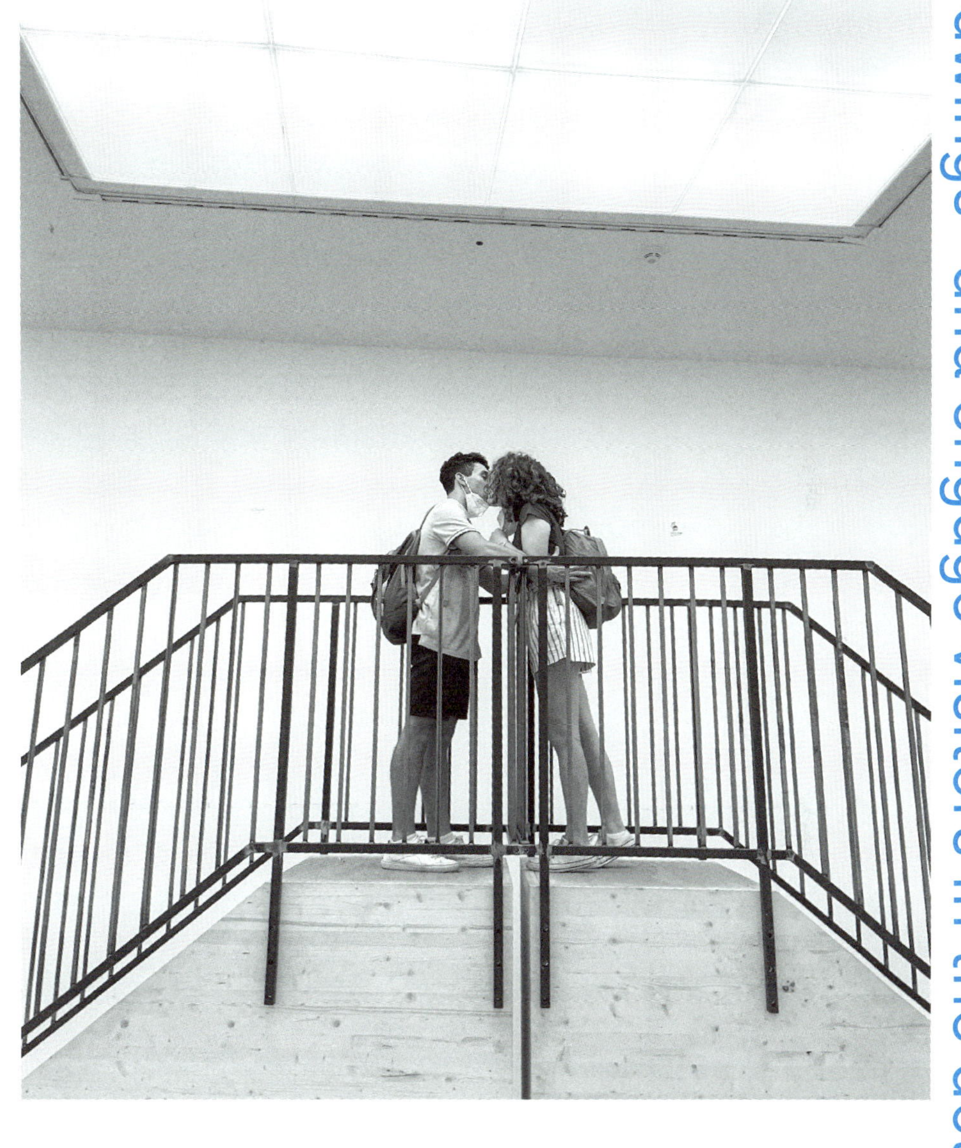

part of this exhibition. draw "string

drawings and engage visitors in the activity.

create a sculpture using an chairs in

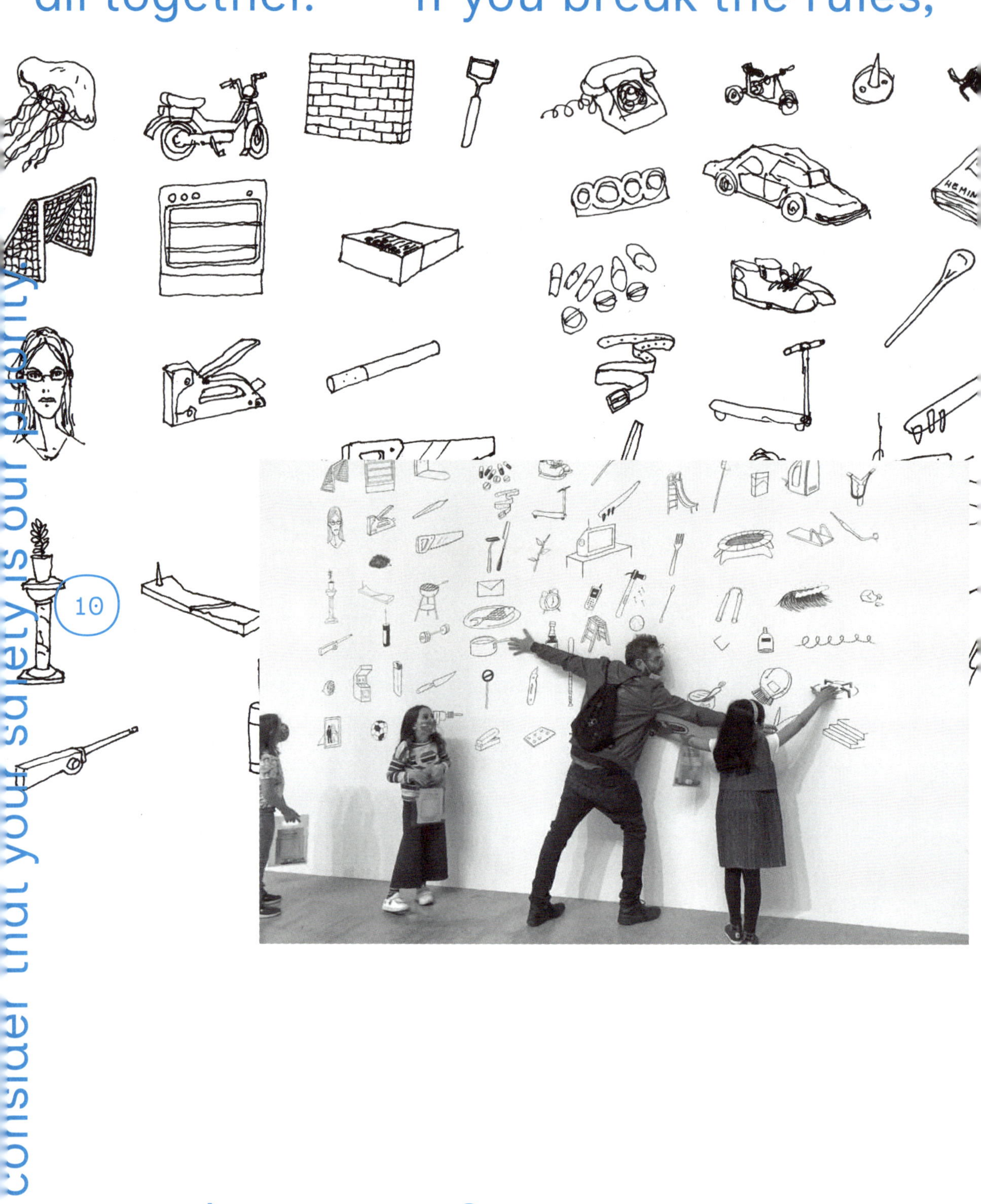

all together.   If you break the rules,
consider that your safety is our priority.
plan to socialize all together.   please
10

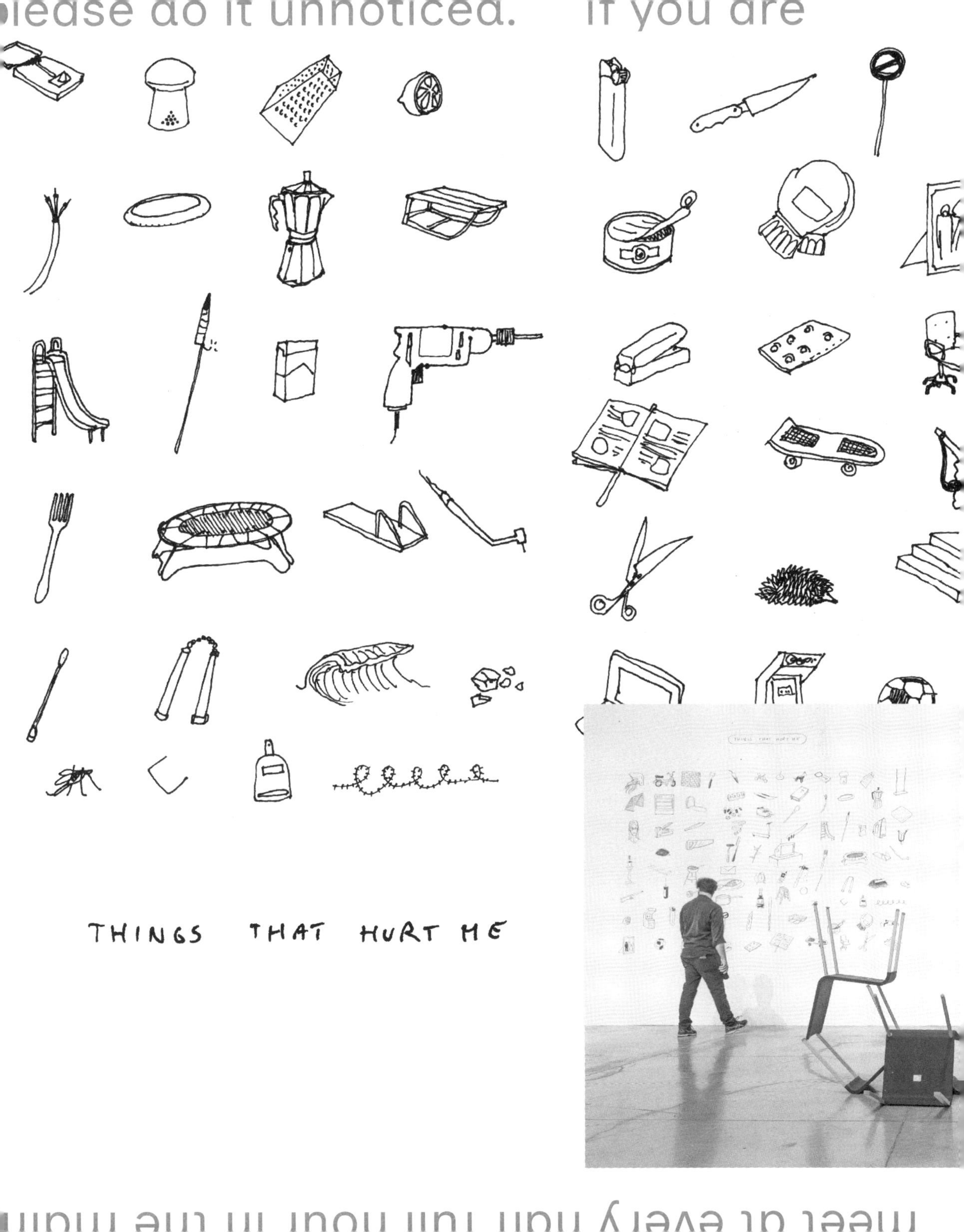
please do it unnoticed.   if you are
THINGS THAT HURT ME
meet at every half full hour in the main

you are planning to take a risk, please

take an unusual

my position for 5 minutes?

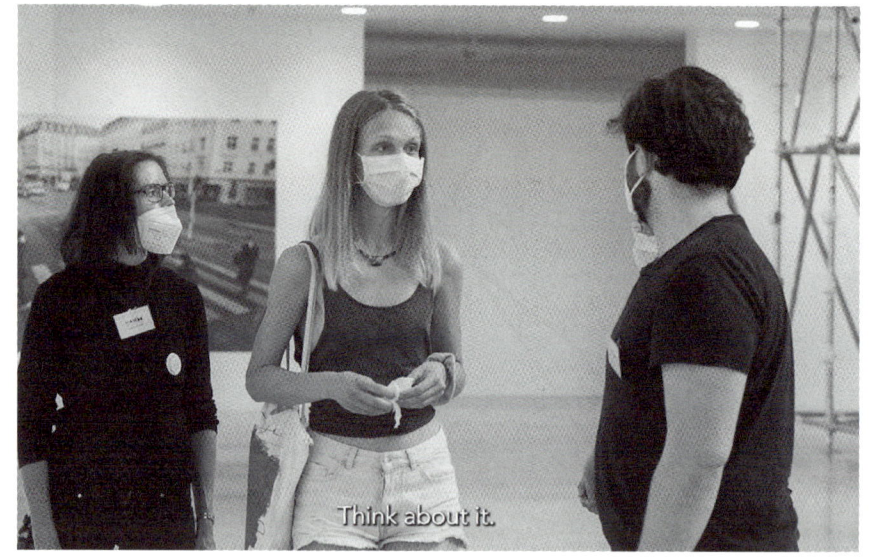

priority.   would you mind taking over

involve me.   meet at every half full

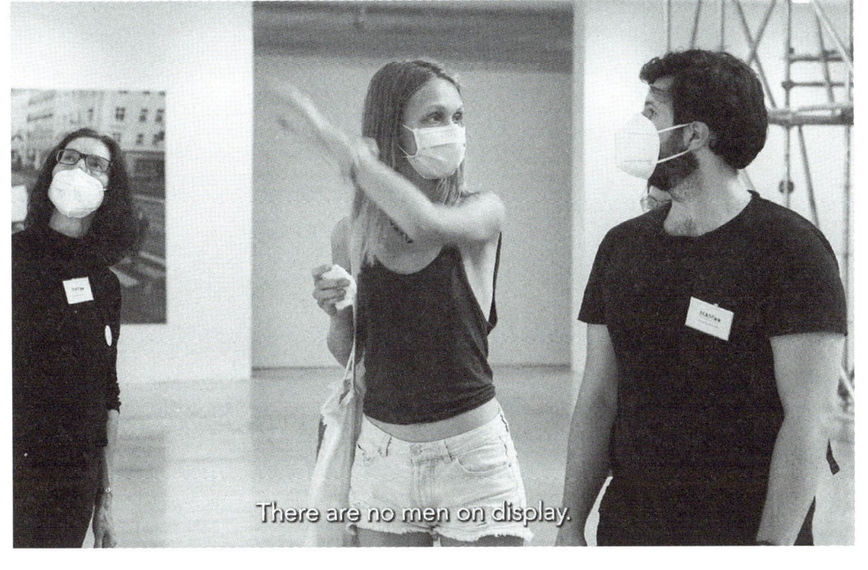

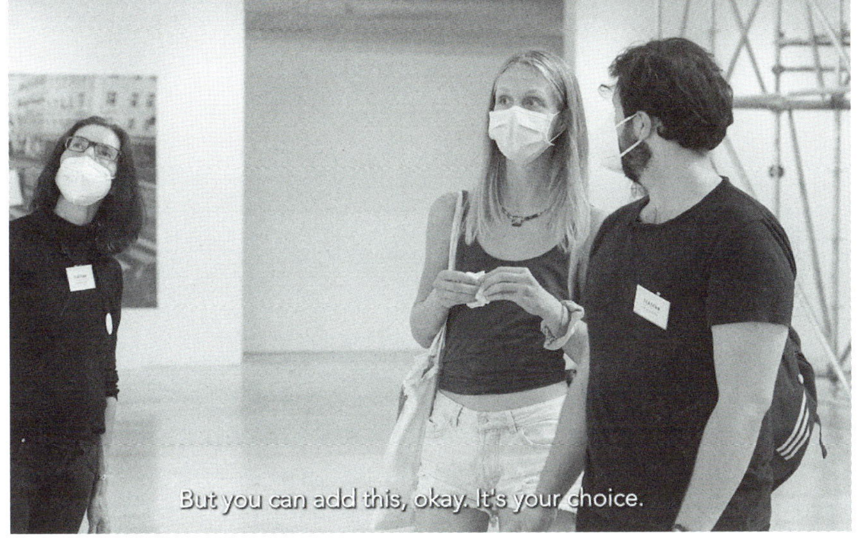

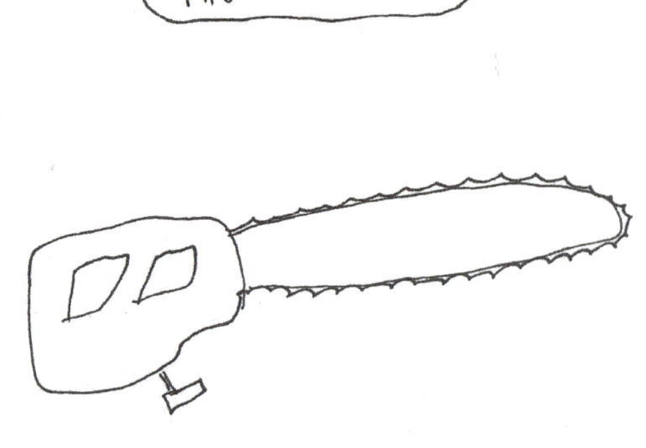

11

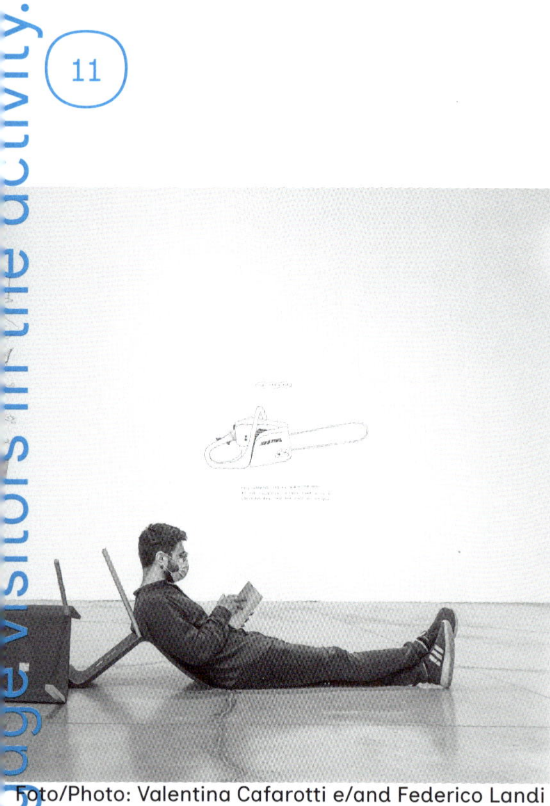

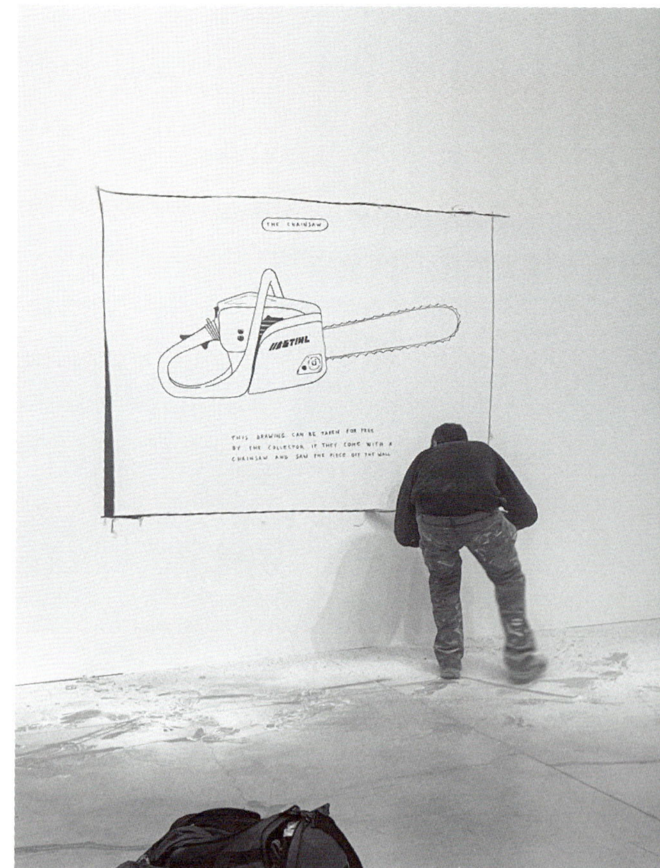

Foto/Photo: Valentina Cafarotti e/and Federico Landi

on for 5 minutes? take an unusual po-sition in space.

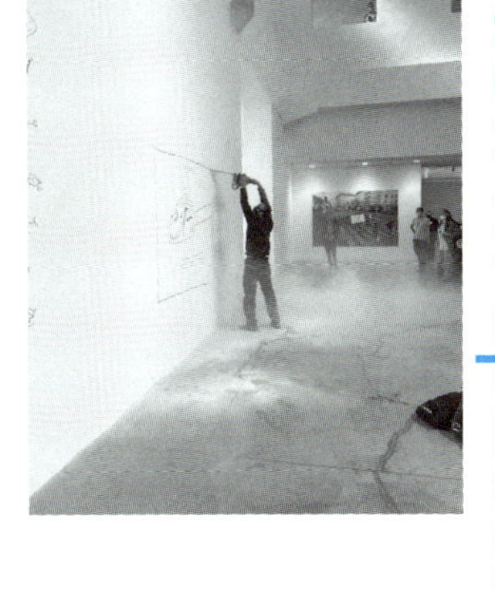

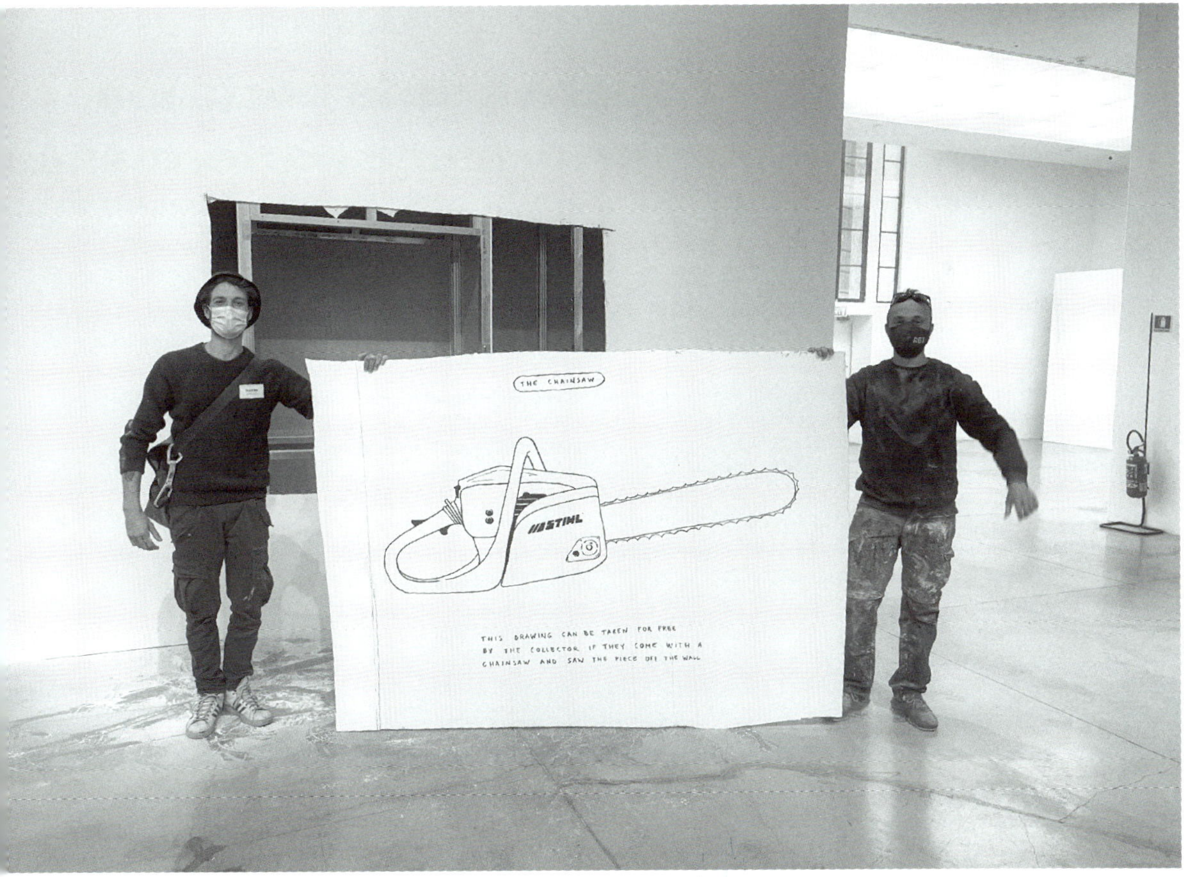

THE CHAINSAW

HASTIHL

THIS DRAWING CAN BE TAKEN FOR FREE
BY THE COLLECTOR IF THEY COME WITH A
CHAINSAW AND SAW THE PIECE OFF THE WALL

in my name is .... please remember me as part of this exhibi-

Con la motosega tra il pubblico Anche il furto è un'opera d'arte

-. Avevamo autorizzato a far entra-re chi si fosse presentato all'ingresso con una motosega, preoccupandoci però che l'operazione si svolgesse in sicurezza per il pubblico». Già, perché entrare in museo con una motosega contraddice ogni forma di salvaguardia, delle opere e dei visitatori, ma d'altra parte l'intera mostra di Giannotti solleva una riflessione proprio sui temi di "safety" e "security" in rapporto ai musei.

La notizia è rimbalzata sul web e alla fine si è venuti a sapere che l'operazione non è stata compiuta da un collezionista ma da un gruppo di artisti e operatori culturali che dichiarano: «Abbiamo staccato l'opera e cercheremo di venderla per sostenere un progetto editoriale indipendente, Moai Press, dedicato all'arte urbana. C'è del concettuale nello staccare

un'opera museale per soster un progetto dedicato all'arte [p]URISMO blica». Esattamente l'opposto quanto avvenne nel 2016 con l scussa mostra "Street Art Ba sy&Co": allora furono staccate muri della città le opere di senza il suo permesso, per app derle a Palazzo Pepoli. E in sorta di strano cortocircuito, fondatori di Moai Press c'è Dav Gavioli, che collaborò con l'o nizzazione di quella mostra.

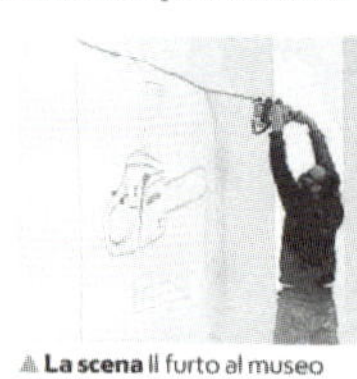
▲ **La scena** Il furto al museo

◫ il Resto del Carlino
Bologna
Dir. Resp.: Michele Brambilla
Tiratura: 122.031 Diffusione: 90.800 Lettori: 1.032.000

Edizi
Es

L'uomo ha raccolto l'invito dell'artista Giannotti

'Ruba' l'opera al Mambo usando una motosega

Gamberini a pagina **30**

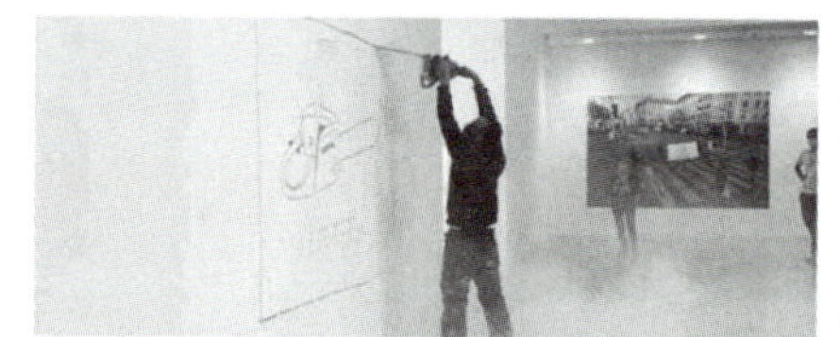

Sega l'opera e se la porta via
Niente furto, è una performance

Al Mambo
Ruba un'opera d'arte con la motosega, ma è una performance

«È successo veramente! A Bologna tagliavano i murales dalle mura della città per portarli dentro i musei. Ieri li abbiamo tagliati fuori dai musei per tirarli fuori». Poche righe sulla pagina Facebook del Mambo, accanto a un video di 30 secondi che ritrae una scena singolare, per spiegare la performance di ieri, quando un uomo armato con una motosega elettrica, ha tagliato un pezzo di muro in cartongesso e ha portato via un disegno di Aldo Giannotti, parte della mostra «Safe & Sound», in corso fino al 5 settembre. Nessun furto spettacolare, ma una mossa suggerita dallo stesso

Giannotti, che sotto all'opera raffigurante una motosega posizionata su una parete aveva scritto: «Questo disegno può essere prelevato gratis da un collezionista che si presenta con una motosega e taglia un pezzo di muro». Al personale del museo erano state date indicazioni di far entrare chi si fosse presentato con una motosega e la performance si è svolta in tutta sicurezza per il pubblico L'annuncio sui social è un riferimento a quanto successe nel 2016 per la mostra «Street Art-Banksy&Co», che venne allestita facendo staccare dai muri opere dell'artista Blu.

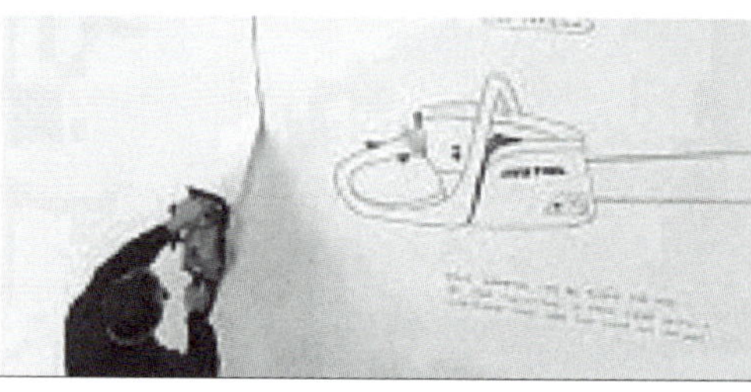

ARTE CONTEMPORANEA

Reo e confesso "Al Mambo ho agito così"

Cesare Bettini, street artist e "rapinatore" racconta la genesi del furto con la motosega

di **Paola Naldi**

Sono entrato al Mambo con la motosega nascosta in un grande borsone pieno di vestiti per giocare a calcetto, ho finto di essere un visitatore e poi quando è stato il momento o tagliato il muro con l'opera di Aldo Giannotti. Il resto è storia».

È ancora emozionato Cesare Bettini, artista di strada e curatore di eventi dedicati al mondo della street culture, chiamato domenica scorsa in fretta e furia dai componenti del collettivo Moai Press, ideatori del "furto", per prelevare il famoso disegno della "Chainsaw" esposto al Mambo.

«I componenti di Moai Press sono tutti miei amici perché si occupano di arte urbana e avendo saputo che ci sarebbe stata la possibilità di segare via il disegno, come scritto dallo stesso Giannotti, mi hanno subito contattato per mettere a segno il colpo – prosegue Bettini –. Io ero in campagna ma sono arrivato di corsa con la motosega di mio padre e un furgoncino. Siamo entrati nella hall e io sono riuscito ad intrufolarmi nella grande Sala delle Ciminiere. Ad un certo punto una guardiasala, insospettita, mi ha pure chiesto se dentro al borsone ci fosse la motosega, ma io le ho fatto vedere la maglietta e i calzini puzzolenti che la coprivano. Poi è arrivato Aldo Giannotti e, una volta capito che eravamo in regola, ho azionato il motore. Alla fine tremavo anche se sono abituato ad operare in fretta sui muri con le bombolette».

Un furto con destrezza legale, ma gli autori della performance non si aspettavano tanto clamore.

«In realtà l'esposizione mediatica è stata il risvolto negativo di una esperienza che altrimenti si sarebbe esaurita con grande positività da parte di tutte le persone coinvolte – spiegano dal collettivo Moai Press –. Ci siamo imbarazzati quando la nostra azione, spontanea, è stata associata alla figura di Banksy o addirittura interpretata come una fantomatica polemica nei confronti di passate mostre bolognesi. Non c'è stato retro-pensiero».

Ma per Bettini è chiaro che non si trattava di una semplice performance. «A posteriori è stato ancora più chiaro che il gesto è stato giusto – aggiunge lui –. Per me è importante che l'arte non sia arroccata dentro ad museo mentre la società, fuori, ha bisogno di cultura. I musei devono finanziare con la cultura lo spazio pubblico, altrimenti rischiano di rimanere autoreferenz[…]

Gli autori del "furto" […] stanno studiando insiem[e …] Giannotti come vendere l'[…] za operazioni speculative. […] do che venga acquistata […] pubblico. Il ricavato fin[…] progetto editoriale di Moa[i …]

Post Scriptum: il colle[ttivo Moai] Press e Cesare Bettini ci h[anno rila]sciato le dichiarazioni c[he …] qui sopra. Successivament[e, dopo es]sersi confrontati con Aldo […] ci hanno detto di volersi […] all'esposizione mediatica» […] deciso di pubblicare ugual[mente le lo]ro dichiarazioni.

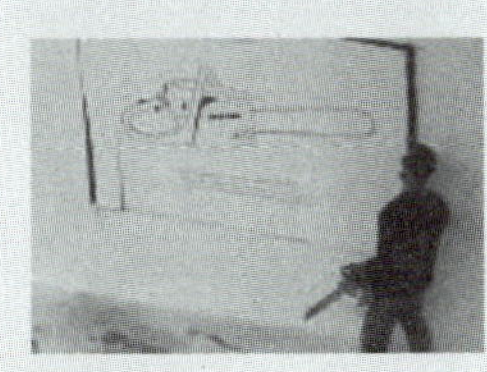

Ruba opera d'arte con la motosega: è una performance

Un uomo con una motosega elettrica taglia un pezzo di muro in

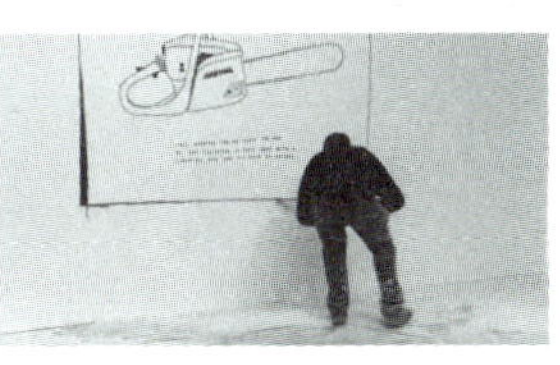

la Repubblica

Assoldato da Moai Press, ha seguito alla lettera le istruzioni lasciate dall'autore, Aldo Giannotti

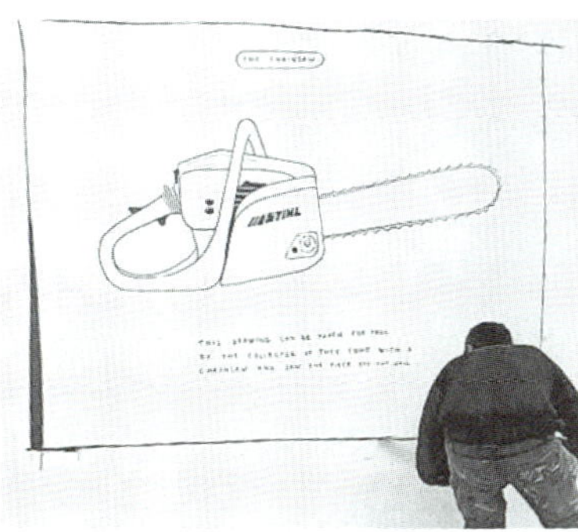

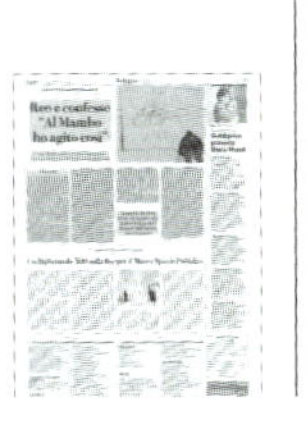

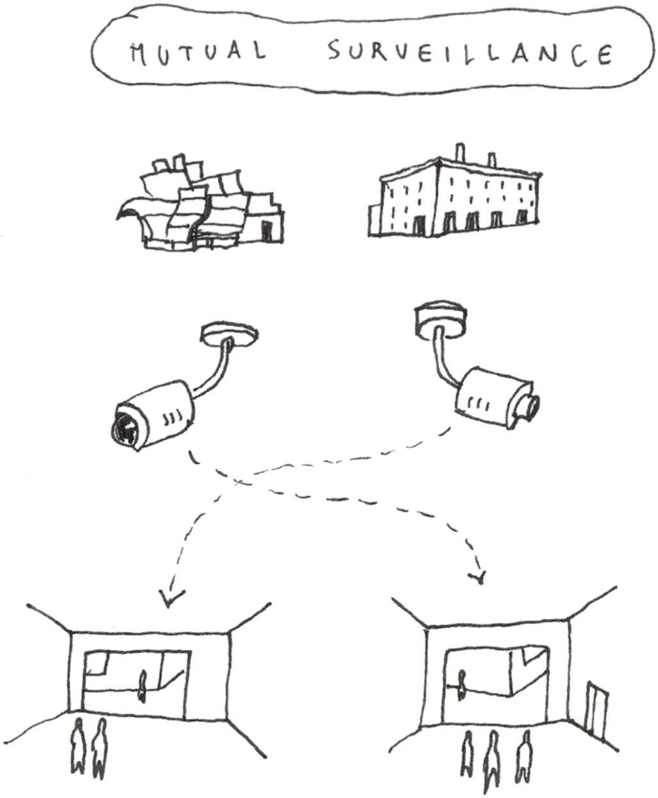

FOOTAGE FROM THE INSTITUTION'S
SECURITY CAMERAS IS STREAMED
LIVE TO ANOTHER INSTITUTION
AND VICE VERSA

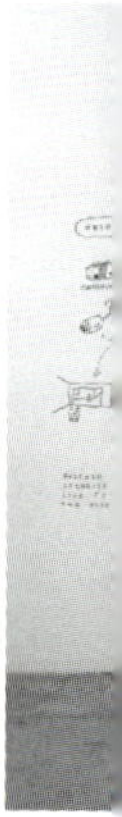

14

my name is .... please remember me as part

an unusual position in space.   in

gether.   please consider that your

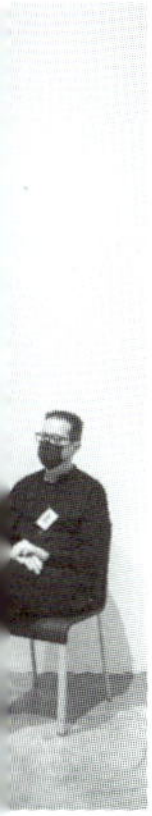

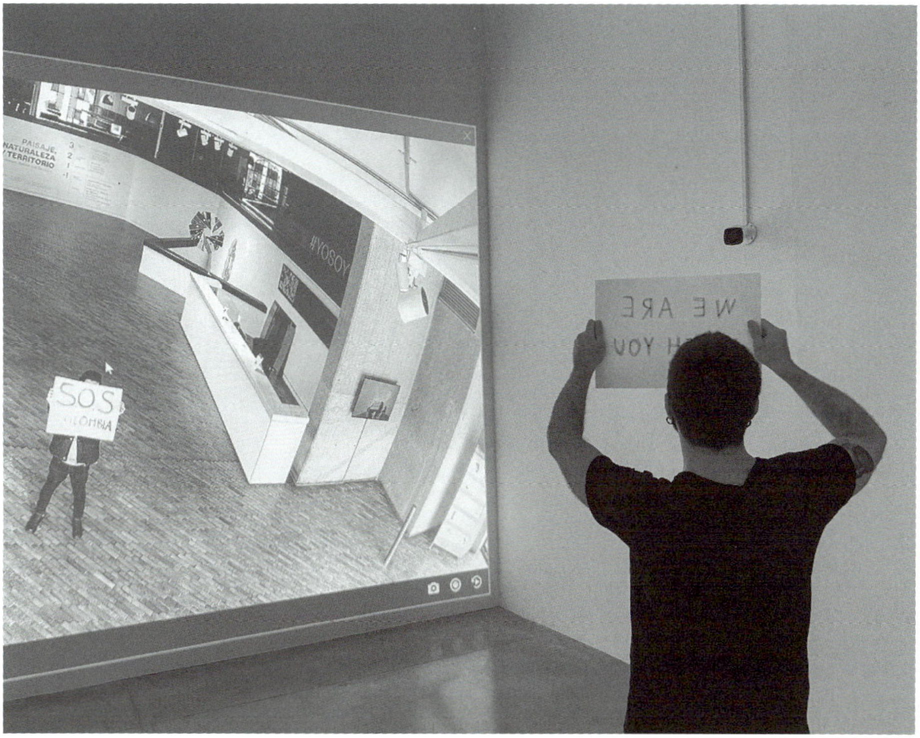

safety is our priority.

would you mind taking

over my position for 5 minutes?   take

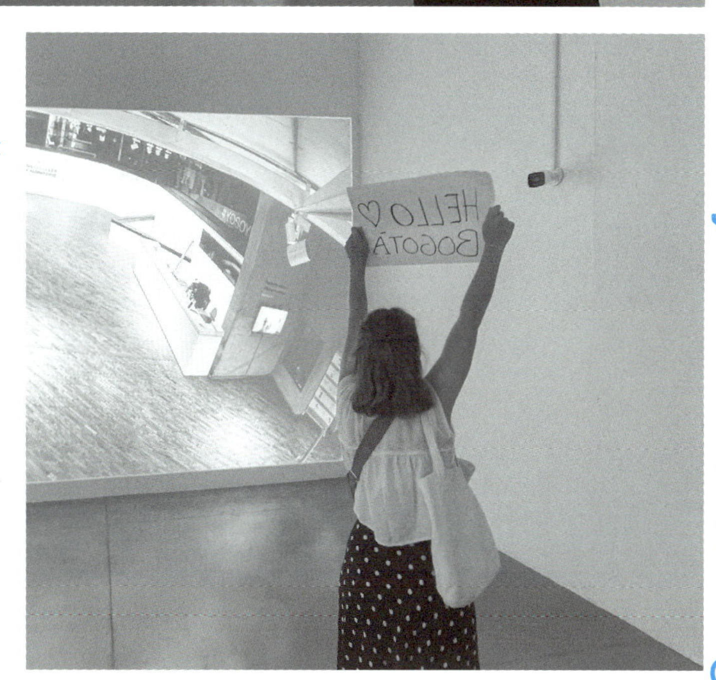

As the exhibition was up at the MAMbo in Bologna (Italy), it was only logical to connect cameras with the MAMBO in Bogota (Colombia).

If you break the rules,

And when the social and political unrest in Bogota rose, the security guards and museum visitors found one another in solidarity and exchange.

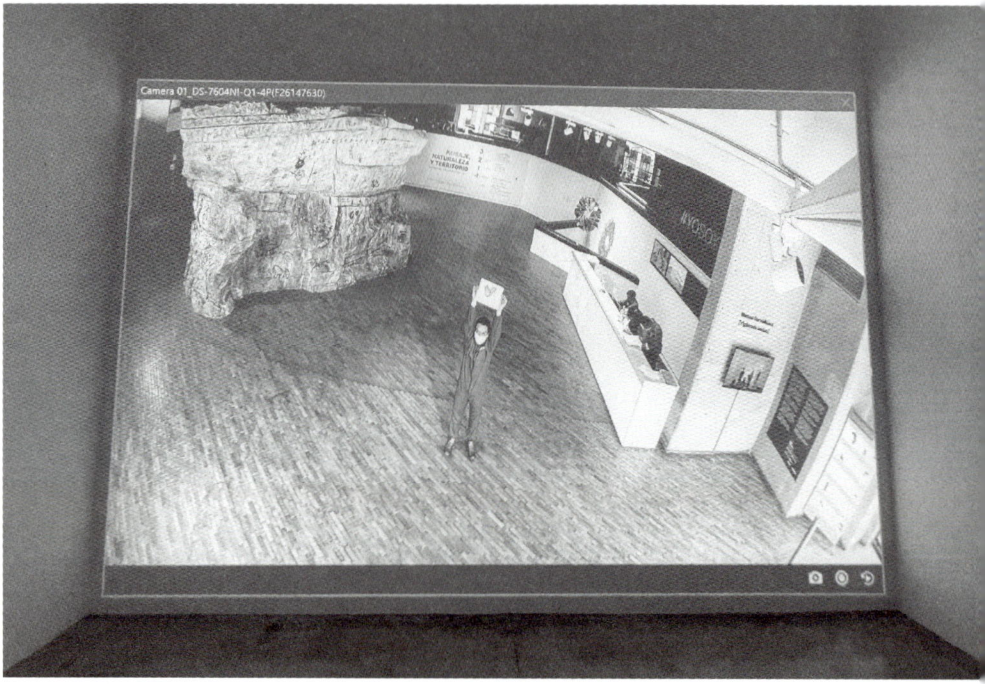

socialize all together.

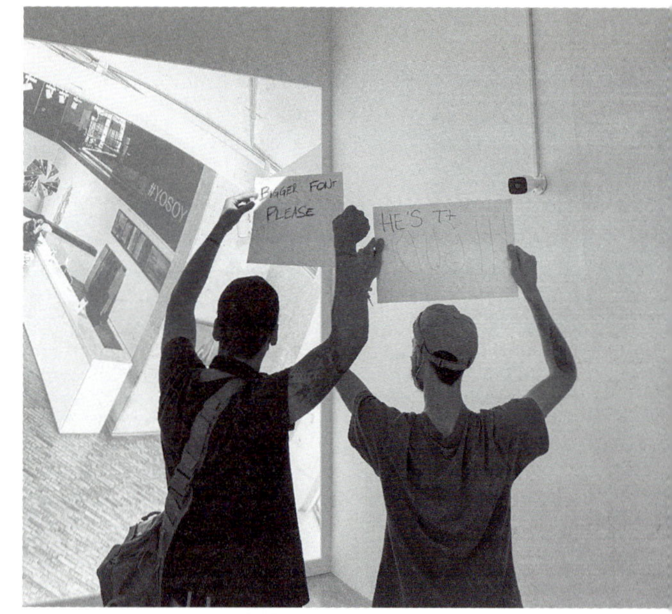

drawings and engage visitors in the

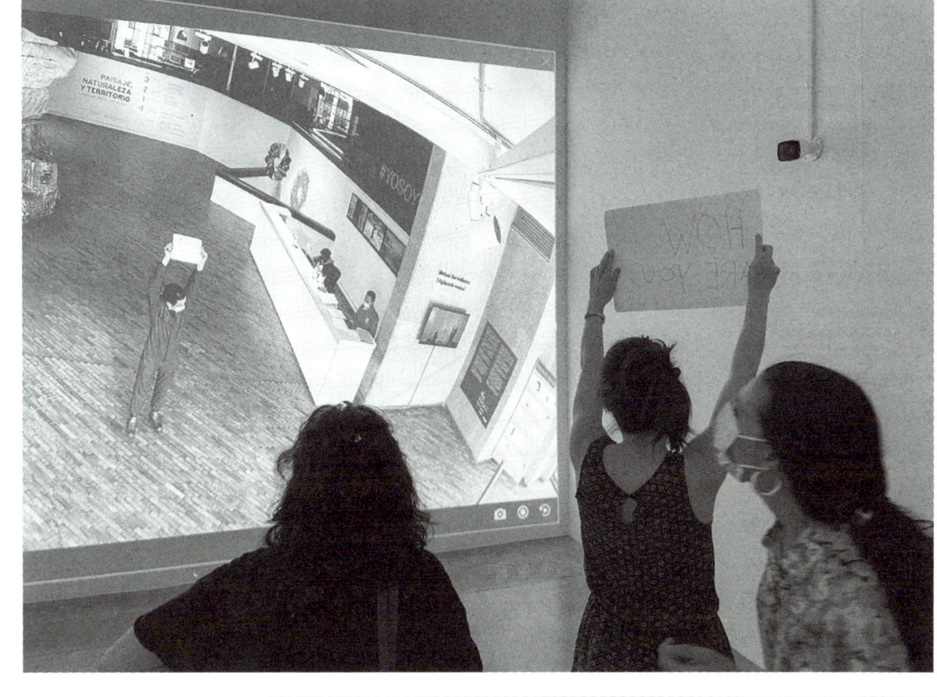

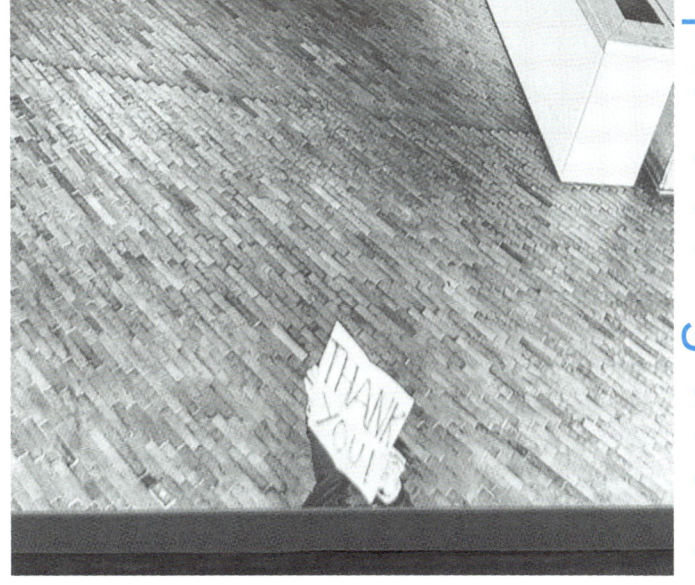

activity. create a sculpture using all chairs in the center of the space. meet at

6

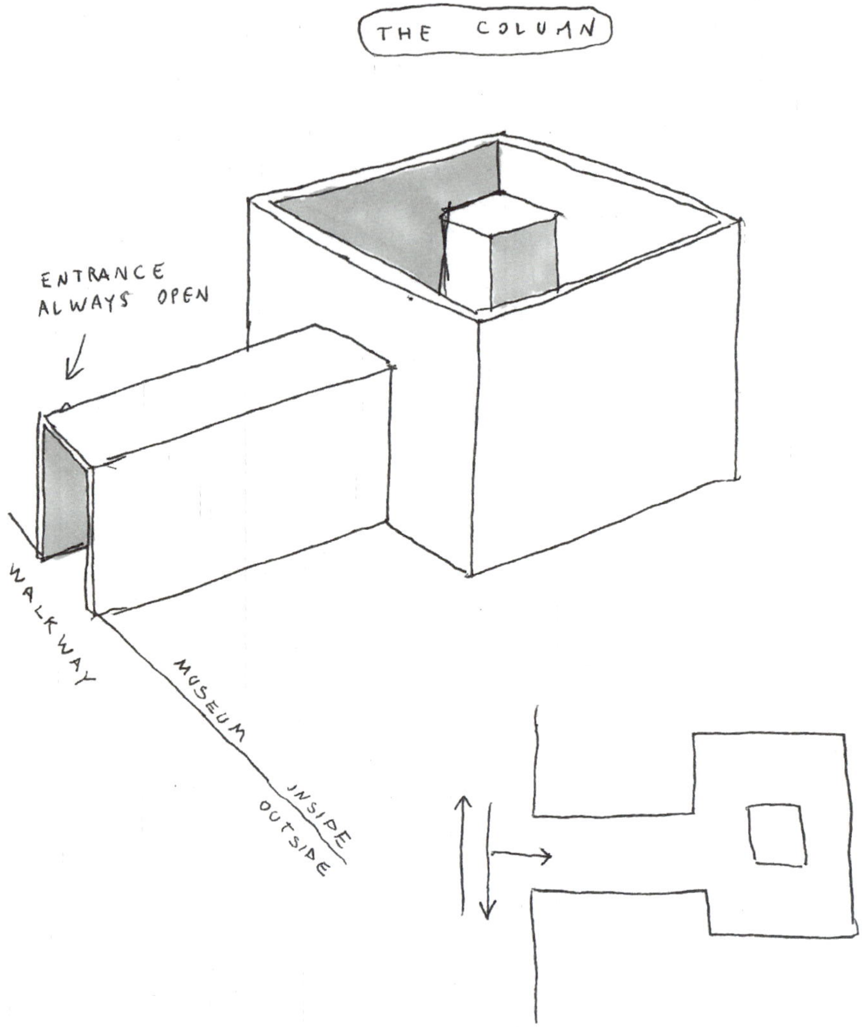

The Column, a distinct yet interconnected space, was intentionally constructed for exclusive access from the street, remaining open around the clock. It extended an open invitation for visitors to contribute graffiti, which built up over the course of the exhibition, while being surveilled by security cameras.

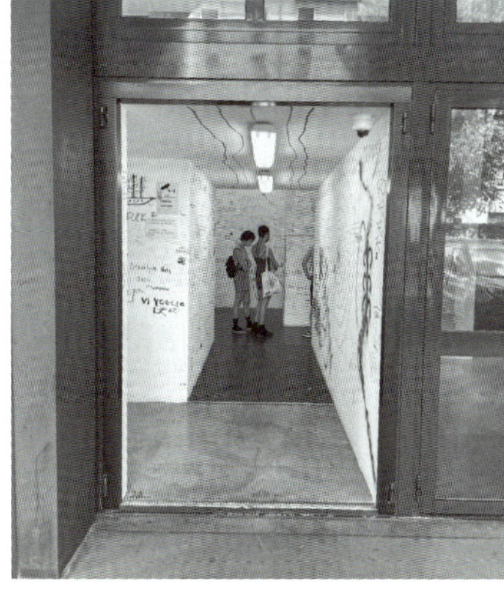
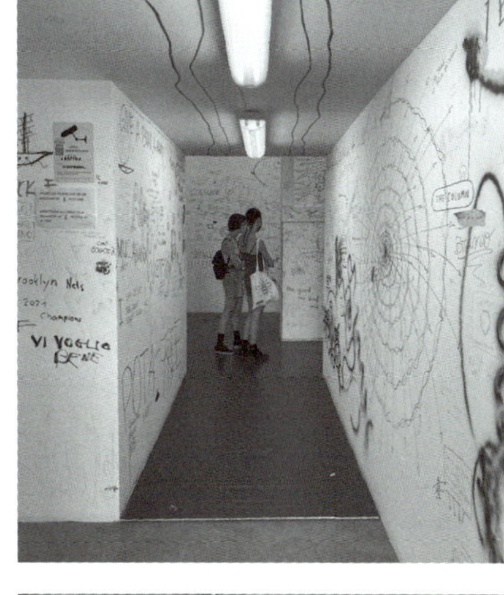
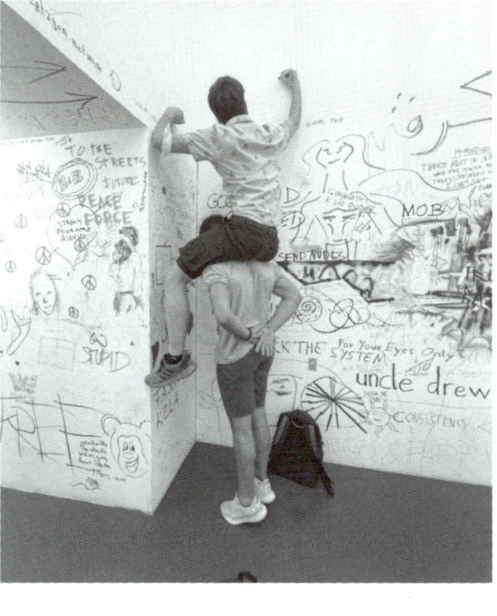

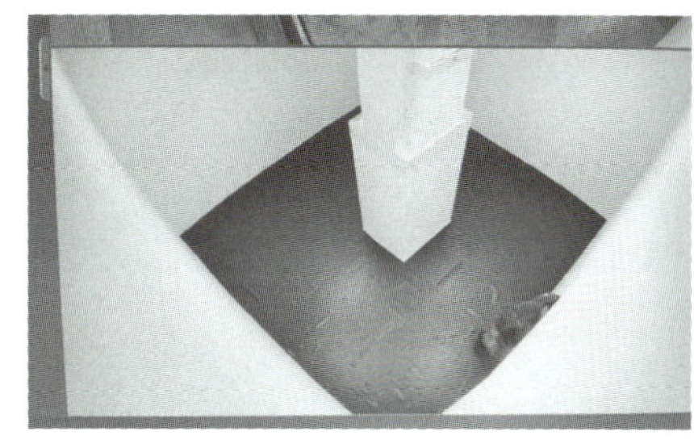

This separate room was crafted by reconstructing a segment of the main hall to have direct connection from the street yet no access to the exhibition's interior, a design which recast the traditional boundaries between the museum's internal space and the external world.

a sculpture using all chairs in the center of the

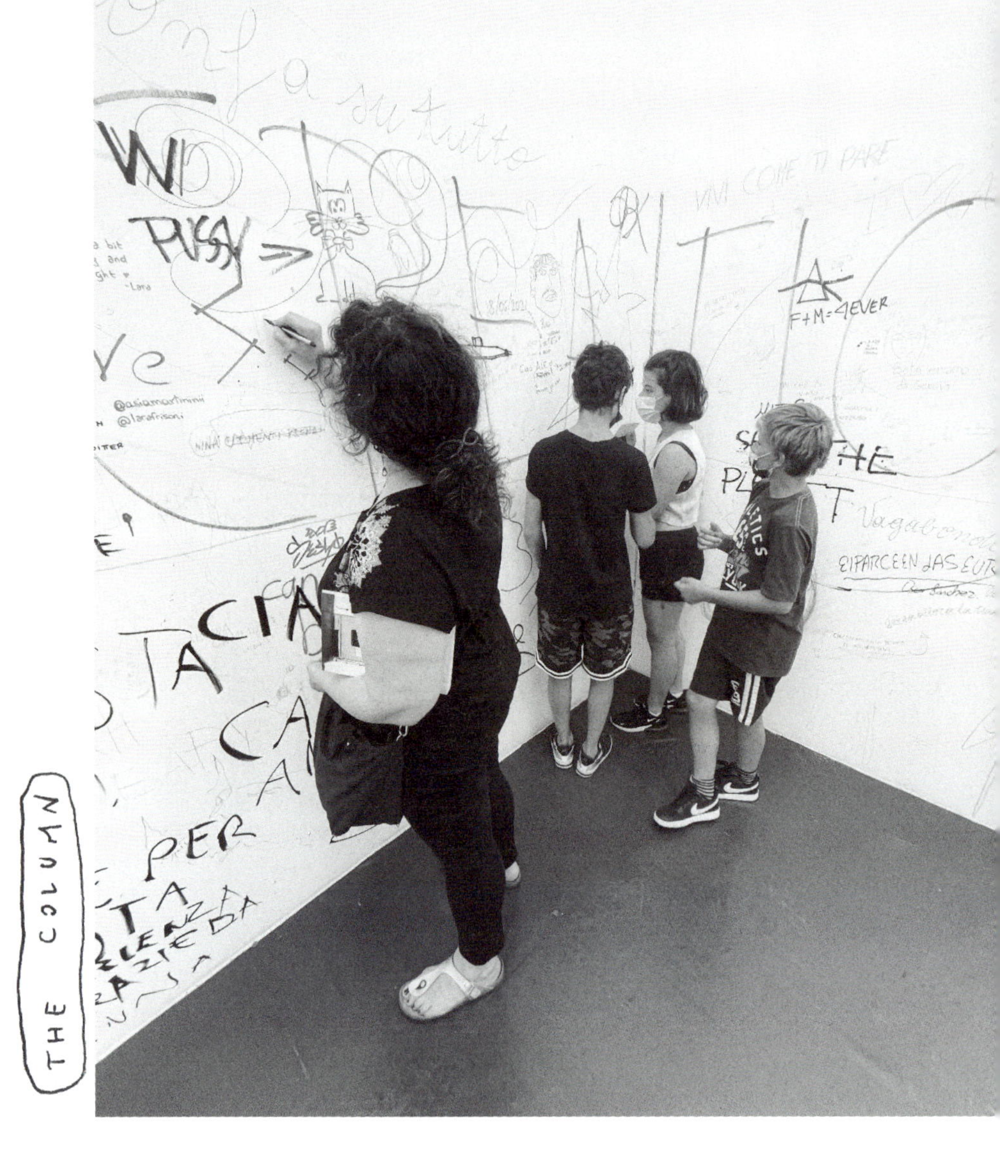

space.   hi my name is ....

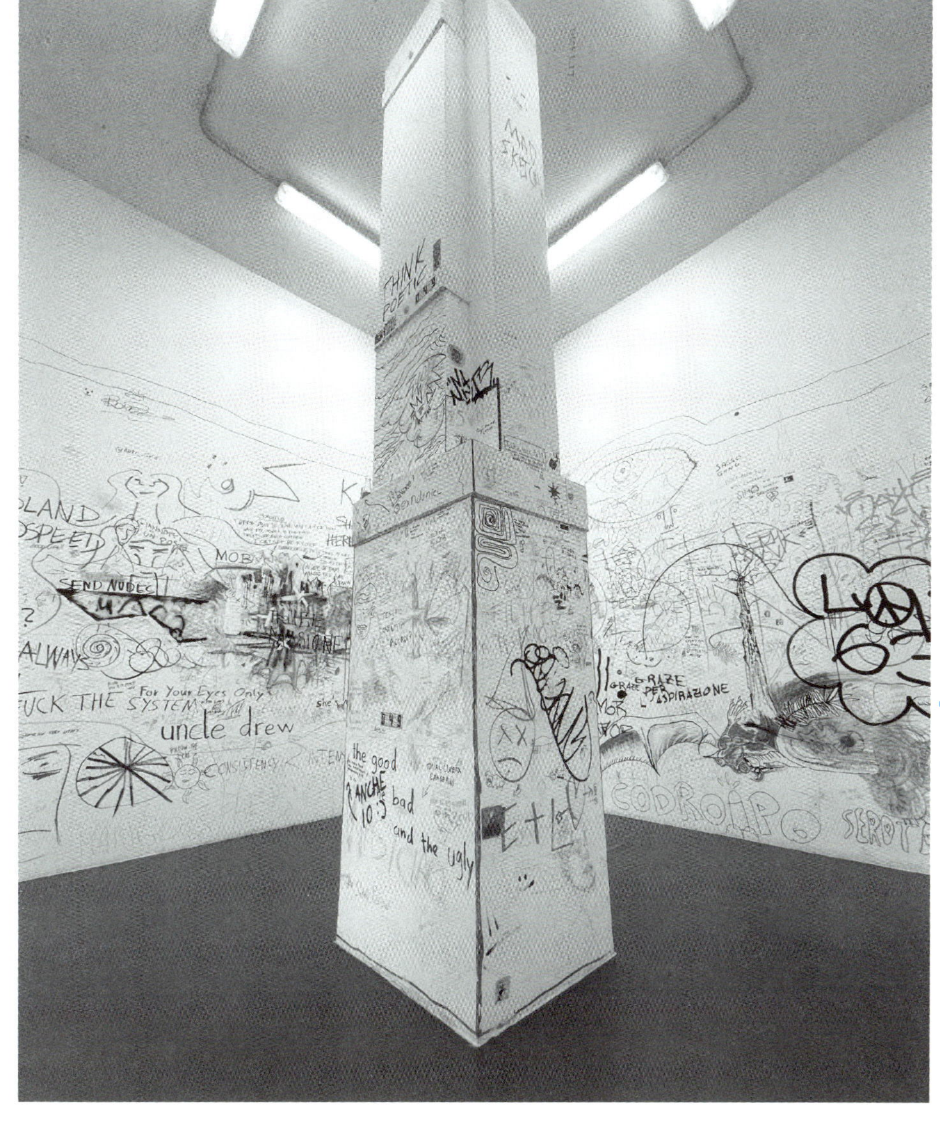

please remember me as part of this exhibition.

space.

meet at every half full

meet at every half full hour in the main hall to

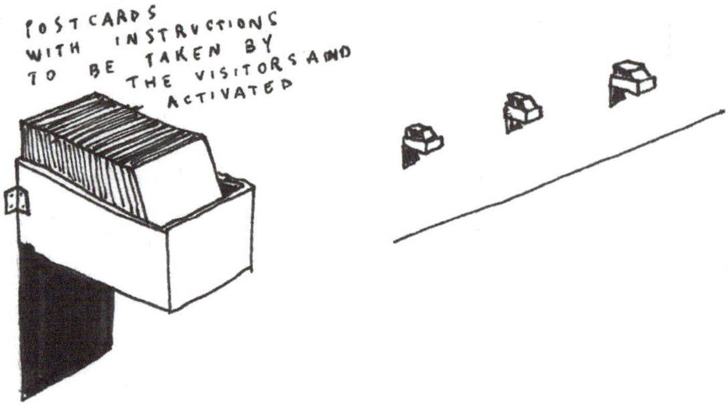

POSTCARDS WITH INSTRUCTIONS TO BE TAKEN BY THE VISITORS AND ACTIVATED

INSTRUCTION:

→① GIVE THIS CARD TO A STRANGER
② YOU AND THE STRANGER WILL ONE DAY START A REVOLUTION

→① GIVE THIS CARD TO ___ ONE OF YOUR PARENTS
② THIS CARD THEN READS: THANK YOU

→① OVERCOME YOUR SHYNESS AND TRY FEW DANCE STEPS
② IGNORE THE ABOVE TEXT AND HOPE NOBODY SAW YOU

→ FIND THE NEXT BOX COINTAINING THES SAME MESSAGES AS THIS ONE AN LEAVE THIS POSTCARD THERE

→ FOLLOW THE INSTRUCTIONS ON THIS CARD TO CREATE THE SHAPE OF THIS ROOM ON THE WALL

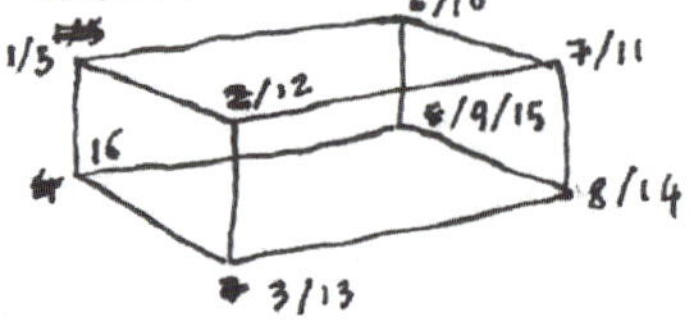

6/10
1/5
7/11
2/12
8/9/15
16
8/14
3/13

take a risk, please involve me.

hour in the main hall to socialize all to-

gether. if you break the rules, please do it

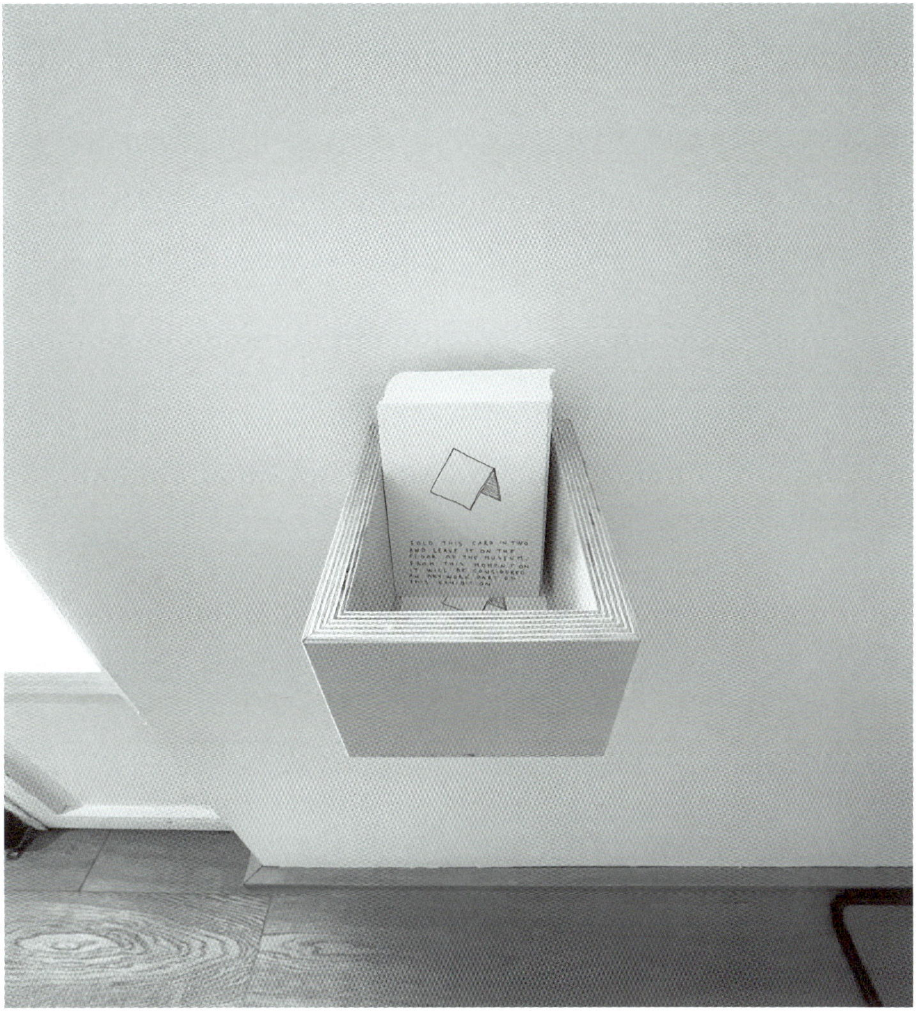

unnoticed. if you are planning to

This cardbox with instructions was placed behind the
breached entrance to the collection presentation
at the top floor.

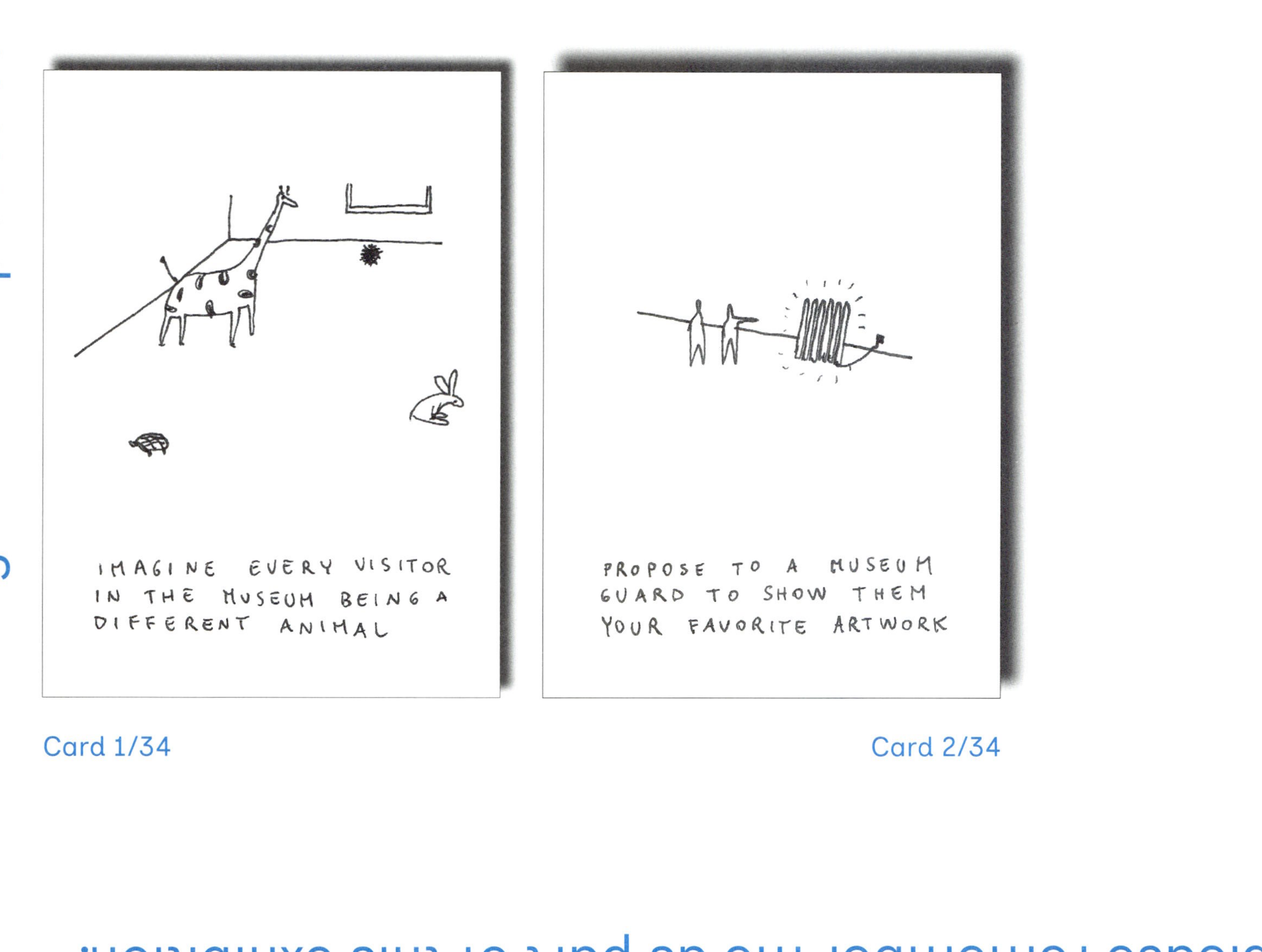

IMAGINE EVERY VISITOR
IN THE MUSEUM BEING A
DIFFERENT ANIMAL
Card 1/34
PROPOSE TO A MUSEUM
GUARD TO SHOW THEM
YOUR FAVORITE ARTWORK
Card 2/34
please consi-
socialize all together.
on in space.
in my name is ....
please remember me as part of this exhibition.

Card 3/34

Card 4/34

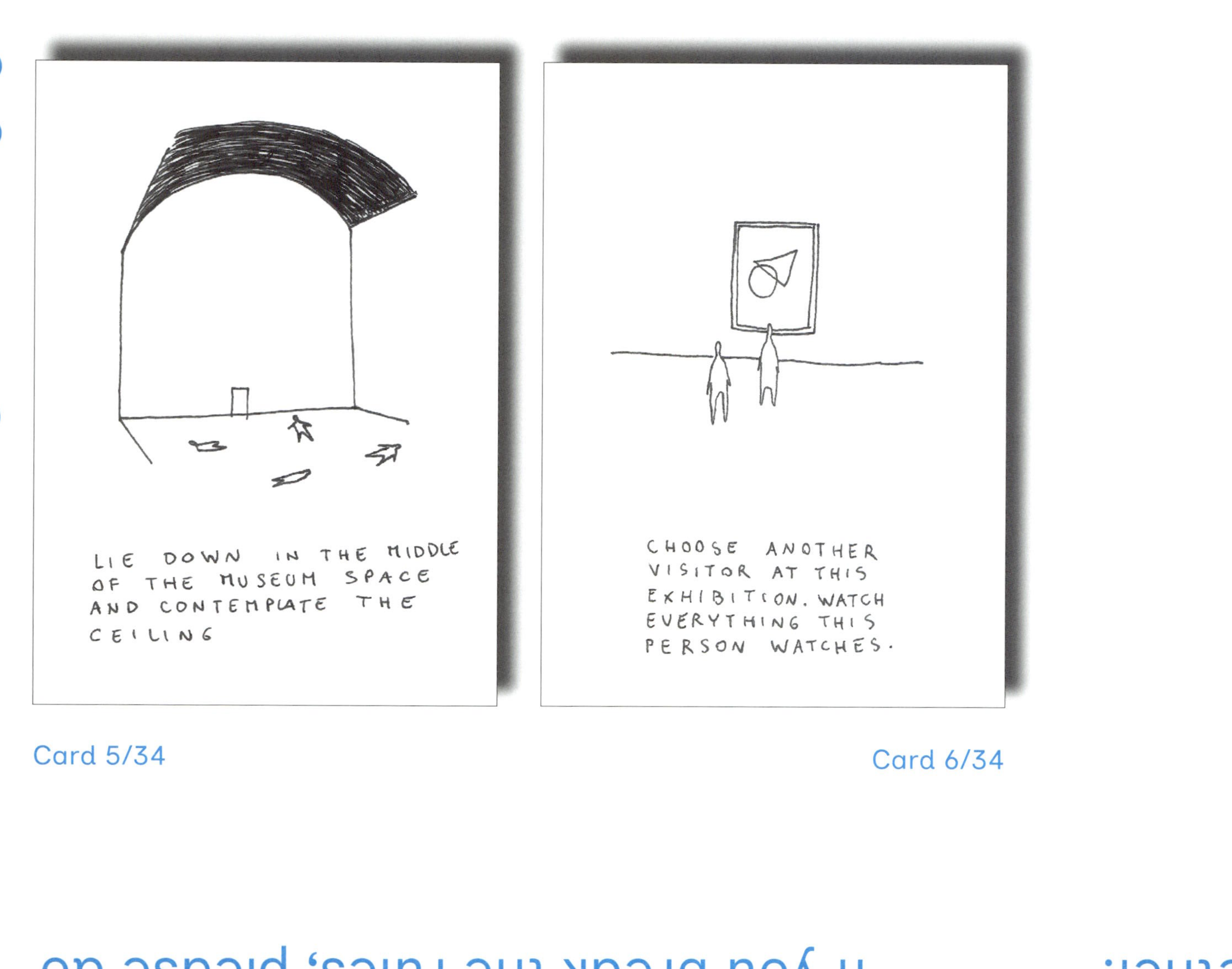

Card 5/34

Card 6/34

draw "string drawings" and engage vi-

hour in the main hall to socialize all to-

if you break the rules, please do

gether.

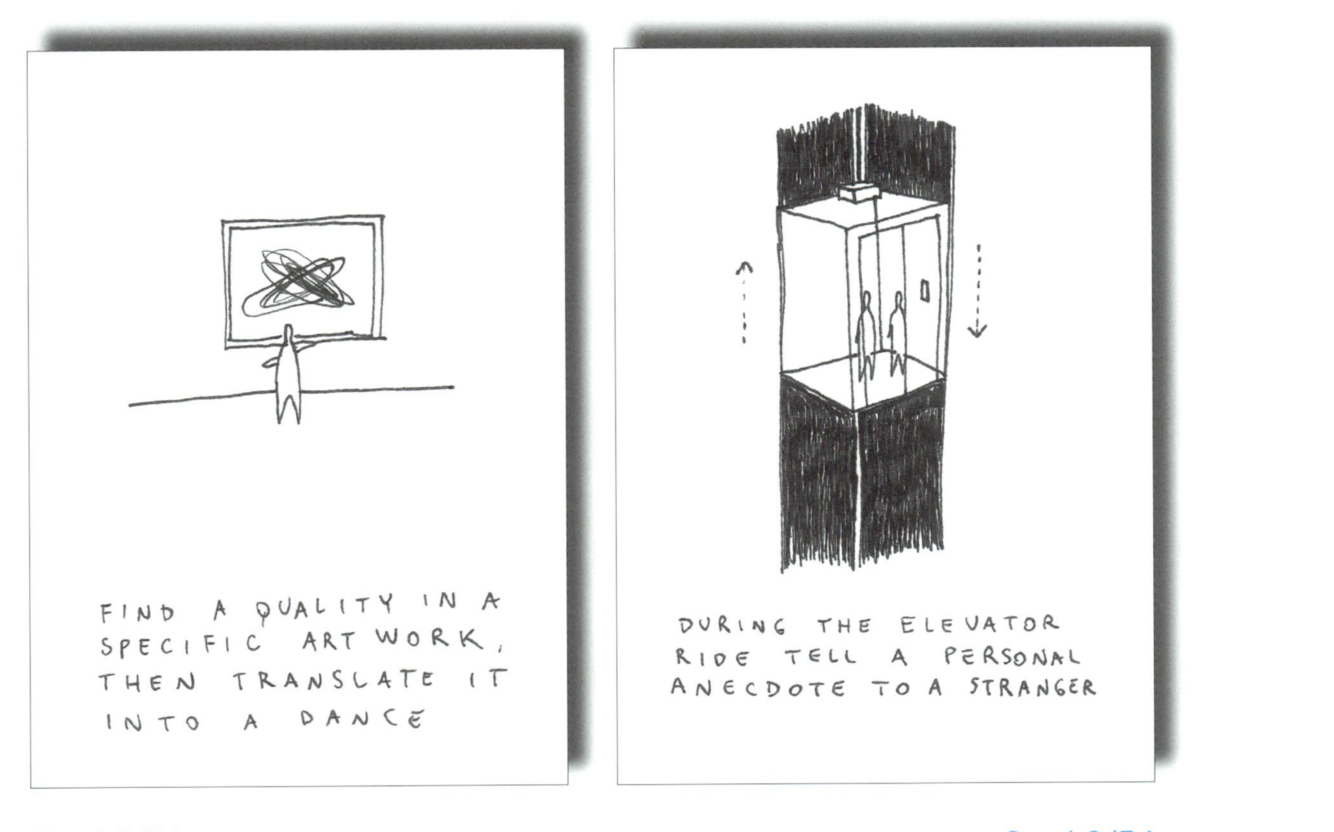

Card 7/34

Card 8/34

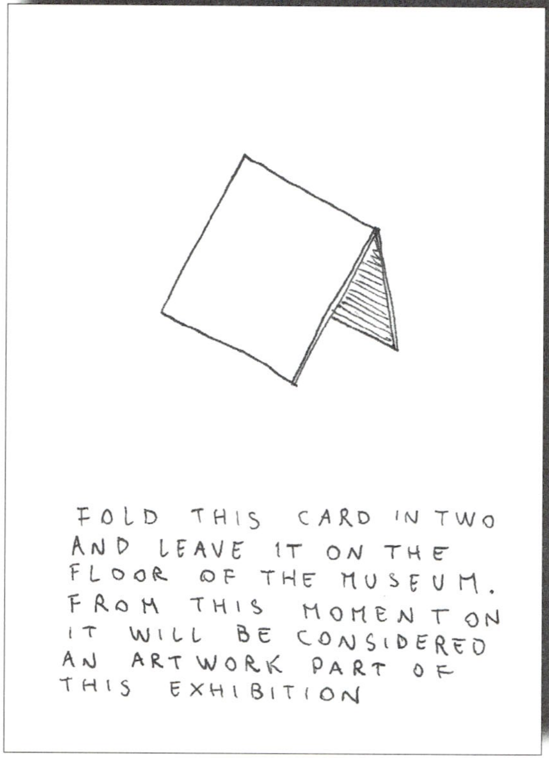

FOLD THIS CARD IN TWO
AND LEAVE IT ON THE
FLOOR OF THE MUSEUM.
FROM THIS MOMENT ON
IT WILL BE CONSIDERED
AN ARTWORK PART OF
THIS EXHIBITION

Card 9/34

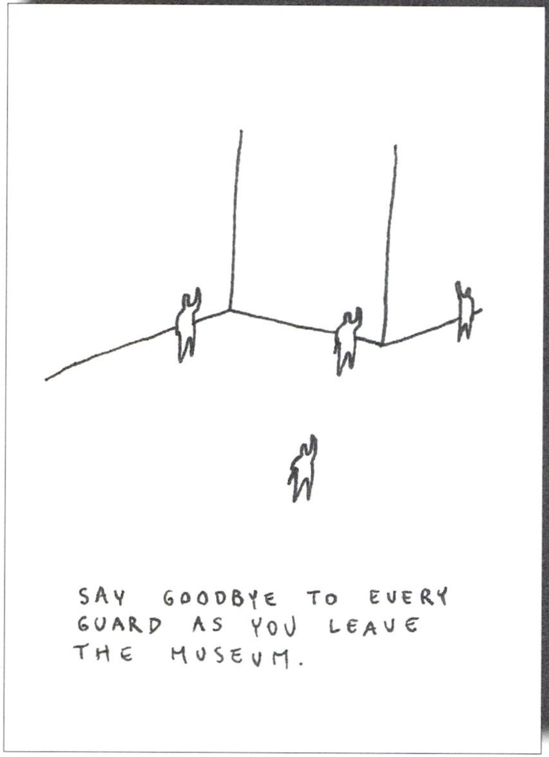

SAY GOODBYE TO EVERY
GUARD AS YOU LEAVE
THE MUSEUM.

Card 10/34

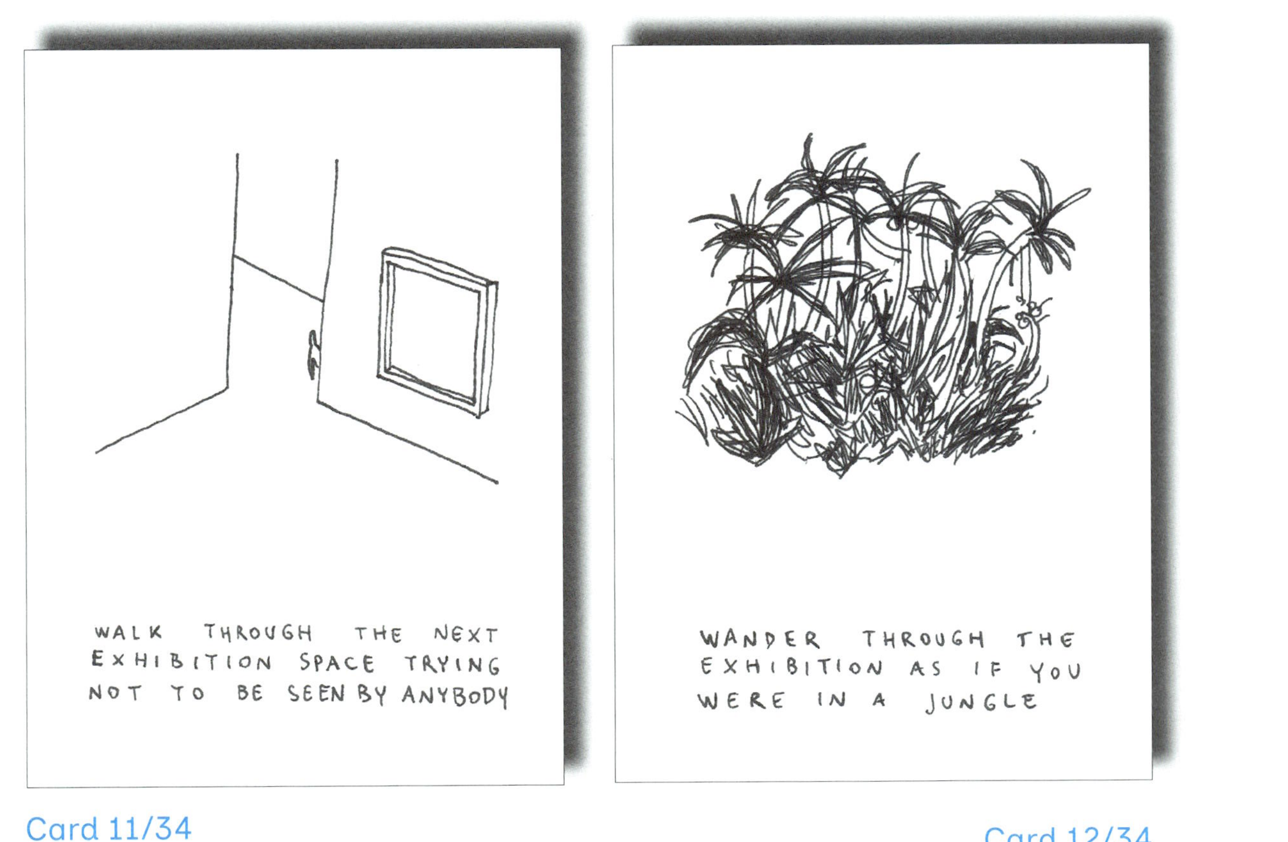

Card 11/34

Card 12/34

take an unusual position

minutes?

stiors in the activity.   create a

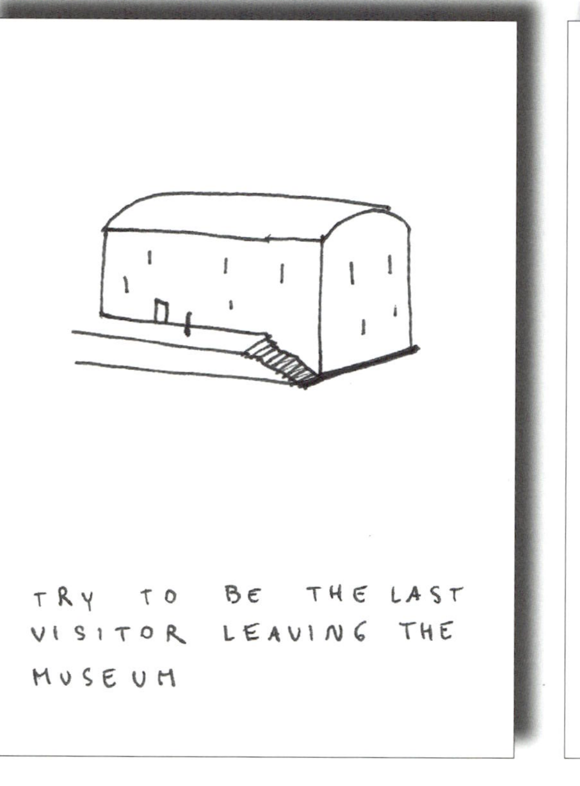

Card 13/34

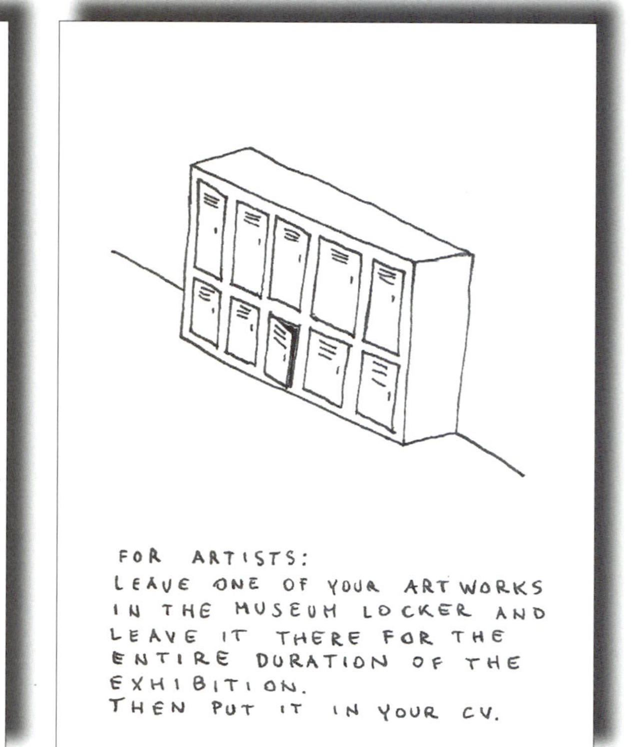

Card 14/34

sculpture using all chairs in the center of the

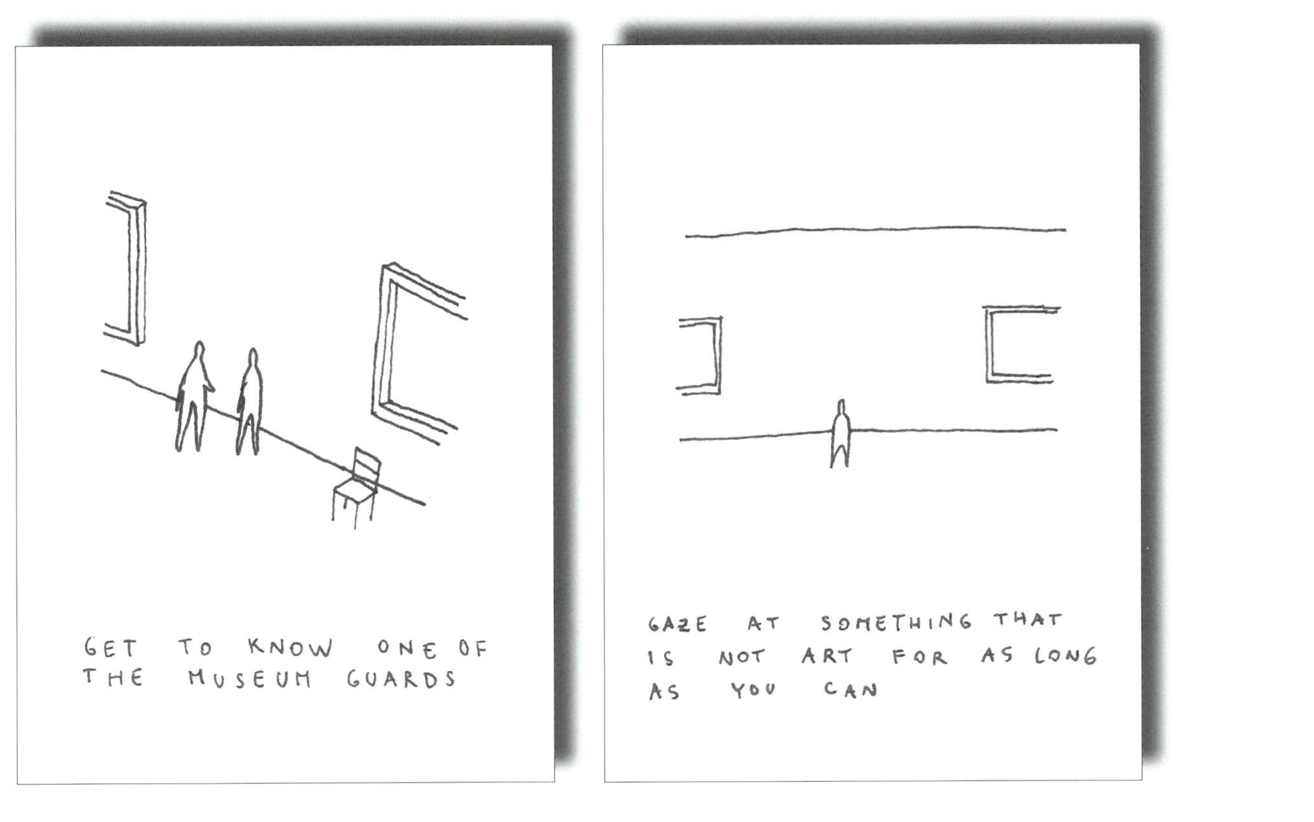

Card 15/34

Card 16/34

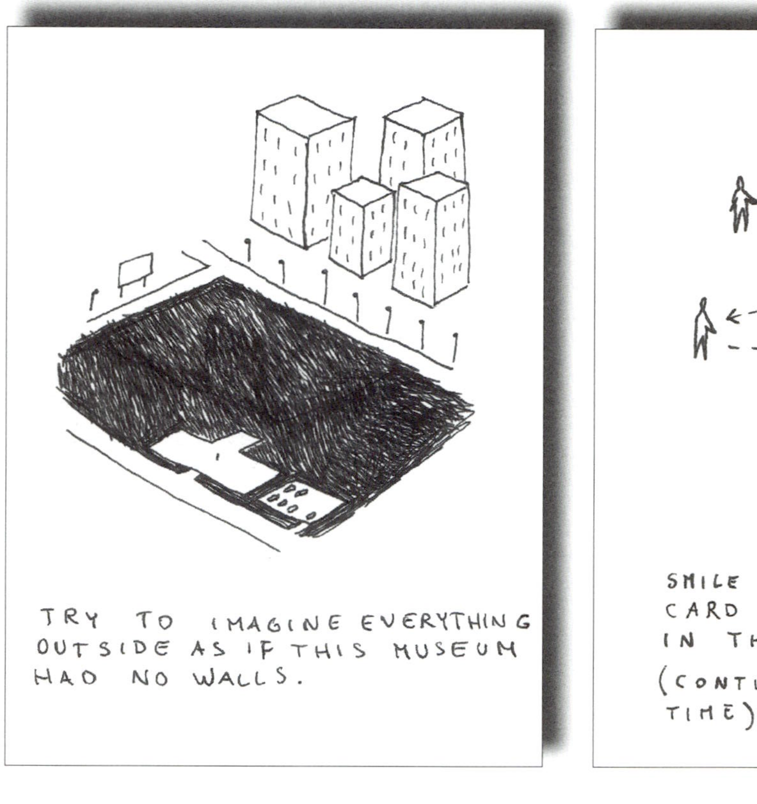

Card 17/34

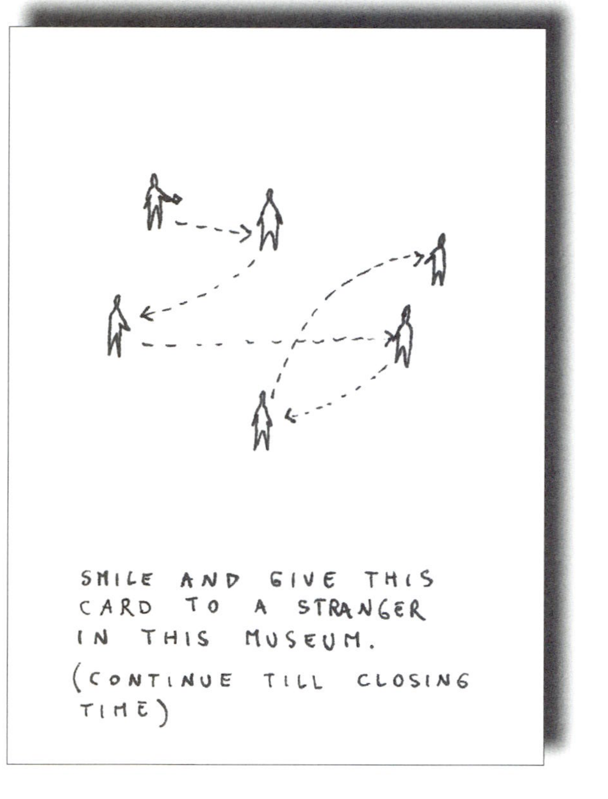

Card 18/34

gether.   if you break the rules, please do it

our in the main hall to socialize all to-

unnoticed.   if you are planning to

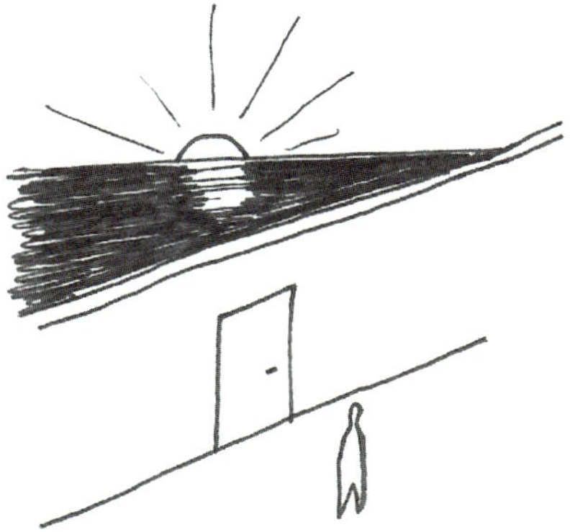

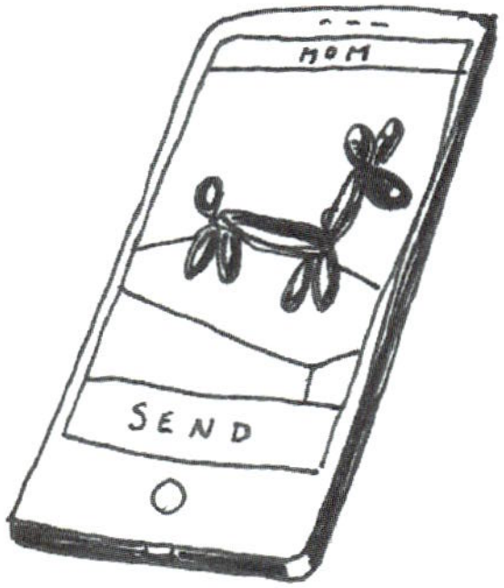

Card 19/34

Card 20/34

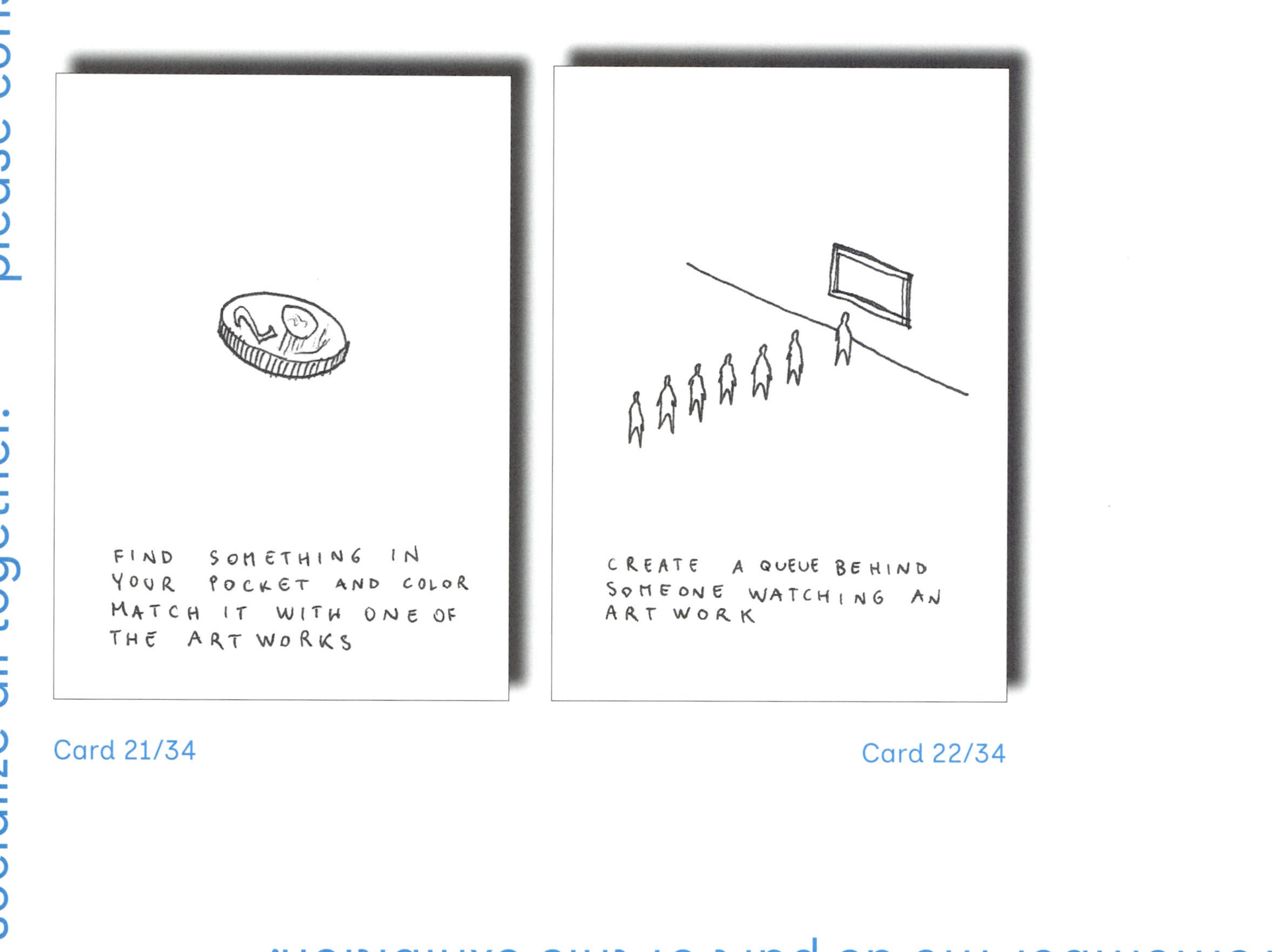
please consi-
socialize all together.
remember me as part of this exhibition.
on in space. in my name is .... please

FIND SOMETHING IN
YOUR POCKET AND COLOR
MATCH IT WITH ONE OF
THE ARTWORKS

Card 21/34

CREATE A QUEUE BEHIND
SOMEONE WATCHING AN
ARTWORK

Card 22/34

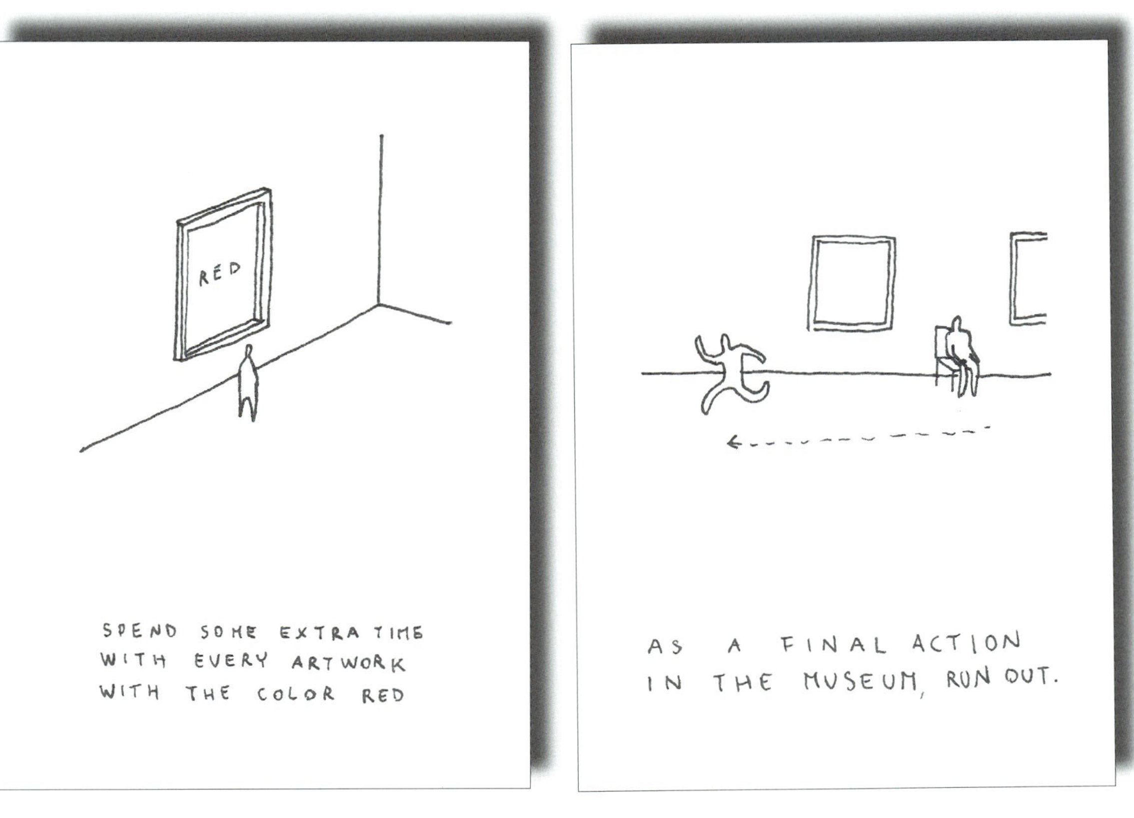

Card 23/34

Card 24/34

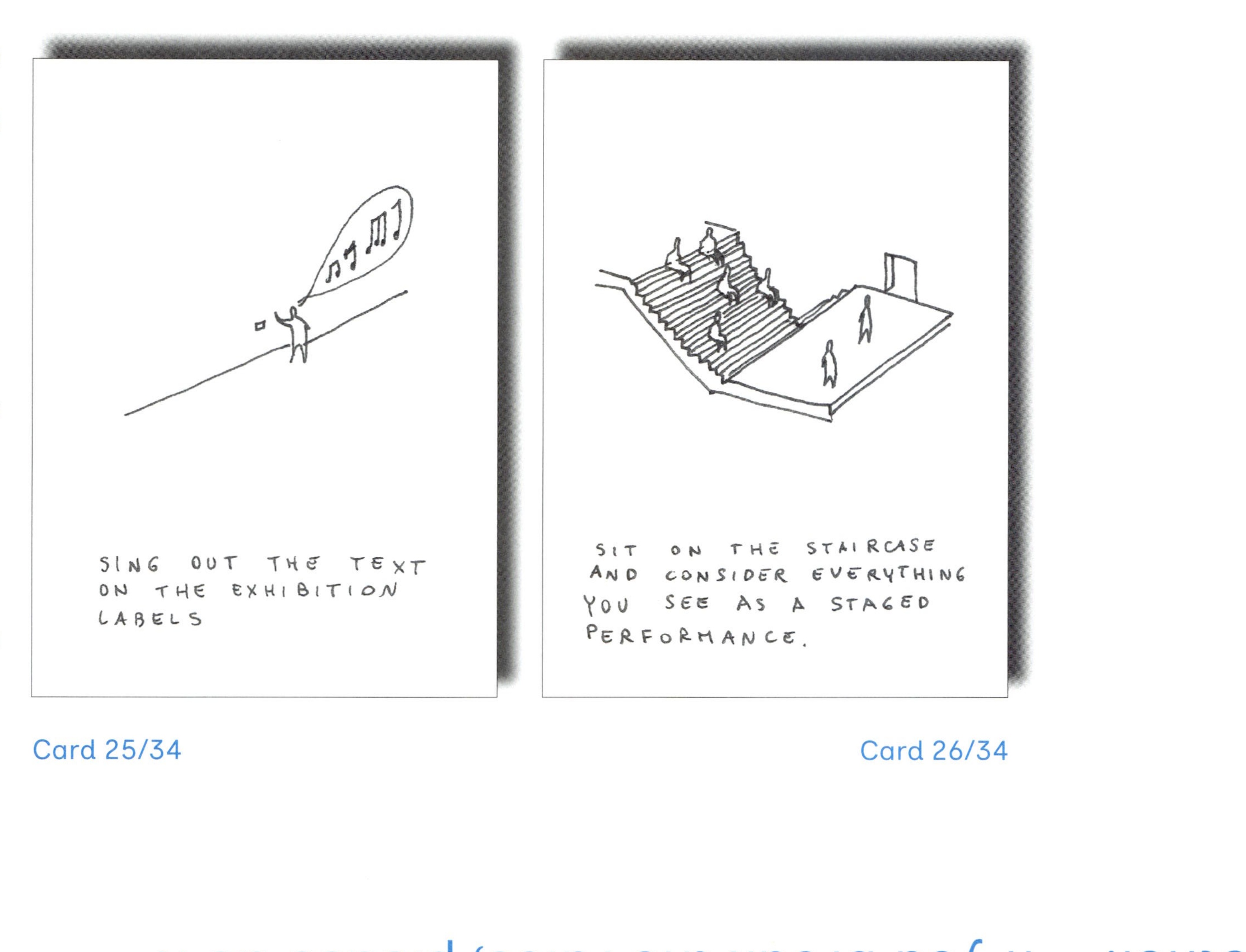

Card 25/34

Card 26/34

Card 27/34

VISIT THE MUSEUM WITH
A FRIEND AND AT THE
END COMPARE THE
NUMBER OF STEPS YOU TOOK

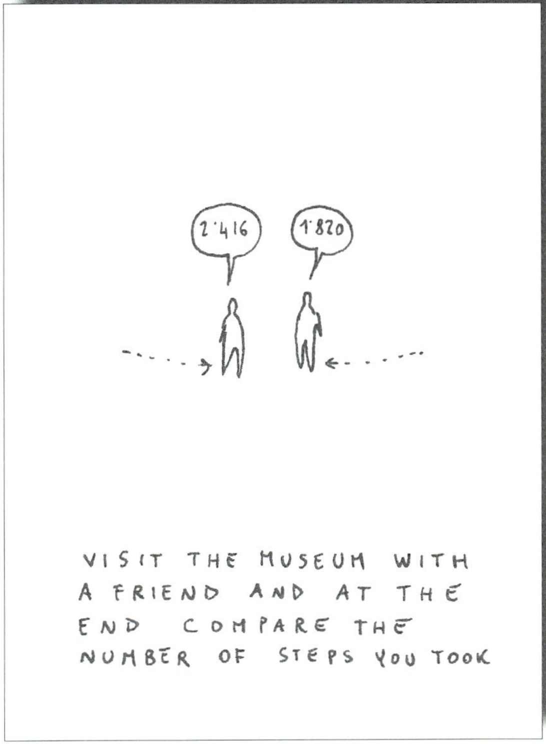

Card 28/34

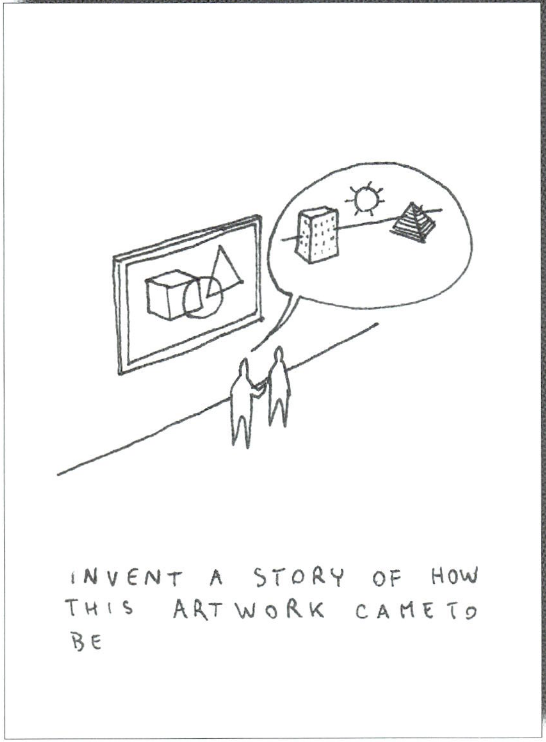

INVENT A STORY OF HOW
THIS ARTWORK CAME TO
BE

unnoticed.

if you are planning to

would you mind taking over my position for a mi-

er that your safety is our priority.

Card 29/34

ONCE HOME FRAME YOUR
TICKET AS A REMINDER
OF YOUR EXPERIENCE

Card 30/34

FIND A GROUP OF TOURISTS
AND IMPROVISE YOURSELF AS
A MUSEUM TOUR GUIDE

Card 31/34

Card 32/34

...ake a risk, please involve me.

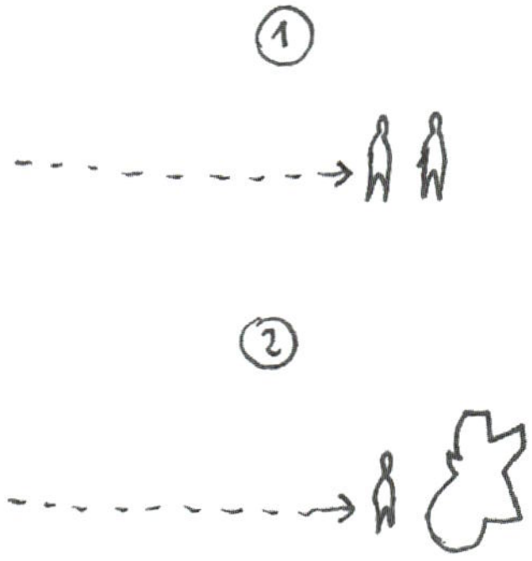

please cons-

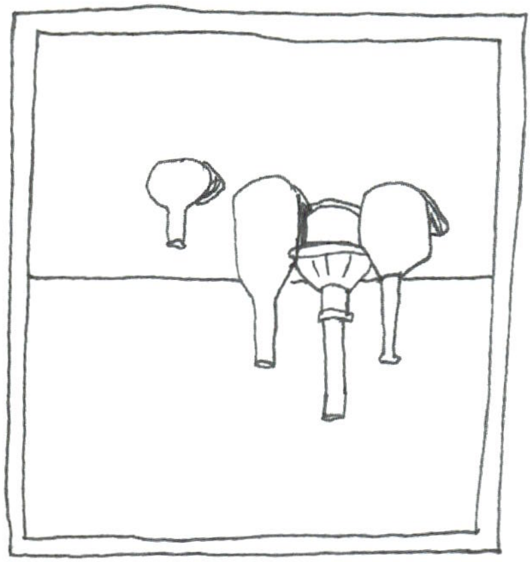

Card 33/34

Card 34/34

n space.   hi my name is .... please

remember me as part of this exhibition.

draw string drawings and engage vi-

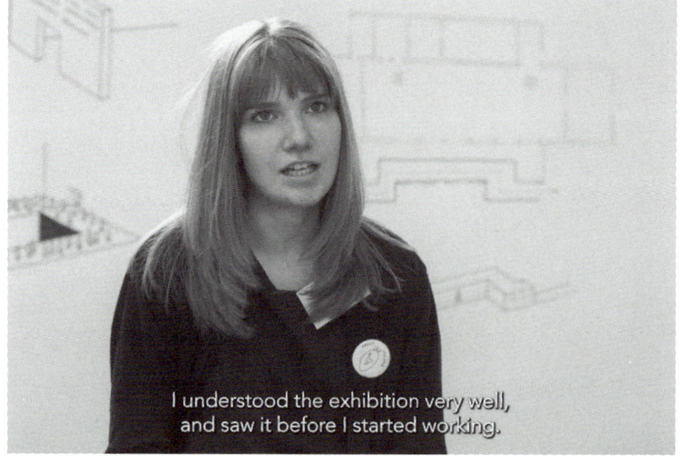
I understood the exhibition very well,
and saw it before I started working.

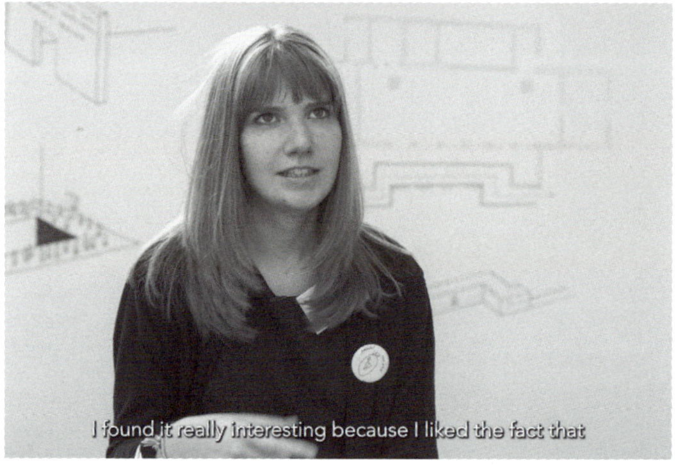
I found it really interesting because I liked the fact that

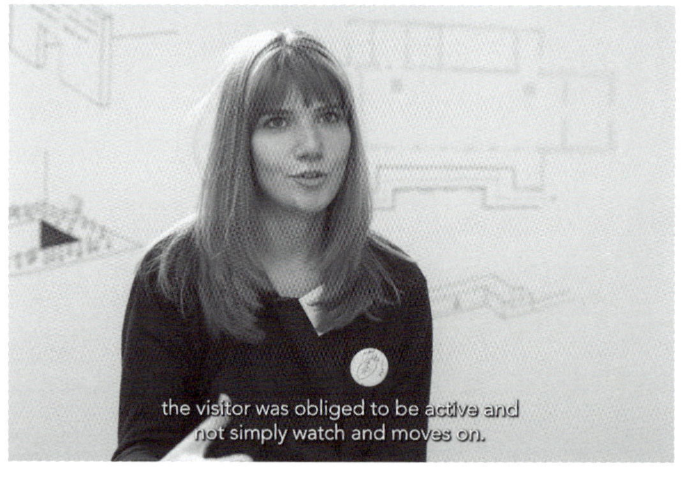
the visitor was obliged to be active and
not simply watch and moves on.

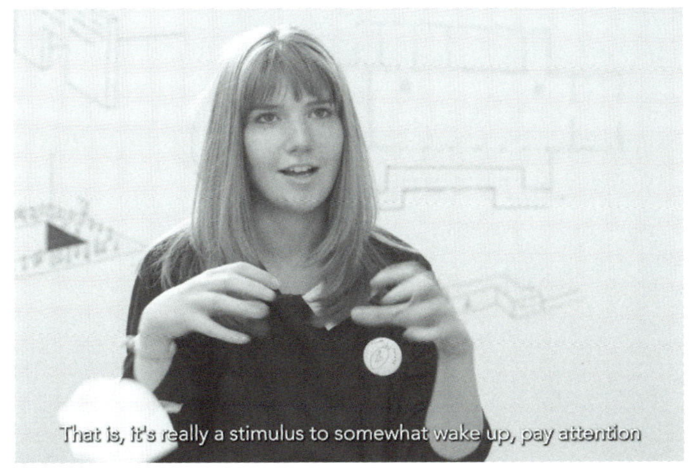

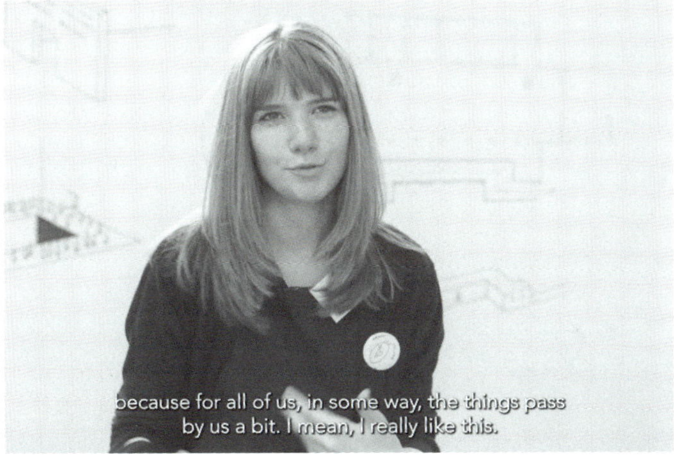

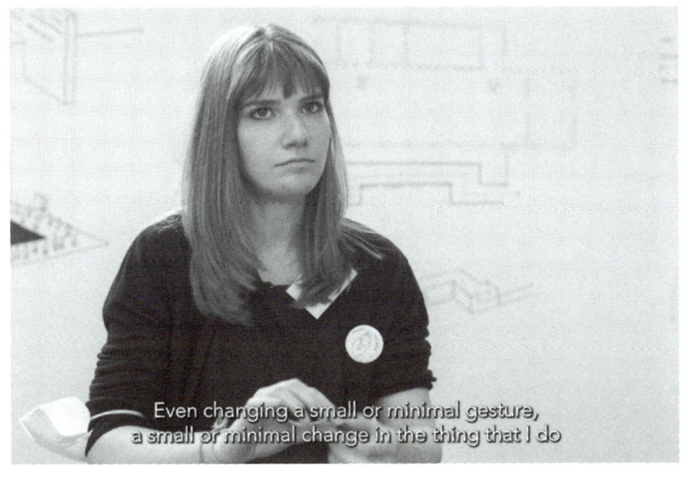

If you break the rules, please do it unnoticed.

If you are planning to take a risk,

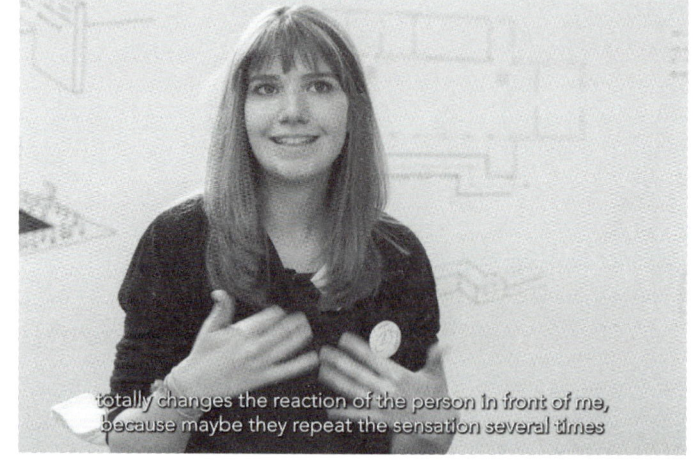
totally changes the reaction of the person in front of me,
because maybe they repeat the sensation several times

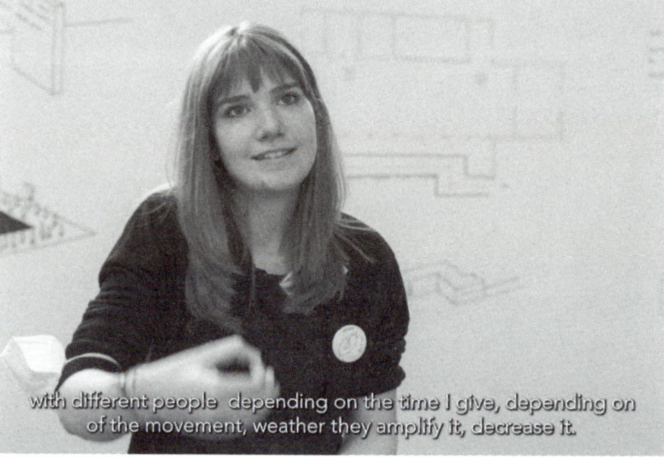
with different people depending on the time I give, depending on
of the movement, weather they amplify it, decrease it.

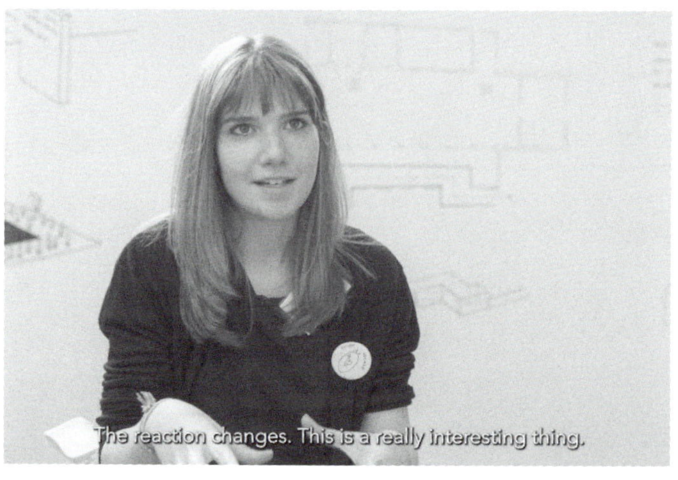
The reaction changes. This is a really interesting thing.

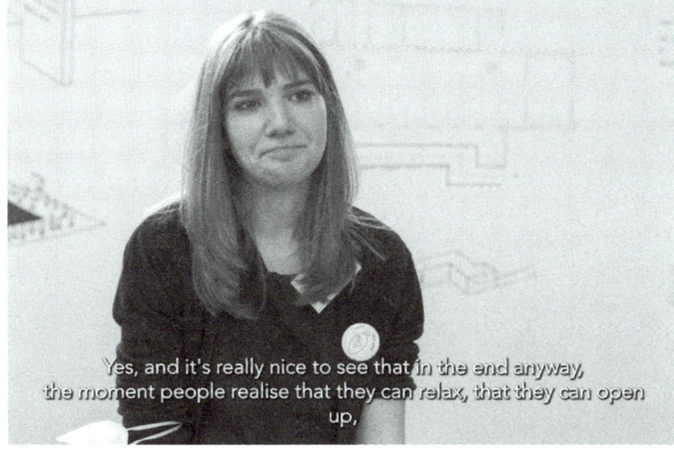
Yes, and it's really nice to see that in the end anyway,
the moment people realise that they can relax, that they can open
up,

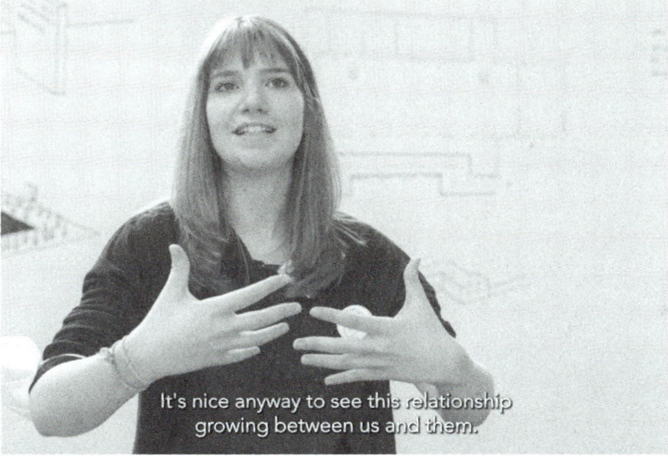
It's nice anyway to see this relationship
growing between us and them.

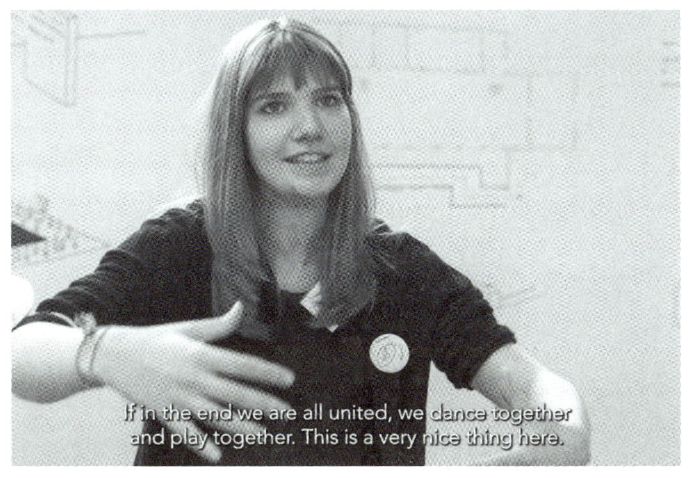
If in the end we are all united, we dance together
and play together. This is a very nice thing here.

drawings" and engage visitors in the

you break the rules, please do it unnoticed. it

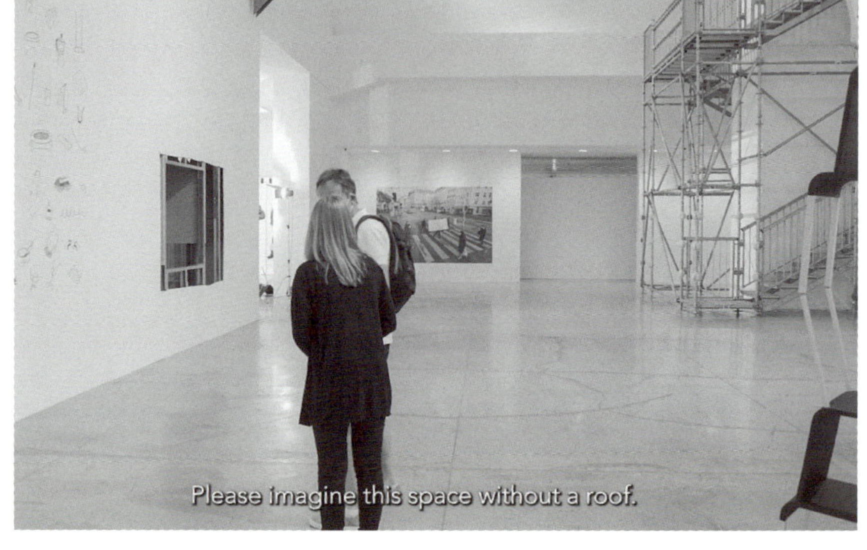

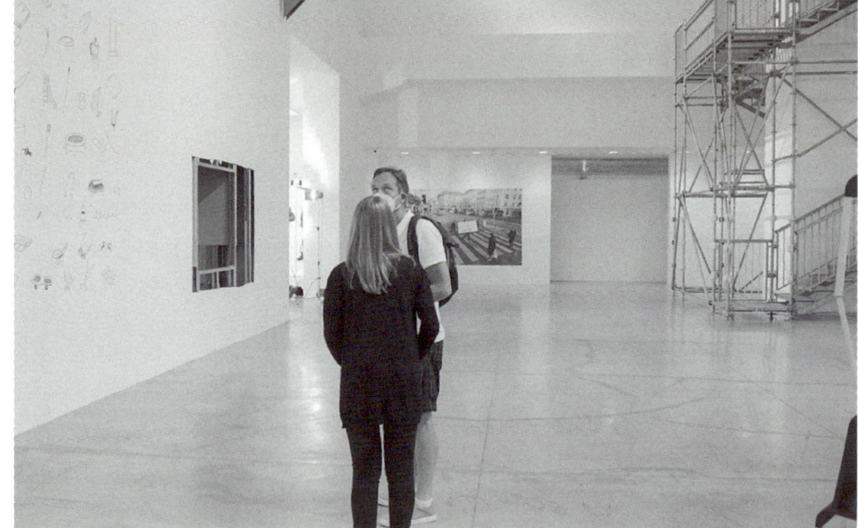

rian to socialize an together. If

activity.

create a sculpture

using all chairs in the center of the space.

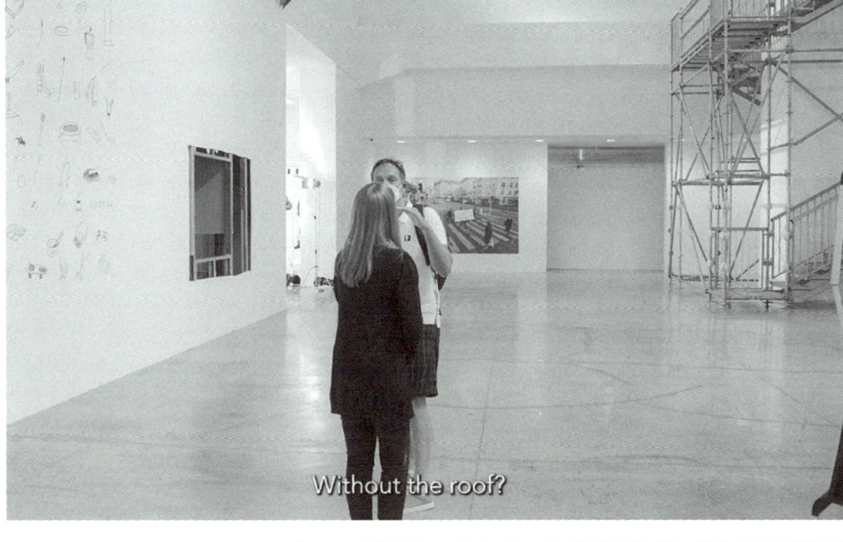
Without the roof?

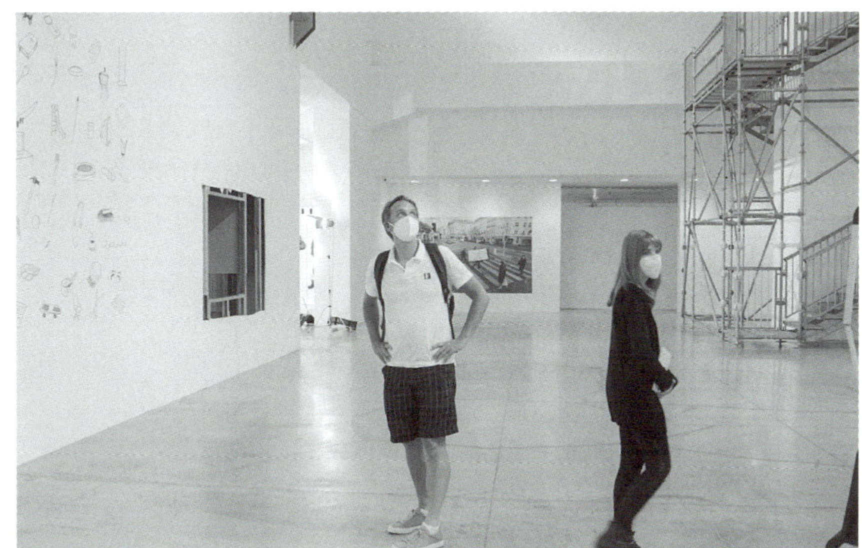

meet at every half hour in the main

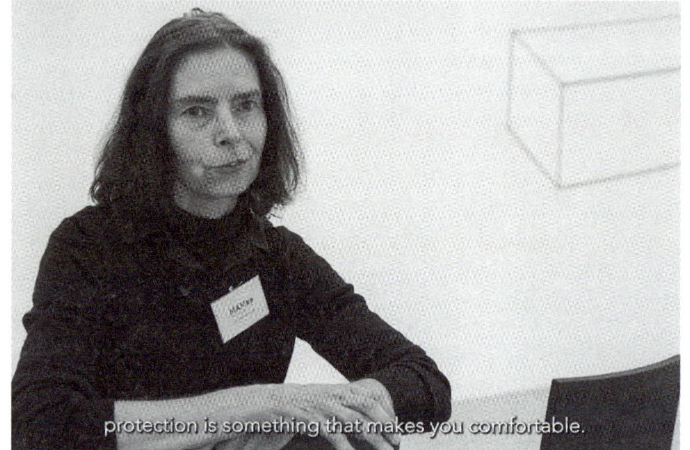

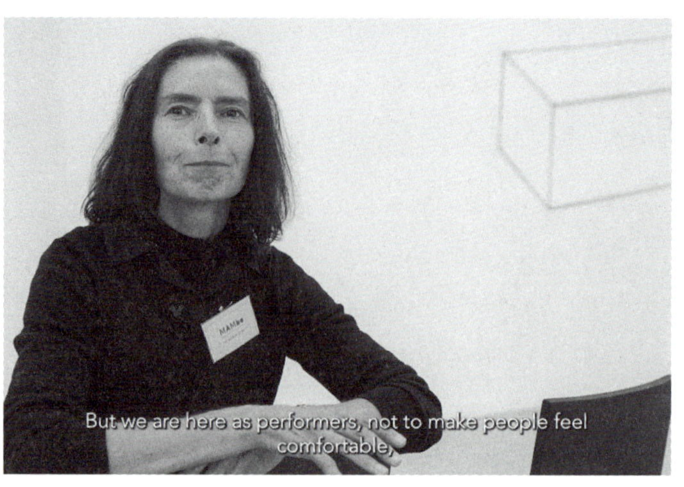

If you are planning to take a risk,

unnoticed.

If you break the rules, please do it

a sculpture using all chairs in the center of the space. meet at every hair full hour in the main hall to socialize all together.

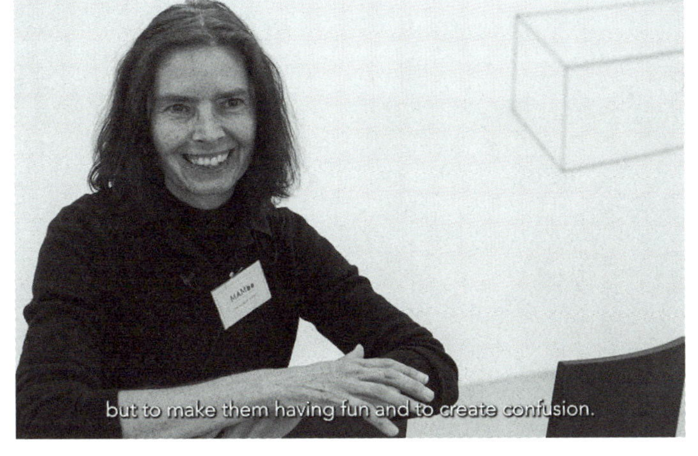

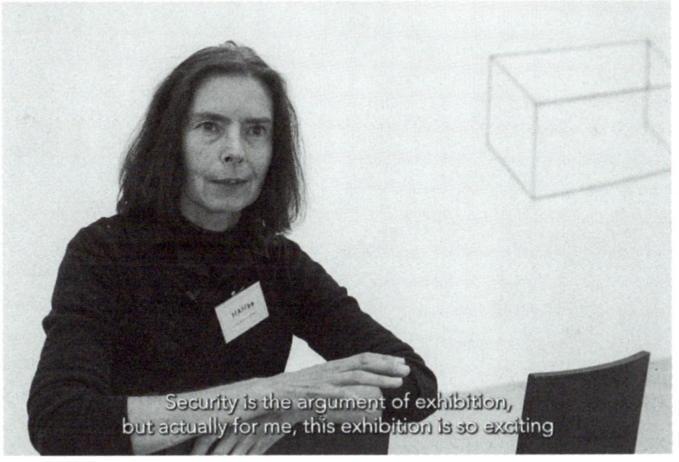

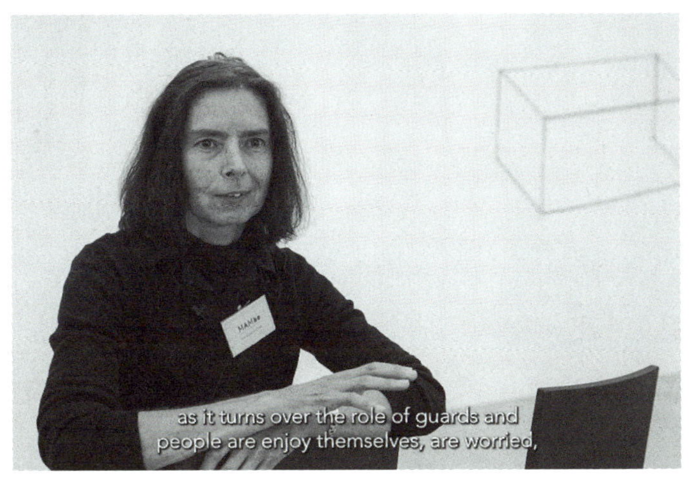

please involve me.   meet at every

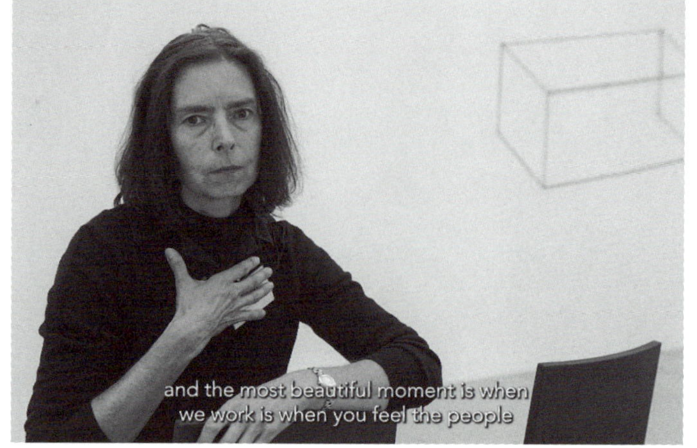
and the most beautiful moment is when
we work is when you feel the people

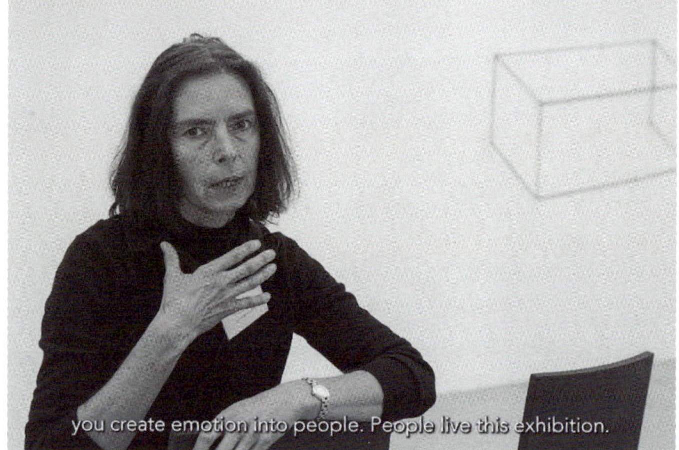
you create emotion into people. People live this exhibition.

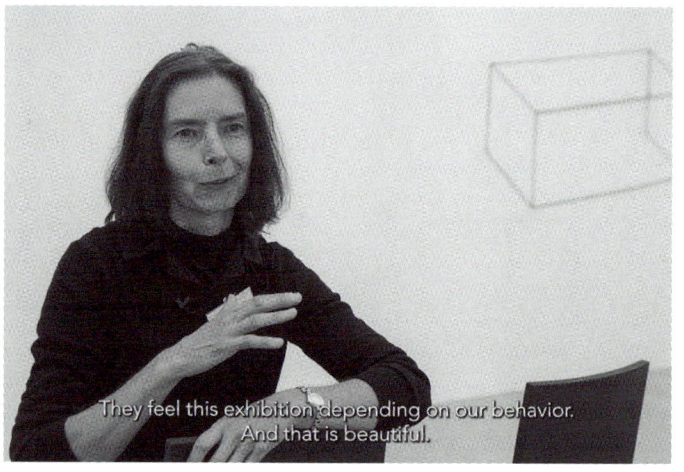
They feel this exhibition depending on our behavior.
And that is beautiful.

take an unusual position in space.

nutes?

-nind taking over my position for 5 mi-half full hour in the main hall to socialize all together. please consider that your safety is our priority. would you

If you break the rules, try not to be noticed.

position in space.   hi my name is

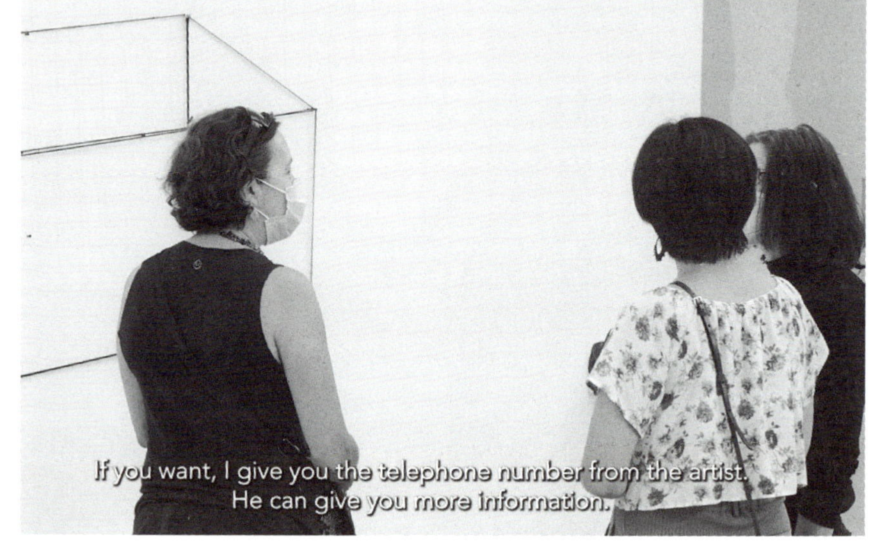

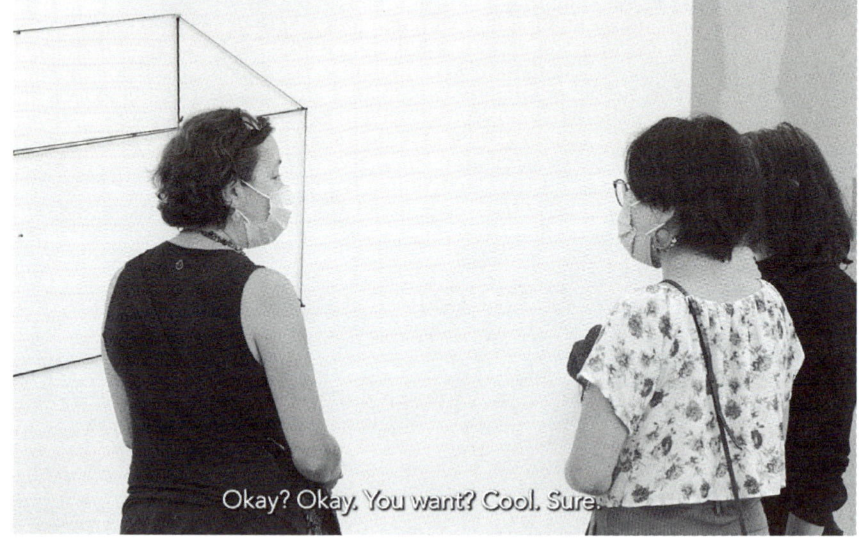

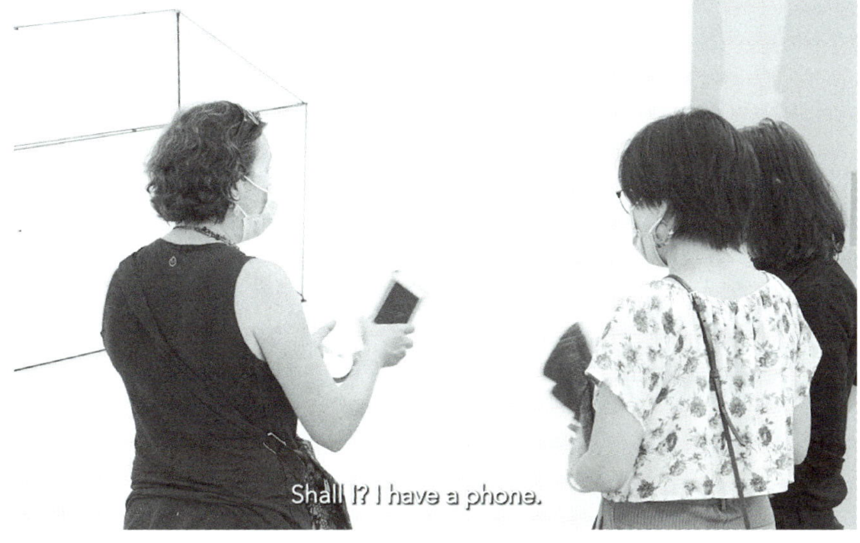

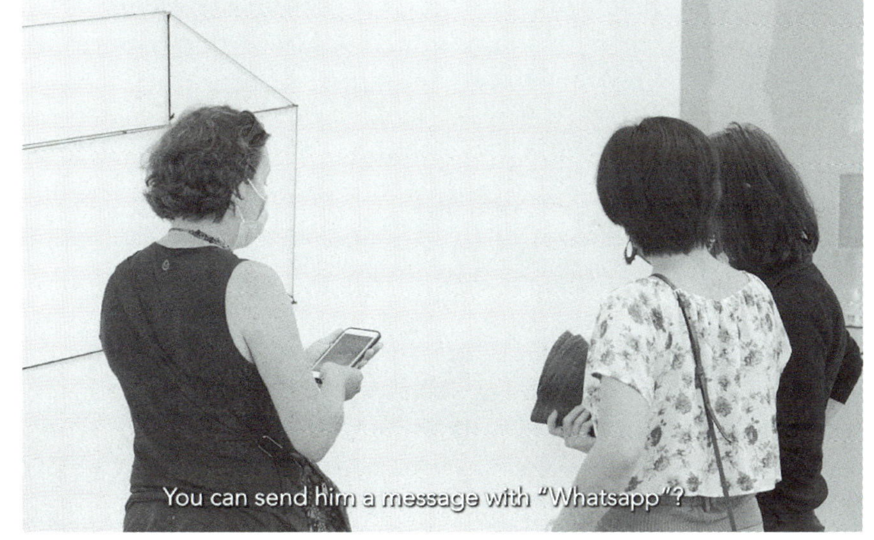

this exhibition. draw string drawings and

engage visitors in the activity. cre-

that your safety is our priority.   would

Aldo Giannotti
(Genova, 1977)

is an Italian artist who has lived and worked in Vienna since 2000. Often departing from the medium of drawing as a tool for imagining, planning, and visualizing possibilities, he works across modes of installation, performance, and the construction of situations to explore topics such as personal/cultural identity, collectivity, and structures of power. He frequently stages situations involving visitor participation. By shifting and rearranging, he challenges the meaning of terrains and spaces such as nations, institutions, and individual positions, unpacking power structures and producing new possibilities.

He studied at the Accademia di Belle Arti in Carrara, Italy, the Wimbledon University of Arts in London, England, and the Fine Arts Academy in Munich, Germany. His work has been presented and realized in collaboration with various institutions, such as Albertina in Vienna, Kunsthalle Wien, Lentos Museum in Linz, Kunsthaus Graz, Kunstraum Niederösterreich in Vienna, Ar/ge kunst in Bolzano, Künstlerhaus Dortmund, Museum der Moderne in Salzburg, Austrian Cultural Forum in London, Donaufestival in Krems, Museum of Contemporary Art in Zagreb, MAMbo in Bologna, among others.

He is the recipient of numerous prizes and awards, including a 2020 Pollock Krasner Foundation Grant, The Austrian Graphic Art Award (2019), Pomilio Blumm Prize, Milano (2017) and a Golden Lion at the Biennale di Venezia for Chris Haring's & Liquid Loft's "Posing Project B – The art of seduction" (2007).

He is represented by Projektraum Viktor Bucher in Vienna.

take an unusual position in

minutes?

you mind taking over my position for a

Lorenzo Balbi
(Turin, 1982)

(lives and works in Bologna) is an art historian and curator. Since 2017, he has been artistic director of MAMbo - Museum of Modern Art in Bologna.

Ivan Carozzi
(Massa, 1972)

served as editor-in-chief of Linus and authored TV programs such as "Le invasioni barbariche," "Lessico amoroso," and "Dilemmi." He has written books like "Figli delle stelle" (Baldini and Castoldi, 2014), "Teneri violenti" (Einaudi Stile Libero, 2016), "L'età della tigre" (Il Saggiatore, 2019), and "Fine lavoro mai" (Eris, 2022). Additionally, he produced podcasts such as "Frigo!!!" (Chora Media, with Nicolò Porcelluzzi) and "Substance of hoped-for things. Voices and stories from the April 7 trial" (Radio Three, with Massimo Carozzi).

Andrea Steves
(Michigan, USA, 1983)

is a curator, researcher, and organizer based between Vienna, Austria and New York, USA, whose recent projects explore capitalism, climate change, public history, museums and monuments.

Freek Lomme
(The Netherlands, 1979)

founder and owner of Set Margins' publications, is an editor, publisher, producer, graphic designer, writer, lecturer, curator, poet, administrator, entrepreneur, and janitor. Lomme is dedicated to promoting awareness through diverse topics that explore visual culture, tolerance, and autonomy.

Colophon

Set Margins' #31
the upside-down museum
by Aldo Giannotti

ISBN: 978-90-833501-7-2

Editor: Aldo Giannotti, Andrea Steves, Freek Lomme
Contributing authors: Andrea Steves, Ivan Carozzi
Graphic design: Freek Lomme
Lithography: Sebastiaan Hanekroot / Color & Books
Text editor: Andrea Steves
Proofreader: Rose Linke
Printer: PlatformP
Font: Inclusive Sans by Olivia King

Made possible thanks to the generous support of the Federal Ministry
Republic of Austria

Special thanks to the guards, Lorenzo Balbi (Director, MAMBo and
Curator of Safe and Sound), Sabrina Samorì (Assistant Curator,
MAMBo).

Every effort has been made to contact copyright holders and to obtain
their permission for the use of copyright material. If inadvertent
infringement has occurred please contact the publisher.

This publication is licensed under a Creative Commons Attributon-Non-
Commercial-ShareAlike 4.0 International Licence (CC BY-NC-SA 4.0).
To view a copy of this license, visit
 https://creativecommons.org/licenses/by-nc-sa/4.0/

January 2024, first edition

www.aldogiannotti.com
www.setmargins.press

Federal Ministry
Republic of Austria
Arts, Culture,
Civil Service and Sport

Image
credits

All photo's by Aldo Giannotti, the MAMbo guards and the MAMbo museum, except from:
- Aldo Giannotti Safe and Sound veduta della mostra /installation view MAMbo – Museo d'Arte Moderna di Bologna Foto/Photo: Valentina Cafarotti e/and Federico Landi
- Photography of *The Museum Score* by Annette Behrens
- Video stills are taken from the film *The Guards* by Viktor Schaider, subtitled by Andrea Steves.
- the photo's of the removal of the staircase by Aldo Rossi are taken from *MAMbo Al Forno Del Pane*, Skira Editore 2007, photography by Raffaello Scatasta

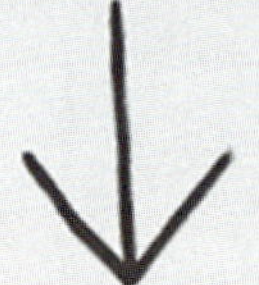
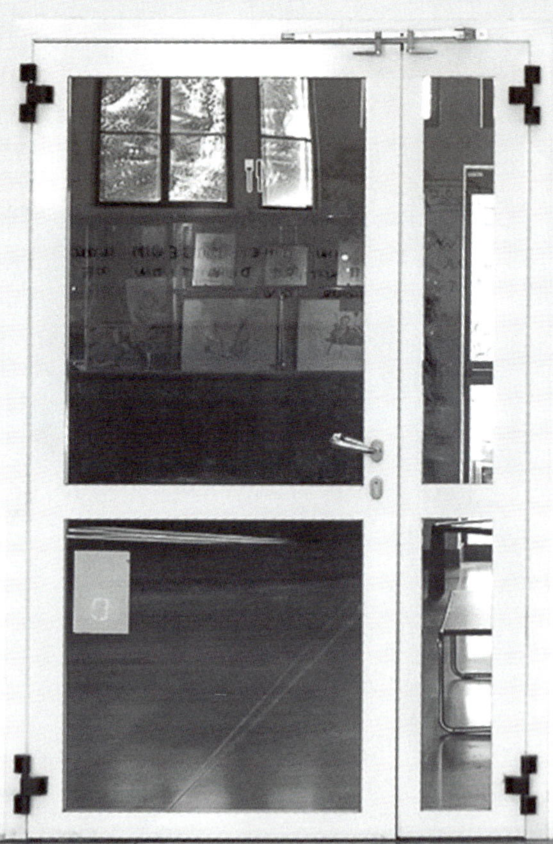

.3

DANGEROUS
EXIT

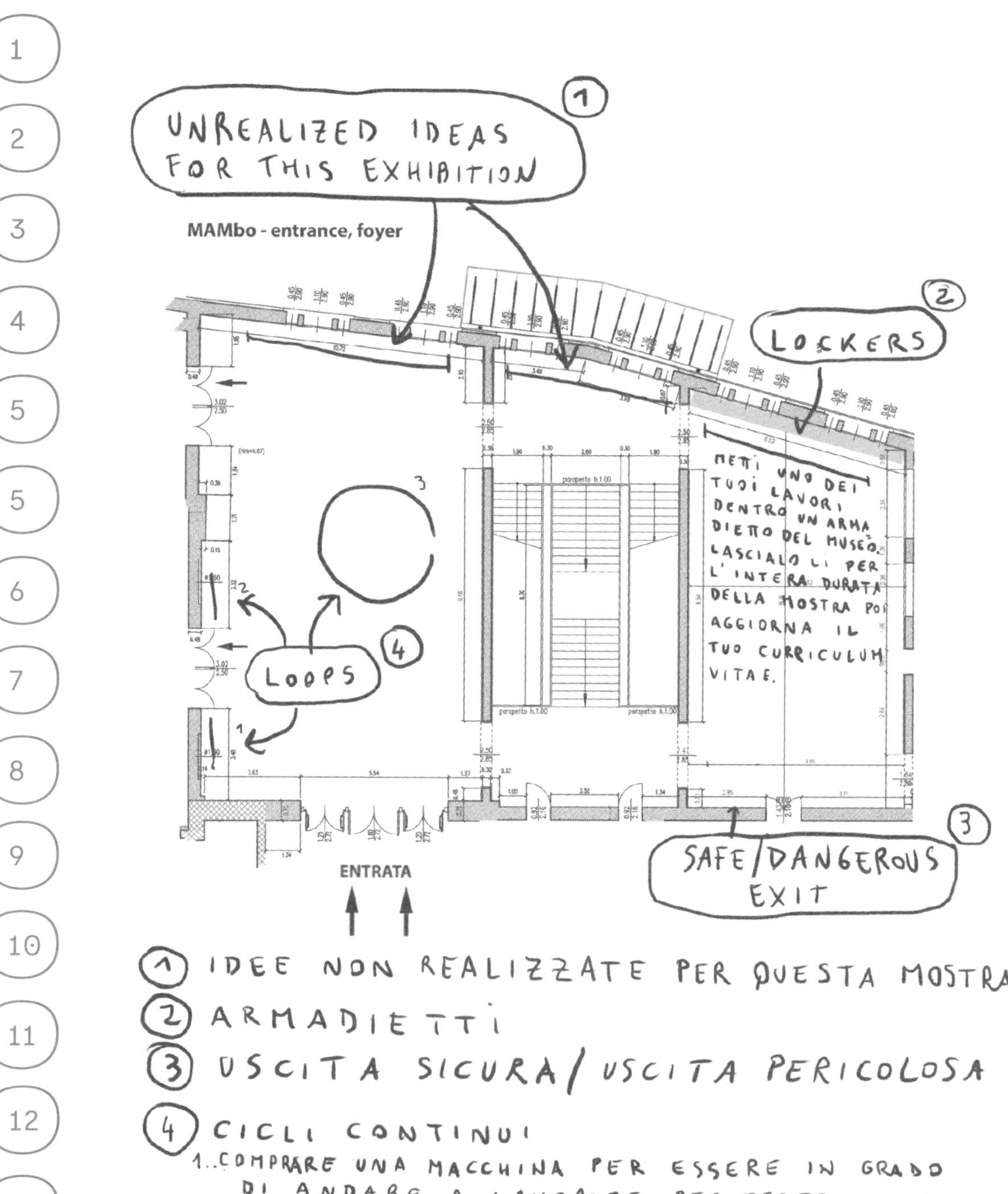

1 IDEE NON REALIZZATE PER QUESTA MOSTRA

2 ARMADIETTI

3 USCITA SICURA / USCITA PERICOLOSA

4 CICLI CONTINUI

1..COMPRARE UNA MACCHINA PER ESSERE IN GRADO DI ANDARE A LAVORARE PER ESSERE IN GRADO DI

2...EDIFICI CONTENENTI STANZE CONTENENTI DISEGNI CONTENENTI...

3...FARE UNA MOSTRA PER ESSERE IN GRADO DI..

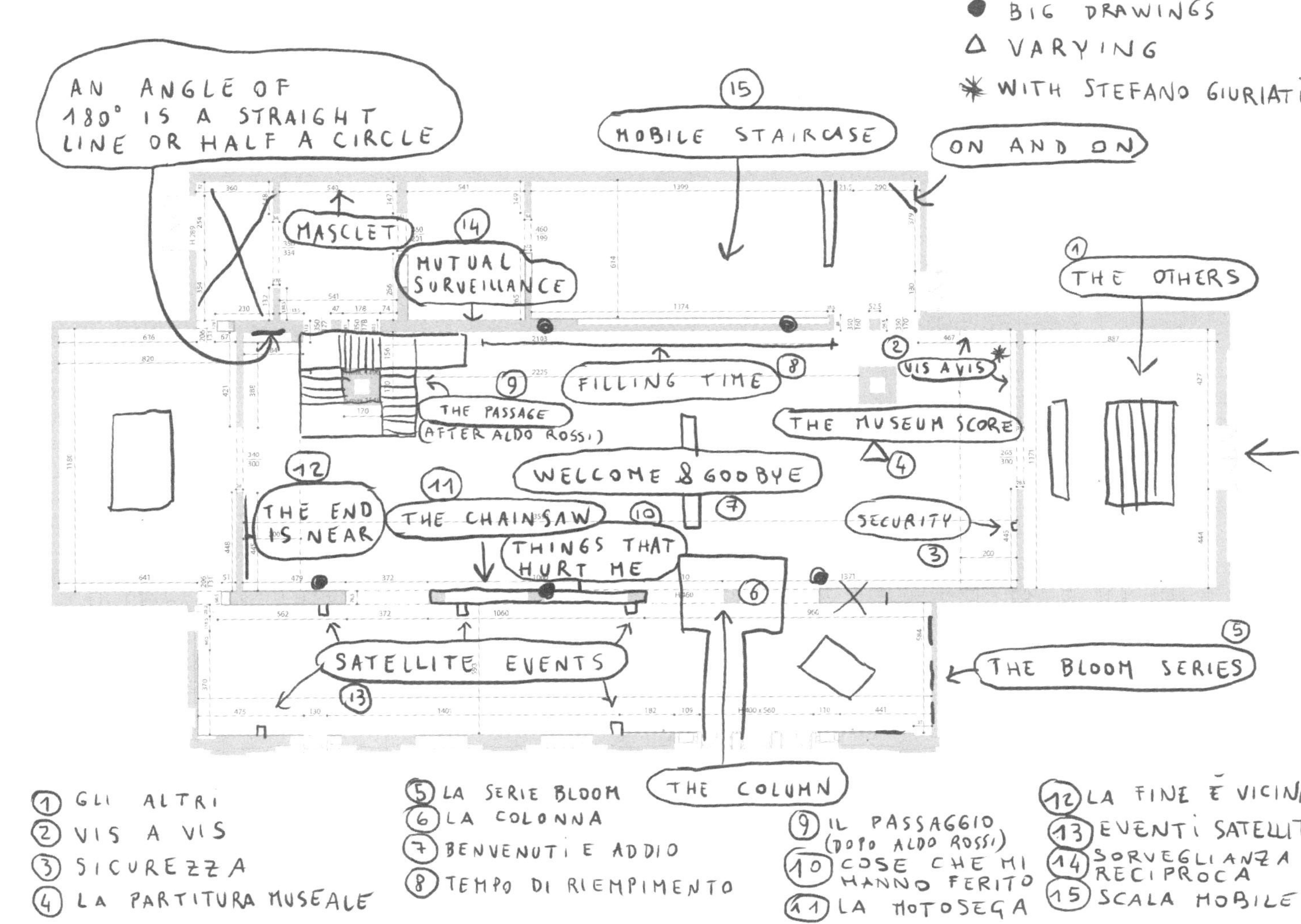

AN ANGLE OF 180° IS A STRAIGHT LINE OR HALF A CIRCLE
● BIG DRAWINGS
△ VARYING
✳ WITH STEFANO GIURIATI
15 MOBILE STAIRCASE
ON AND ON
MASCLET
14 MUTUAL SURVEILLANCE
1 THE OTHERS
9 THE PASSAGE (AFTER ALDO ROSSI)
8 FILLING TIME
2 VIS A VIS
THE MUSEUM SCORE
4
12 THE END IS NEAR
11 THE CHAINSAW
10 THINGS THAT HURT ME
WELCOME & GOODBYE
7
SECURITY
3
6 THE COLUMN
SATELLITE EVENTS
13
5 THE BLOOM SERIES
1 GLI ALTRI
2 VIS A VIS
3 SICUREZZA
4 LA PARTITURA MUSEALE
5 LA SERIE BLOOM
6 LA COLONNA
7 BENVENUTI E ADDIO
8 TEMPO DI RIEMPIMENTO
9 IL PASSAGGIO (DOPO ALDO ROSSI)
10 COSE CHE MI HANNO FERITO
11 LA MOTOSEGA
12 LA FINE È VICINA
13 EVENTI SATELLITE
14 SORVEGLIANZA RECIPROCA
15 SCALA MOBILE

hour in the main hall to socialize all to-

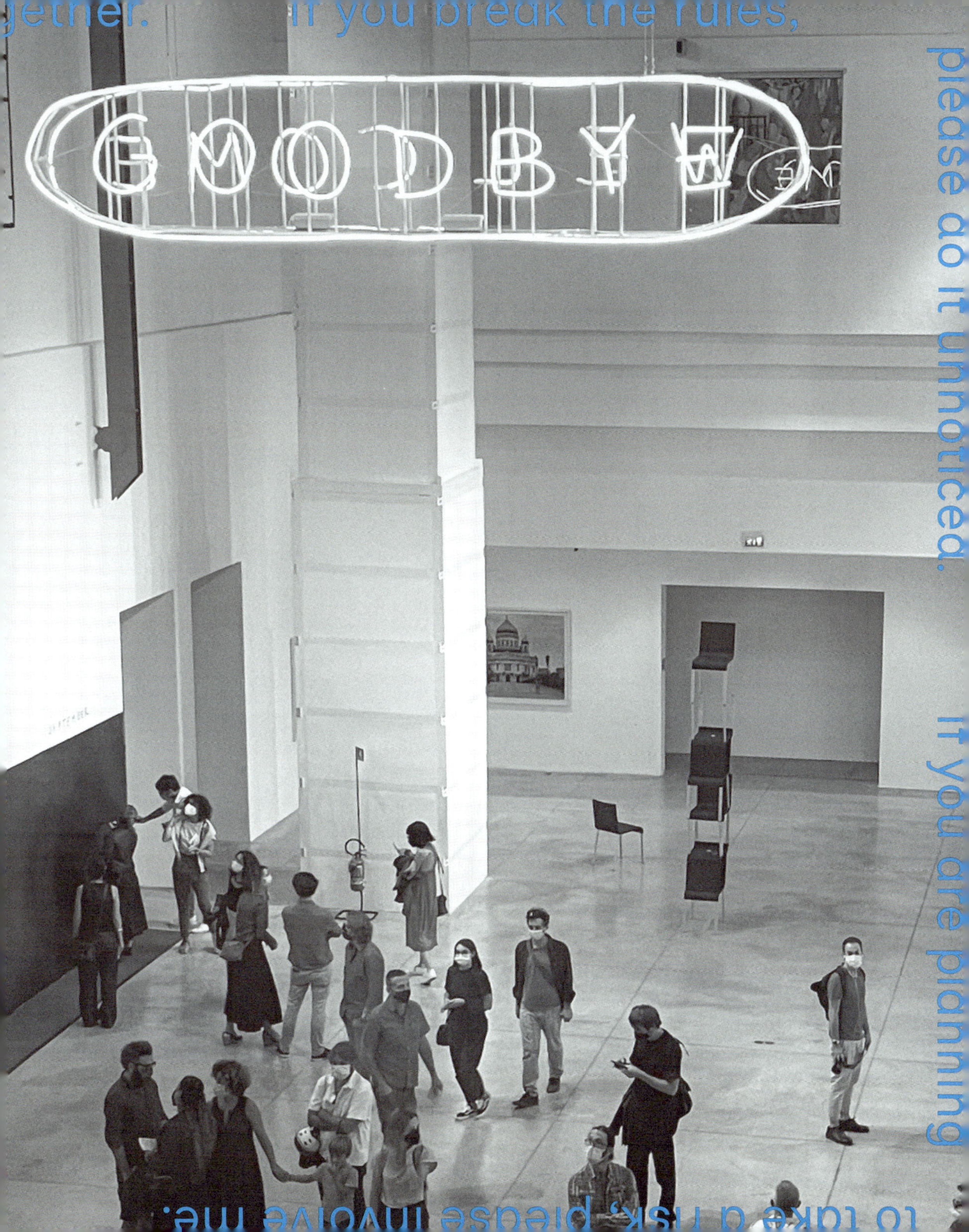
gether. ...if you break the rules,
please do it unnoticed.
if you are planning
to take a risk, please involve me.
GOODBYE